Sport in Europe

This book presents an overview on sport history research in Europe by giving insights into various topics between Europe's south and north. Examples are physical activities in the middle ages in Córdoba, bullfighting in Spain, aspects of football in various countries to winter sports in France. Football is mainly looked at in the period of the late 1930s to the 1940s, a period of dictatorship in many European countries. This is shown at the example of the German press coverage of German–Danish sport collaborations and the identity of Spanish football during this time.

A further focus are the Olympic Games. This topic is taken up in two articles: One discusses as its main subject the famous painting 'Sport Allegory/The Crowing of the Athletes' created by the father of Pierre de Coubertin, the other one has a more current content and shows stakeholders and challenges of the European Youth Olympics in 2015.

Besides these broad topics, a focus is put on research in sport history by reflecting on historical frameworks and various methodological approaches.

The chapters in this book were originally published as a special issue in *The International Journal of the History of Sport*.

Annette R. Hofmann, Professor for Sports Studies at the Ludwigsburg University of Education in Germany, and head of the sport department. President of the International Society for the History of Physical Education and Sport (ISHPES) and Vice President of the German Gymnastic Federation (Deutscher Turner-Bund). Academic Editor Europe of the IJHS. Main research areas in sport history: German–American Sports, Gender and Sport, History of Skiing.

T0347163

Sport in the Global Society: Historical Perspectives

Edited by
Mark Dyreson, *The Pennsylvania State University, USA*
Thierry Terret, *University of Lyon, France*
Rob Hess, *Victoria University, Melbourne, Australia*

Titles in the Series

For more information about this series, please visit:
https://www.routledge.com/Sport-in-the-Global-Society---Historical-perspectives/book-series/SGSH

Sport in Europe

Edited by
Annette R. Hofmann

Routledge
Taylor & Francis Group

LONDON AND NEW YORK

First published 2018 by Routledge

2 Park Square, Milton Park, Abingdon, Oxfordshire OX14 4RN
52 Vanderbilt Avenue, New York, NY 10017

Routledge is an imprint of the Taylor & Francis Group, an informa business

First issued in paperback 2020

British Library Cataloguing in Publication Data
A catalogue record for this book is available from the British Library

ISBN13: 978-0-8153-6094-0 (hbk)
ISBN13: 978-0-367-53076-1 (pbk)

Typeset in MinionPro
by diacriTech, Chennai

Publisher's Note
The publisher accepts responsibility for any inconsistencies that may have arisen
during the conversion of this book from journal articles to book chapters, namely
the possible inclusion of journal terminology.

Disclaimer
Every effort has been made to contact copyright holders for their permission to
reprint material in this book. The publishers would be grateful to hear from any
copyright holder who is not here acknowledged and will undertake to rectify any
errors or omissions in future editions of this book.

Contents

CONTENTS

Citation Information

The chapters in this book were originally published in *The International Journal of the History of Sport*, volume 33, issue 10 (May 2016). When citing this material, please use the original page numbering for each article, as follows:

Chapter 1

Medieval Córdoba: From Umayyad Recreations to Competitive Christian Sport
José Antonio Funes-Pérez, Juan Rodríguez-López and Alfonso Manas
The International Journal of the History of Sport, volume 33, issue 10 (May 2016)
pp. 1009–1027

Chapter 2

Art Works as Sources for Sport History Research: The Example of 'Sports Allegory/The Crowning of the Athletes' by Charles Louis Frédy de Coubertin
Natalia Camps Y Wilant
The International Journal of the History of Sport, volume 33, issue 10 (May 2016)
pp. 1028–1045

Chapter 3

Salvador López Gómez: Apostle of Gymnastics in Spain
Gonzalo Ramírez-Macías and José P. Sanchís Ramírez
The International Journal of the History of Sport, volume 33, issue 10 (May 2016)
pp. 1046–1064

Chapter 4

Sport Versus Bullfighting: The New Civilizing Sensitivity of Regenerationism and its Effect on the Leisure Pursuits of the Spanish at the Beginning of the Twentieth Century
Antonio Rivero Herraiz and Raúl Sánchez-García
The International Journal of the History of Sport, volume 33, issue 10 (May 2016)
pp. 1065–1078

For any permission-related enquiries please visit:
http://www.tandfonline.com/page/help/permissions

Notes on Contributors

Natalia Camps Y Wilant earned her PhD from the Institute for Sport and Exercise Sciences at the University of Muenster, Germany. Her research focuses on the Olympic art competitions. She is Secretary General of the German Pierre de Coubertin Committee.

José Antonio Funes-Pérez has a PhD in History of Sport ascribed to the Department of Physical Education and Sport of the University of Granada, Spain. His PhD dissertation is entitled 'Evolución de las actividades deportivas de las provincias de Granada, Córdoba y Jaén entre los siglos X y XVII'.

Carlos García-Martí is currently finishing his PhD at the Instituto Nacional de Educación Física de Madrid on the changes Spanish football identity underwent in the 1980s. His interests are media influence in sport, the commodification process and sporting national cultures and identities.

Doriane Gomet, Senior Lecturer in Sports Sciences and History, is working in the research center "Violence, Identities, Politics and Sports" (VIPS, EA 4636) of the University of Rennes II, France. Research Associate of the IFEPSA (Angers), she is particularly interested in the history of the practices of vulnerable people, notably those in situations of captivity during nineteenth and twentieth centuries. Her thesis bears the title 'Sport and body practices of the French prisoners of war, deported people and the forced workers during the Second World War'.

Annette R. Hofmann, Professor for Sports Studies at the Ludwigsburg University of Education in Germany, and head of the sport department. President of the International Society for the History of Physical Education and Sport (ISHPES) and Vice President of the German Gymnastic Federation (Deutscher Turner-Bund). Academic Editor Europe of the IJHS. Main research areas in sport history: German–American Sports, Gender and Sport, History of Skiing.

Gary James is a member of International Sport and Leisure History at Manchester Metropolitan University, UK, where he is also a Lecturer. He has published extensively since 1989, and he has been commissioned to write a monograph on the emergence of footballing cultures for Manchester University Press.

Christian Tolstrup Jensen holds a master degree in History with a minor in German from the University of Copenhagen, Denmark. Currently, a PhD student at the University College of Southeast Norway, he studies how stakeholders in recent major sport events in Denmark and Norway justify such events. Other areas of interest are youth organizations and their role in the civil society and sports and it's political use in recent history.

Elsa Kristiansen is a Professor of Management at the University College of Southeast Norway. Her research interests are sport event management, youth sport, motivation, organizational and media stress.

Alfonso Manas is a Lecturer in History of Sport. He has written several articles, chapters and book reviews on the subject. His most recent book is *Gladiadores: el gran espectáculo de Roma* (Barcelona: Ariel, 2013).

Gonzalo Ramírez-Macías (PhD) is an Assistant Professor and a Research Fellow of Sport History in the Seville Faculty of Education, University of Seville, Spain. His research interests are physical education and sport history. He has published widely in these areas.

Antonio Rivero Herraiz is a sport historian specializing in the analysis of the development of modern Spanish sport. He is the current Dean of the Sports Science School (INEF) of the Universidad Politécnica de Madrid, Spain.

Juan Rodríguez-López is a Lecturer in History of Sport at the University of Granada, Spain, a subject that is taught at the Faculty of Sport Sciences of that university. He has written over 20 articles, chapters and book reviews in the field of History of Sport. He is the author of the books *Deporte y ciencia: teoría de la actividad física* (Barcelona: Inde, 1995) and *Historia del deporte* (Barcelona: Inde, 2000).

Raúl Sánchez-García is a sport sociologist specializing in the historical development of martial arts and Spanish sport pastimes such as bullfighting. He teaches Sociology of Sport at the Sports Science School of the Universidad Europea de Madrid, Spain.

José P. Sanchís Ramírez (PhD) has been an Assistant Professor and a Research Fellow of Sport History in the Seville Faculty of Education, University of Seville, Spain, for 20 years. His research interests are physical education and sport history, especially during the nineteenth century.

Pierre-Olaf Schut is Associate Professor at the laboratory ACP (Comparative Analysis of Powers), University Paris-Est, France. His research interests are related to the history of outdoor activities and the link between sport and tourism since the nineteenth century. More specifically, he has published articles about caving, mountaineering and skiing.

Berit Skirstad is an Associate Professor Emerita in Sport Management at the Norwegian School of Sport Sciences, Norway, and research interests are volunteers, leadership, sport organizations and gender.

Anna-Maria Strittmatter, PhD, is Associate Professor and Head of Sport Management at the Norwegian School of Sport Sciences, Norway. Her research interests are youth sport, sport policy, sport governance and sport event management.

Series Editors' Foreword

Sport in the Global Society: Historical Perspectives explores the role of sport in cultures both around the world and across the time frames of human history. In the world we currently inhabit, sport spans the globe. It captivates vast audiences. It defines, alters, and reinforces identities for individuals, communities, nations, and empires. Sport organises memories and perceptions, arouses passions and tensions, and reveals harmonies and cleavages. It builds and blurs social boundaries – animating discourses about class, gender, race, and ethnicity. Sport opens new vistas on the history of human cultures, intersecting with politics and economics, ideologies and theologies. It reveals aesthetic tastes and energises consumer markets.

Our challenge is to explain how sport has developed into a global phenomenon. The series continues the tradition established by the original incarnation of *Sport in the Global Society* (and in 2010 divided into *Historical Perspectives* and *Contemporary Perspectives*) by promoting the academic study of one of the most significant and dynamic forces in shaping the historical landscapes of human cultures.

In the twenty-first century, a critical mass of scholars recognises the importance of sport in their analyses of human experiences and *Sport in the Global Society: Historical Perspectives* provides an international outlet for the world's leading investigators on these subjects. Building on previous work in the series and excavating new terrain, our series remains a consistent and coherent response to the attention the academic community demands for the serious study of sport.

Mark Dyreson
Thierry Terret
Rob Hess

Medieval Córdoba: From Umayyad Recreations to Competitive Christian Sport

José Antonio Funes-Pérez, Juan Rodríguez-López and Alfonso Manas

ABSTRACT

In this article, we study the evolution of competitive sport and sporting recreations in medieval Córdoba, from the Umayyad Muslims (756–1236) to the Christians (since 1236). In this diachronic study, firstly we compare the competitive sport and sporting recreations of the Muslim East (especially those of the Abbasid period) with those of Muslim Córdoba, in order to know the level of Arabization of those practices in Córdoba, and if competitive sport is more predominant than recreations or vice versa. Secondly, we study if competitive sport and sporting recreations had the same presence in Muslim Córdoba and Christian Córdoba (or if one predominated over the other), and the possible reasons for it. We conclude: (1) that in Muslim Córdoba, sporting recreations were more important than competitive sport, unlike what happened in the great Muslim cities of the East; (2) Arabization is almost total regarding the types of sport and recreations implanted in Córdoba but low regarding horse sports and the importance of competitive sport; and (3) that Christian Córdoba shows a very different character, since competitive sport is very important (largely because by that time Córdoba had become a frontier city).

Introduction

The historical period of Muslim Córdoba starts in 711, when an army of Arabs and Berbers begins the conquest of the Iberian Peninsula. In 716, Córdoba is chosen as the capital of al-Andalus (the territory of the Iberian Peninsula under Muslim rule), the new province of the Umayyad Caliphate. In 929, the Emir of Córdoba (Abd-ar-Rahman III) proclaims the Caliphate of Córdoba, achieving thus full independence from the Abbasid Caliphate of Bagdad. Thus starts the most glorious period in the whole history of Córdoba, becoming one of the most beautiful, advanced and prosperous cities of the world, with an estimated population of around 500,000 inhabitants by the year 1000. From 1009 onwards, Córdoba starts to suffer a series of civil wars that greatly weakens it; of the 21 neighbourhoods (arrabales) that existed in the tenth century, only five survived in the twelfth century.[1]

Finally, in the year 1031, the Caliphate of Córdoba is abolished, and al-Andalus becomes a territory formed by several independent Muslim kingdoms (taifas) that, nonetheless, continued to be inspired by the cultural and political model of the Caliphate of Córdoba. In 1236, Córdoba is conquered by the Christians.

In this paper, we study the evolution of sport practices in medieval Córdoba from the beginning of the Emirate of Córdoba (756) until the end of the Middle Ages. The cultural impact of the Muslim rulers of Córdoba resulted in the Arabization of recreational and sport practices, though Cordoban sport practices (as we will see) were never the same as those of the Muslim East, always keeping distinguishing features. One of the main differences was that horse sports were never very important in Córdoba, due to the well-known low warlike spirit of the inhabitants of that city. In 1236, Córdoba was re-conquered by the Christians, which meant a total change in the sport practices of the city. The new settlers' wide geographical origin, their search for identity as a newly founded society, the city's character as frontier between two worlds, and the prospect of social promotion via entering the people's cavalry shaped the new sport practices dominant in the city, with chivalric sports now becoming paramount.

From the point of view of methodology, the joint study of recreations and sport is a frequent resource in social history (for example, about the medieval history of the Muslims, Ahsan, Mez, or Arié).[2] Marshall, when studying sport and recreations in the Middle Ages, defines them jointly: 'By sports and recreations we mean any activity engaged in by people that took them outside of their everyday occupational activities.'[3] In the same way, here we will also study them jointly, but distinguishing between competitive sports (those requiring great physical effort, with or without the participation of animals) and sporting recreations (practices that require a lower physical effort, or that though requiring almost no physical effort – such as chess – or no competitive element, they had been traditionally classified within this category). This distinction between competitive sport and sporting recreations finds its justification in the fact that one of the main aims sought by medieval competitive sport was to serve as preparation for war (something especially evident in the case of horse sports),[4] an aim that sporting recreations did not seek.

Due to the great importance of war in the Middle Ages, competitive sport (especially horse sports) was generally considered very important in most societies, whereas recreations were not deemed so essential. Competitive horse sports were seen as the perfect means to create good soldiers, by developing their masculinity. As Mangan says: 'throughout recorded human history sport in various forms, but invariably competitive, confrontational and aggressive in nature, has been a preparation, to use Gilmore's term, for "real" manhood'.[5] Thus, competitive horse sport would have been an excellent means to exhibit and develop masculinity, especially warrior masculinity – something which societies are generally interested in, though not always (as we will see in the case of Muslim Córdoba).[6] That there exist societies less interested in this type of masculinity has often been noted, for example, by Lehfeldt: 'As recent scholarship has argued, masculinity, like femininity, is a mutable category. There is no universal standard of manhood that transcends time and place.'[7] Thus, this may help us understand why, unlike the Muslim societies of the East, in Muslim Córdoba, sporting recreations were more important than competitive sport. It seems that they did not share the same standard of masculinity as Eastern societies.

A total change occurred with the Christian re-conquest of the city, with competitive sport becoming extraordinarily important. Hence, in this paper, we will also study (among other things) if there exists a predominance of sporting recreations over competitive sport in the sources that document Muslim Córdoba and (if it exists) if it can be interpreted as a sign that society was not interested in war, as an indication of a low military compromise on the part of that society, and –alternatively– if the predominance of competitive sport in Christian Córdoba might indicate a high interest in war, a high military compromise on the part of that society.

Low Presence of Horse Sport and Competitive Sport in Muslim Córdoba in Comparison with the Great Cities of the Muslim East

The Muslim East, Origin of Córdoba's Sport Practices

The favourite pastimes of the ruling elite are the most widely recorded in art and written sources. They mainly consist of feasts, hunts and several sport games, most of them characterized by their high cost.[8] The Muslims of the Medieval East were peoples who loved recreations and sports that, in general, were of pre-Islamic origin. They particularly distinguished themselves by their passion for horsemanship.[9]

A systematic exposition shows the abundant list of sporting recreations and competitive sports that were practised in the Muslim East during the period of the emirate and caliphate of Córdoba (756–1031):[10]

(1) Sports related to cavalry: horse-racing (*sibāq al-khayl* or *ijrā' al-khayl*[11]), polo (*ṣawlajān*),[12] a variety of polo (*ṭabṭāb*), *djerid*[13] (a kind of mock tournament with canes instead of lances),[14] archery on horseback (*birjās*),[15] hunting, lion hunting.[16]

(2) Armed sports without horses: fencing, the lance game (*la'b al-rumḥ*), archery (*rami al-nushshāb*), cross-bow shooting (*rani bi'l-bunduq*).[17]

(3) Athletic sports: foot racing, wrestling (*muṣāra'a*),[18] swimming, weightlifting, rowing.

(4) Intellectual games: chess (*shaṭranj*).

(5) Animal entertainments: fights of all kinds of animals (cocks, dogs, rams, he-goats, pigeons, quails, elephants, lions),[19] and races of camels, donkeys, dogs, and pigeons.

Many of those practices predated Islam (e.g. polo), whereas others were borrowed from neighbouring regions (*djerid*, as we will see). Ahsan explains the extraordinary importance for war of cavalry and the sports related to it.[20] Such military and social importance of horse sports – especially horse races, polo and *djerid* – and the abundance of sources documenting them in the great cities of the East do not appear with the same strength in Umayyad Córdoba.

In the East, horse races were the most popular form of races until the eleventh century,[21] indeed, there existed a successful literary genre specializing in producing 'books of horses'. It seems clear that the favourable opinion of the Prophet about horse races was very influential in their success.[22] In Rusafa, the Umayyad held races of the type 'out-and-back' over a distance of around 10 kilometres, the same distance as the races that the Abbasids held later in the tracks of Samarra.[23]

Horse racing was a sport of princes[24] that reached its climax between the late seventh century and the early ninth century (691–809, between the reign of the Umayyad Hishan – owner of 4,000 horses[25] – and the Abbasids).[26] By the beginning of the Abbasid period, horse racing and the ownership of horses seems to have extended to the upper nobility too.[27] Thus, in Samarra, four tracks were built between c. 833 and 861,[28] with an imaginative and capricious route in three of them, over a distance of 10,577, 10,500, 5,300 and 9,780 metres. Those colossal tracks are, however, an exception in the history of Muslim horse races, since they were normally held over the open steppe.[29]

During the ninth century, horse racing ceased to be a sport of princes, but still they continued to be held for centuries, even today.[30] In eleventh-century Bagdad, the sport that replaced horse racing as the favourite one was polo, a sport that had already been important in Samarra with the Abbasids of the ninth century.[31]

The lack of interest of Umayyad Córdoba for those horse sports may have its explanation in the low warlike spirit of its inhabitants, together with the fact that, in the case of horse racing, by the ninth century (when Córdoba starts its Golden Age), its popularity among the princes had already started to decrease in the East.

Focusing on polo, its earliest attestation is a pre-Islamic text (the *Ka-rna - mak-e Ardashir-e Pâpaka-*) of the early seventh century (still under the Sassanid dynasty, 224–651).[32] The Muslims conquered Syria and Iraq and the Umayyads (661–750) kept on patronizing the game.[33] We know that polo was played in Damascus under the second Umayyad caliph (Yazid I, 680–3), and that later the Abbasids continued practising it in Bagdad during the reign of Ha-run al-Rashid (r. 786–809). His son and successor, Ma'mun (r. 813–33), built a polo field near his palace, in Bagdad,[34] and in Samarra a large polo field can be seen to this day.[35] The local Iranian dynasties, once they got their independence from their Arabian conquerors, continued practising polo. In *The Book of Kings* (*Sha-hna-meh*), the national epic of Iran, written between 977 and 1010, princes and heroes are forever playing polo.[36]

Polo was characterized as being a princely game, as serving as preparation for war and, notably too, for its dangerousness; Abd al-Malik (954–61) broke his neck falling from a horse and the eleventh-century handbook of the art of ruling (*Qa-busna-meh*) advises youngsters to play the game just once or twice a year and to stay at the end of the field, to prevent hits and collisions.[37] The poet Farrokhi, from the court of sultan Mahmud (998–1030), wrote that there were four things that a king should do: feasting, hunting, playing polo, and warfaring.[38] For the mystic poet Rumi (1207–73), polo was a form of achieving the skills needed for war.[39] That enthusiasm for polo continued with the Safavids (rulers of Iran since 1501).[40]

About *djerid*, the sole source documenting its practice in Córdoba is curiously older than the first source that attests its practice in the East, although this sport also has its origin in the East. The source that documents its practice in Córdoba says that in 1008, the son of Almanzor, Abd al-Malik, played that game with other youngsters in his father's palace of Madinat al-Zahira.[41]

Djerid was a horse sport that was played by two teams that threw short javelins at each other 'made of either dried oak or peeled date tree branches'.[42] The game was probably introduced in Anatolia by the Seljuks as early as the eleventh century, as they moved from Central Asia to the West.[43] In fact, we know that the Anatolian Seljuk Sultan Alaeddin Keykubad I (1220–1237) liked playing *djerid*, and the game became still more important with the Ottomans (from 1299 onwards, especially with the Janissaries), with several varieties of it existing. Since the times of the Sultan Orhan Bey (1324–1362), *djerid* was the activity most earnestly supported by the Ottoman dynasty. In 1933, Carl Diem still could watch it played in Ankara, and he noted that it was 'a game with no binding rules'.[44]

Thus, summing up, three main features stand out in the Muslim East sport practices of that period: 1) they had been practised for a long time, had a deep tradition by that time (many pre-dated Islam) [45], 2) they had great social importance, 3) there was an important presence of horse sports (polo, horse races, djerid) and athletic sports (e.g. wrestling). In Muslim Córdoba, on the other hand, there is little evidence of horse races, polo, djerid, or athletic sports, maybe due to the special character of the inhabitants of Córdoba within the Muslim world.

The Cordoban Character

Despite the efforts of the Umayyads and Fuqahā' to impose the orthodoxy of Islam in Cordoban society, it was always distinguished by having more relaxed customs than the East.[46] In al-Andalus, and especially in Córdoba, they lived in an exotic and indulgent environment,[47] the reason for this largely being that Córdoba was a melting pot of races and cultures, and there was a lack of military threats (in the first centuries of the Muslim occupation).

Very few Arab conquerors arrived at al-Andalus, less than half a million (c. 50,000 from Yemen, Syria, Iraq and c. 400,000 berbers) for a total native population of around four million (Hispano-Romans and Visigoths).[48] The Arabs reserved for themselves the best lands (occupied by those who preferred an austere way of life) and the big cities (occupied by those who liked a luxurious way of life), and they also brought with them slaves, mostly black people from Africa and Slavs (they called anyone from beyond the Pyrenees Slavs).

The original Christian population converted in their great majority to Islam, becoming the Muladies – the great majority of the population. Those Christians who did not convert to Islam, and who continued living in the area, were called Mozarabes. We know that Abd-ar-Rahman III showed a lot of religious tolerance and that mixed marriages and families of Muslims and Christians were abundant, which explains the celebration of sport competitions on Christian festivities, attended by Christians and Muslims alike.[49]

In fact, the poets Ibn Hazm, al-Maqqari and Ibn al-Galib say that the Cordobans were a happy mix of races and praise their many virtues.[50] According to Levi-Provençal, that mix of races, cultures and the relaxed conditions of the place resulted in the character of the Cordobans being distinguished by their lack of warlike spirit,[51] being more apt instead for trade. This is evidenced by a tenth-century traveller from the East, Ibn Hawqal, who criticized the Muslims of al-Andalus for their lack of fighting spirit and their inexperience in riding horses.[52]

Thus, the soldiers from Córdoba and al-Andalus lacked warlike spirit and preparation, as evidenced by the fact that the Cordoban caliphs brought soldiers from the Christian kingdoms and from Africa to form their personal guards. Indeed, Abd-ar-Rahman III suppressed the conscription of Cordoban men, and his son Al-Hakam II eventually included more and more Berbers in the army. With Almanzor, almost the whole of the army was formed by Berbers.

That low warlike spirit and lack of preparation for war of the Cordobans agrees with the scarcity of sources about horse sports and competitive sports in Córdoba. On the contrary, there exist abundant sources about sporting recreations such as hunting, falconry and chess.[53]

Horse Sports

Among the few testimonies of horse races in Córdoba, we know that Abd-ar-Rahman III organized that kind of entertainment for his Mozarabes (Christian) subjects on the day of Saint John, compelling orators and poets to attend.[54] It is also attested that some jurists from the time of Al-Hakam I (770–822) warned about the impropriety of attending those races held on Christian festivities.[55] In any case, according to Levi-Provençal, horse races would not become really important before the tenth century.[56]

About polo (*ṣawlajān*), one source suggests its practice in Muslim Córdoba, some verses by the poet Abul-l-Mugira Ibn Hazm describing the crescent moon as a curved polo stick (*ṣawlajan*) on the point of hitting the ball.[57] We have not found a single reference to hippodromes in Córdoba or the south of the Iberian Peninsula, only a poetic fragment about two Slav princes from Valencia (east of the Iberian Peninsula) in the eleventh century.[58] This is in sharp contrast with the abundant record of hippodromes and horse races in the Near East.[59]

The Palatine Annals of the Caliph Al-Hakam II (that records the public and private activities of that tenth-century caliph) contains only two references related to sport, both of them referring to horse sports:[60]

(1) in the Marble Courtyard of the alcazar of Córdoba, the caliph watches horse exercises performed by Berbers. Out of admiration, he says that 'they seem to have been born already on horses'.[61]

(2) A kind of horse game consisting in riders 'attacking each other mockingly', a kind of primitive tournament, is watched by the caliph and his son from the balcony of the palace of Madinat al-Zahira. Several riders get hurt, one of them a Berber warrior.[62]

The scarce corpus of sources documenting horse sport in Córdoba would be complete if we add the above-mentioned reference to *djerid* in 1008 and information about youngsters playing warriors with horses made of canes, also from that date.[63]

Archery

About archery, another important military sport in the East, its evidence in Córdoba is also scanty (only one reference in Cordoban poetry). Ibn Hazm, the eleventh-century Cordoban poet, says: 'I hit the target I choose with such an aim that, if it were widely known, Wahriz [a famous archer] would not aspire to the primacy among archers'.[64]

Now that we have seen the situation of competitive sport in Córdoba, let us next examine the situation of non-competitive recreations in Córdoba.

Abundance of Non-Competitive Recreations in Muslim Córdoba

Hunting

In the East, hunting was not just an important activity, but also a pictorial topic and a literary genre (and it had been so since even before the appearance of Islam). In Muslim Córdoba, unlike what happened with horse sports, hunting was as important as in the East, since it is abundantly attested by the sources that even show that hunting was considered as an exercise almost morally indispensable for the Cordoban nobility.[65]

Of the fondness of Cordoban emirs and caliphs for hunting in Sierra Morena and for practising falconry in the Guadalquivir valley, we have plenty of testimonies.[66] Abd-ar-Rahman II, on several occasions, went to rural estates (*munyats*) near Córdoba to practice hunting: once he ascended to the throne, he decided to spend one day hunting, going to the state of Rabanales, near the *llano del Pabellón*, the famous Fahs al-Suraqid'.[67] On his part, the Cordoban poet Ibn 'Abd Rabbihi praises Abd-ar-Rahman III the first time he went hunting after ascending the throne. He went to the state of Muniat al-yanna, to the east of Córdoba, on 13 January 913.[68]

Hunting with animals was another extraordinarily popular mode of hunting in the East, where the preferred animal for hunting was the cheetah (*fahd*), followed by the leopard (*panthera pardus*), hounds, wolves, caracals, ferrets, weasels, jungle cat (*Felis chaus*) and many other analogous species.[69] In Córdoba, on the other hand, hunting with animals was far less developed, with the hound as the only documented animal used for that purpose.[70]

Falconry

The Muslims were very fond of falconry, an art they supposedly learned from the Persians, as suggested by the fact that Persian words were sometimes used (instead of their Arab equivalents) by the Muslims when talking about falconry (e.g. *sahin* 'falcon', *dastaban* 'glove').[71] The great importance falconry had in the East was equally present in Córdoba.

The falcon (*bāzi*) was the bird typically used in falconry in the East,[72] though there they also used the goshawk, the sparrowhawk, the peregrine falcon, the Saker falcon and the eagle.[73] The falcon was supposedly introduced into the Iberian Peninsula from the East by the Muslims.

A diversity of species was also used in Cordoban falconry, such as the vulture (*nasr*), the eagle (*'uqab*),[74] and the sparrowhawk. The sources talk about an important consumption in Córdoba of bird meat – partridges, pheasants, wild ducks, wood pigeons, wild geese – captured by means of falconry.[75]

The existence in several cities of the south of the Peninsula of neighbourhoods of falconers (some of them still bearing that name today, e.g. Albayzin in Granada) prove the social importance of falconry in al-Andalus.[76] Falconry with sparrowhawk was widely extended in Córdoba because sparrowhawks were cheaper than genuine, bigger, falcons.[77] This custom extended into Christian times, since the fourteenth-century poet Pero López de Ayala states that the best sparrowhawks are bred in the Cordoban shire of Los Pedroches.[78]

Animal Entertainments

As already stated, Muslims from the East were very fond of animal fights and animal races,[79] and though that passion was probably also shared in the West of Africa (today's Magreb),[80] it seemingly did not extend into Córdoba during the three first centuries of Muslim rule (from the eighth to the tenth century).

The first spectacle of this kind is documented in the year 1070; the king of the taifa of Seville conquers the taifa of Córdoba and, in order to try to become popular among the inhabitants of the city, his new subjects, he presents them with feasts and spectacles that included animals, something the Cordobans (apparently) were not used to.[81]

It is attested that Abd-ar-Rahman III (912–961) had in his palace of Madinat al-Zahira (near Córdoba) a menagerie (*hāyr*) that included lions and birds,[82] copying the menageries that existed at that very time in the palaces of Bagdad, or those that had existed in the palaces of Samarra during the ninth century,[83] though those animals were not used in any kind of public entertainment, their sole function being – in the case of the lions – simply to try to frighten enemies (so say the sources, specifying that no prisoner was ever thrown to the lions).[84]

Regarding bullfighting (fights between man and bull), no clear evidence exists either in the Muslim sources of the Iberian Peninsula. The Cordoban poet Yahya al-Saraqusti – he worked as a butcher – has some verses ('and we do not go away from the race of the bulls [*ṭawri*] until we have mixed their saliva to their red blood. That ox that one could imagine that will resist, fatally falls under our sharp swords')[85] that some scholars have tried to interpret as allusive to bullfighting, although it is more logical to understand them as referring to his profession as butcher (the use of the word ox is rather illuminating, since oxen –as castrated males– lack the fighting spirit (bravura) needed in bullfighting, so that no bullfight is possible with oxen).

Chess

In the same way as hunting and falconry, chess is also abundantly attested in Cordoban sources, and it enjoyed a great social importance too. In the tenth and eleventh centuries, chess became especially popular in the Muslim world,[86] with a total of 23 treatises on the game produced in the East (16 of them have survived until today[87]). The first reference to chess in the Iberian Peninsula (and Europe) is found in a book about laws by the Cordoban jurist Yahyà, written in the early ninth century, a very early date.[88]

The wide diffusion of chess throughout al-Andalus is well attested by the discovery, in several parts of the Iberian Peninsula, of pieces carved in rock crystal (a Muslim mine of rock crystal has been found in Badajoz). The chess board of Al-Mutamid (king of Seville from 1069 to 1090) is famous, with pieces of precious woods and gold. This chess board was used in the famous game between Al-Mutamid's prime minister and the Castilian king, Alfonso VI.[89]

There is a high number of literary references by authors from al-Andalus to the chess treatises written in the East. There are also seven references to players belonging to all social classes,[90] which bear testimony to the popularity of the game in all ranks of the society of al-Andalus. For example, the Cordoban poet al-Ramadi composed a poem in 1012 citing chess (he probably liked to play the game).

That the Muslims were the introducers of chess in the Iberian Peninsula was also recognized by the Christians, since the thirteenth-century *Book of Chess*, the first treatise about the game written in Spanish, ordered by king Alfonso X the Wise, clearly states the Muslim origin of the game.[91]

Kuraj

The game of *kuraj* (of clear Eastern origin too) was a kind of dance known in the East since the seventh century, that seems to have involved a kind of wooden horse, although the exact shape of this horse remains uncertain, since it is never clearly described in the sources (modern scholars have proposed several interpretations, such as a little wooden horse replica, a stick horse, a hobby horse and a skirted hobby horse).[92]

The name comes from the Old Persian *kurrag* (colt), so that it seems clear that – from the first moment – some kind of horse replica was used in that dance. Ahsan describes the practice, as performed in the East during the Abbasid period, in the following terms:

> On special occasions, such as wedding ceremonies, a game known as *kuraj* was played by young girls. They took a wooden horse and covered it with a beautiful tunic, put a rope around its neck and pulled it about, playing and shouting.[93]

As we can see, for Ahsan, the practice is more a game than a dance (actually, he never uses this term).

Although evidence shows that it was a game typically for girls, some episodes are also documented where it is played by effeminate men (*mukhannathun*).[94] Yet, this does not change the character of the game as a typical one for girls, but it simply documents exceptional isolated episodes. According to the sources, adults and children were fascinated watching this dance.[95]

In Córdoba (and al-Andalus), the earliest recorded evidence of *kuraj* is an episode that occurred in January 1075. A captain of the army was killed while he was watching his slave-girls performing *kuraj* (sadly, the source does not specify the shape of the 'horses').[96]

That *kuraj* came to be performed by female slaves in Córdoba is not strange, since the city had (in the eleventh century) the monopoly in al-Andalus of the trade of female slaves specializing in chanting and dancing (actually, the slave trade was one of the pillars of the economy of the city).[97] One written source attests the sale of a female slave with special skills in dancing, acrobatics and the use of weapons.[98]

Water Recreations

The wars that brought to an end the Caliphate of Córdoba (from the year 1010 to 1031) destroyed palaces (Madinat al-Zahra and Madinat al-Zahira) and places of recreation of the city. We know that by that time it became fashionable to go out to the reservoirs (*sudd*) near the city, especially to the reservoir of Malik. There, the men drank in the mills and practised swimming and rowing.[99] Rowing races disputed on *mihrayān* (Saint John's Day) were especially popular. Some verses by Ibn al-Labbana recall those rowing races of *mihrayān*, comparing the boats to gyrfalcons.[100] Those eleventh-century sources about animal entertainments, *kuraj*, swimming and rowing are the last attestations we have of sporting recreations and sports in Muslim Córdoba. As we see, whereas in Muslim Córdoba the sources about competitive and horse sport are scarce in comparison with those of the East, there is an abundance of sources about non-competitive recreations.

Arabization of the Recreations and Sport Practices of Córdoba

Due to the heterogeneous origin of the culture of al-Andalus, since the first moments, the Umayyad Cordobans – due to their Arabic origins and their political aims – exhibited with intensity their Arab and Islamic condition, and thus they managed to consolidate – albeit gradually – the Arabization of material culture, language and daily life.[101]

During the ninth and tenth centuries, many elements from the culture of the Muslim East were introduced in al-Andalus, to the point that Córdoba seemed almost a replica of the East. The total Arabization of the natives of Córdoba was achieved, including those who practised Christianity. As regards the Jews, it seems that though they had some sport practices exclusive to themselves, in general they enjoyed the same practices as the rest of the population.[103]

Some rulers undertook special efforts to achieve Arabization, such as Abd-ar-Rahman II (822–852),[104] who encouraged many intellectuals and artists from the East (e.g. the musician Ziryab, who probably was the introducer of chess in the Iberian Peninsula)[105] to go to Córdoba.

The success of that Arabization process is evidenced by the high popularity that some Eastern practices won in Córdoba, such as falconry, chess, *kuraj* or bathing (the last enjoying an extraordinary social success in Córdoba).[106] Yet it is also true that some other Eastern practices never became popular in Córdoba, such as animal fights and races, wrestling, or foot races.

Importance of Competitive Sport in Medieval Christian Córdoba

When Ferdinand III of Castile conquered Córdoba (1236), Jaén (1246) and Seville (1248), most of the Muslim population that lived in those territories moved to the nearby Emirate of Granada (the only Muslim kingdom that remained in the Iberian Peninsula), whereas a small portion of them went to North Africa.[107] Thus, Córdoba, Jaen and Seville needed to be repopulated, so Christians were brought from Castile and other Christian kingdoms of the Peninsula. Yet, the original number of the Muslim population was never reached (e.g. Córdoba in the eleventh century had c. 500,000 inhabitants, whereas its current population – the highest since 1246 – is 328,000).

Since those Christian settlers came from different parts of the Peninsula, the resulting society was very heterogeneous.[108] They looked for social integration and social identity, and they adopted new sports practices, necessarily few in number but that were relatively well regulated. The adoption of those new forms of sport could have been determined by reasons of social utility, such as:

- The desire for social promotion by joining the people's cavalry (*cavallería villana*), which required being skilful in riding horses.[109]
- The desire to get a job that required the use of arms (better paid than other jobs).[110]
- The need to protect oneself: to carry weapons was allowed, so that in order to be able to protect oneself, one needed to know how to use (at least) a sword.[111]
- Besides all that, since Córdoba was now a frontier city (bordering with the Muslim kingdom of Granada), military preparations and expeditions were very frequent,[112] which explains the high interest of its rulers in promoting among its population sports related to war; the inhabitants of Córdoba had to know how to use weapons because, in case of conflict, the rulers of the city (*cabildo de jurados*) issued the list of citizens who had to go to the war, citizens that left their respective neighbourhoods (*collaziones*) already perfectly armed and ready, as occurred when the War of Granada broke out.[113]

All this could explain that the sports predominant in Córdoba after the Christian re-conquest were horse races, tournaments, jousting, *juego de cañas* (game of canes, similar to *djerid*), *bofordar* (to throw javelins at a target, normally on horseback), and fencing, and even entertainments with bulls (bullfighting) were performed with men on horseback.

Horse Sports

Texts written in the fourteenth century say that a place in Córdoba called *la Corredera* was normally used by knights for *bofordar*,[114] and for holding horse races (*correr caballos*),[115] whereas texts of the fifteenth century say that bullfights (*correr toros*) were staged there.

That change of function of *la Corredera*, from being mainly defined as a place for horse sports to a place for bullfighting, may reflect the great importance that bullfighting quickly achieved in that new Christian society.

The manuscript *Descriptio Cordubae*, written c. 1481 by the Cordoban canon Jerónimo Sánchez (aka Jerónimo de Córdoba), describes in detail the sports practised at that time in the city. According to the author, the youths of Córdoba engaged in *juego de cañas*, tournaments, jousting and *bofordar*.[116]

When performing *juego de cañas*, they were equipped with leather shields and went with the head uncovered. When tourneying, they used lances without points and the head was protected by the armet. When jousting, they wore full armour and carried a lance. When they practised *bofordar*, the text says that they threw short javelins at full gallop at targets in the shape of a ship, and that those eager to show that they were stronger than the rest tried to reach the target from the greatest distance.[117]

The *Descriptio Cordubae* is the only source that documents the staging of tournaments and jousts in Córdoba. This is not strange, since the Christian kings always showed a preference for Seville (thus keeping the predominant status this city had already attained in Muslim times, when in the eleventh century it became the most important city of al-Andalus).[118] Hence, it was in Seville that tournaments and jousts were held more frequently. For example, some of the kings that staged tournaments in Seville were Alfonso XI (1324), Henry IV (1455),[119] and the Catholic Monarchs (1490).[120]

Fencing

As regards fencing, there are several references, standing out among them a document from 1481 that certifies a fencing exam,[121] which proves the existence by that date of a formal fencing teaching system. The text specifies that two '*maestres*' (masters) examine another '*maestre*' in the modalities of '*esgrima de espada*' (fencing with one-handed sword), '*esgrima de broquel*' (fencing with wood buckler), '*esgrima de espada de dos manos*' (fencing with two-handed sword), '*esgrima de espada y adarga*' (fencing with sword and leather shield), and '*esgrima de espada, capa, lanza y puñal*' (fencing with sword and cape, lance, and poignard). The result of the exam is '*apto*' (a pass).

Sporting Recreations in Christian Córdoba: The Relevant Role of Bullfighting

Bullfighting

As already mentioned, an area of Córdoba called *la Corredera* (that documents of the fourteenth century relate to horse sports) is described by three texts of the fifteenth century as a place for bullfighting.

The first of those texts is dated 1476 and documents the renting of a house in the square of *la Corredera*, in the neighbourhood (*collazión*) of San Pedro. The woman who owns the house reserves for herself the right to watch from the house 'the feasts of bulls and other celebrations and spectacles' (*'las fiestas del toro, regozijos y demás funciones'*).[122] The second text, dated 1492, says that the royal administration sells some goods 'near *la Corredera*, close to the alley where the bulls are kept' (*'baxo de la Corredera, cerca de la calleja donde ençierran los toros'*).[123] The third document is dated 1499 and is about an ecclesiastical dowry consisting of (among other goods) 'one house in Bulls Street, neighbourhood of San Pedro' (*'una casa en la calle de los Toros, collazión de San Pedro'*).[124]

This change of use of *la Corredera* (from horse sports to bullfighting) documents how after the re-conquest, in one century, the bull became the symbol of identity of Christian Córdoba (and of the Christian kingdoms of the Peninsula in general), to the point of displacing the horse from the first place in what concerned spectacles. By the late fifteenth century, bullfighting had become the main and most popular spectacle of Córdoba, since it was staged in the best place of the city.

Hunting

The importance that falconry (and the falcon as the main bird of prey used in it) had in Muslim Córdoba was maintained in the Christian period. It seems that the Christians originally used mainly the goshawk (and never the falcon),[125] but by the time they conquered Córdoba, with the huge amount of perfectly trained falcons existing in the city, they came to appreciate this bird, adding the falcon to the goshawk in the list of birds used by them in falconry. So it is attested in the *Book of Hunting* by Don Juan Manuel (written c. 1325), who says that before king Ferndinand III conquered the city (together with Seville and Jaén), the Christians did not kill the heron with falcons, but with goshawks.[126]

Yet, the goshawk continued to be highly appreciated, and even some sources suggest that the price of a goshawk was higher than that of a falcon. To be precise, in the above-mentioned book by Don Juan Manuel, he says that the fine for stealing a goshawk is double that for stealing a falcon.[127]

The level of development of falconry in the Christian territories reached such heights that there was a job specific to falconry with falcon (he who fulfilled that job was called a *'falconero'*) and a job specific to falconry with goshawks (the one who fulfilled that job was called an *'açorero'*), as documented by the *Book of Accounts and Charges of King Sancho IV the Brave*, written in 1292–1294.[128]

Together with falcons and goshawks, the sparrowhawk also continued to be important in the falconry of Christian Córdoba and south of Spain, as documented by the already-seen commentary by Pero López de Ayala, that 'the best' sparrowhawks are bred in the Cordoban shire of Los Pedroches.

Hunting was normally performed (by the high classes) in areas specifically reserved for that use (and where only the king and those authorized by him could hunt). One of such reserved areas was near Almodovar del Río, reserved by king John II to provide for the meat requirements of those living in the fortress of that city.[129]

Other Considerations About the Sport of Christian Córdoba

The absence of ball games in Córdoba and in almost the whole of the south of the Iberian Peninsula under Christian rule during this period is remarkable because it contrasts with the situation in the Christian kingdoms of the east of the Peninsula, where ball games (such as *pelota valenciana*) were very popular at that time.[130] In Christian Córdoba, also noteworthy is the absence of athletic sports (e.g. foot races, wrestling). Therefore, the sport programme of Christian Córdoba is characterized by being exclusively formed by chivalric sports, something clearly derived from the city's geographical situation (frontier city) and its Muslim past (some important activities in Muslim Córdoba survived into Christian times, such as falconry, *juego de cañas* [Muslim *djerid*], and chess). Some authors have noted the *maurofilia* (respect and admiration for the Muslim culture) of the Christian kingdoms of the Peninsula.[131]

Conclusions

Muslim Córdoba, especially that of the Umayyads, enjoyed the recreations and sports of the Muslim East, but with a low presence of horse and competitive sports (horse races, polo, *djerid*), which were very important in the East. Thus, we could say that the level of Arabization of the sports and recreations of Muslim Córdoba was almost total regarding the diversity of sports and recreations implanted in Córdoba but low regarding the social importance of horse and competitive sport. That greater presence in Córdoba of recreations that did not require physical competition (hunting, falconry or chess) is in line with the low warlike spirit and scant preparation for war of the people of Córdoba. It seems in fact that the low inclination for war of the Cordobans might be what determined their preference for non-competitive recreations over competitive sports and, hence, it could be concluded that the low interest in competitive sport of the Muslim Cordoban society indicates its lack of engagement with war.

For its part, the sport practices of Christian Córdoba distinguish themselves for being essentially of a military nature, with competitive sports (above all horse sports) being very important. The reason for this may be that, unlike caliphal Córdoba, Christian Córdoba was a frontier city, so that all male citizens had to be prepared to go to war, a preparation that seems to have been fulfilled, in part, by the practice of competitive sports (such as tournaments, jousting and fencing). Thus, it could be concluded that the high interest in competitive sport of the Cordoban society of that time indicates its commitment to war. Regarding recreations, in the fifteenth century, bullfighting becomes the main entertainment of the city. The huge success of bullfighting in Córdoba can be explained by the fact that it served to mark and strengthen the identity of that newly founded society.

Notes

1. María Jesús Viguera, 'Territorio y poblamiento', in Antonio Prieto Martín (ed.), *Andalucía Andalusí: del siglo VIII al XIII*, vol. 3 of *Historia de Andalucía* (Sevilla: Planeta, 2006), 35–6.
2. Muhammad Manazir Ahsan, *Social Life Under the Abbasids* (London: Longman, 1979), 243–62; Adam Mez, *El renacimiento del Islam* (Granada: Universidad de Granada, 2002), 454–88, 499–511; and Rachel Arié, *España musulmana (siglos VIII–XV)*, vol. 3 of M. Tuñón de Lara (ed.), *Historia de España* (Barcelona: Labor, 1984), 312–23.
3. John Marshall Carter, 'Sports and Recreations in Thirteenth-Century England: The Evidence of the Eyre and Coroners' Rolls – A Research Note', *Journal of Sport History* 15, no. 2 (1988), 168. Guttmann and others, when dealing with the Middle Ages, consider entertainments with animals as sports: 'Animal sports like bearbaiting are clearly traditional pastimes and, as such, appear anachronistic to those with modern conceptions'. (Allen Guttmann, 'English

Sports Spectators: The Restoration to the Early Nineteenth Century', *Journal of Sport History* 12, no. 2 [1985], 105).

4. Earle F. Zeigler, 'Chivalry's Influence on Sport and Physical Training in Medieval Europe', *Sport History Review* 24, no. 1 (1993), 156.

5. J.A. Mangan, 'Epilogue: Aggression and Androgyny: Gender Fusion In and Beyond Sport in the Post-Millennium', *The International Journal of the History of Sport* 27, nos 1–2 (2010), 471. Mangan is probably the author who has better explained the connection competitive sport-masculinity-war (see also, for example: J.A. Mangan, 'Duty Unto Death: English Masculinity and Militarism in the Age of the New Imperialism', *The International Journal of the History of Sport* 27, nos 1–2 (2010), 134; David D. Gilmore, *Manhood in the Making. Cultural Concepts of Masculinity* (New Haven: Yale University Press, 1990), 122.

6. Timothy Lockley, '"The Manly Game": Cricket and Masculinity in Savannah, Georgia in 1859', *The International Journal of the History of Sport* 20, no. 3 (2003), 77–98, especially 87–8.

7. Elizabeth A. Lehfeldt, 'Ideal Men: Masculinity and Decline in Seventeenth-Century Spain', *Renaissance Quarterly* 61 (2008), 464.

8. Boaz Shoshan, 'High Culture and Popular Culture in Medieval Islam', *Studia Islamica* 73 (1991), 3.

9. Kirk H. Beetz, 'Sports and Recreation in the Medieval Islamic World', http://www.fofweb.com/History/HistRefMain.asp?, paragraph 2 (accessed 10 August 2014).

10. Ahsan, *Life Under the Abbasids*, 207, 243–62; and Mez, *El renacimiento del Islam*, 454–88, 499–511.

11. The system of transliteration from Arabic used in this paper is adopted from the *Encyclopaedia of Islam*, second edition. Arabic names that have a form generally accepted in English have been rendered in that form. Arabic names that do not have a form generally accepted in English have been rendered in their traditional form in Spanish.

12. Polo (*ṣawlajān*) was invented in Persia (the Arabic word derives from Persian *Čawgān*). (Ahsan, *Life Under the Abbasids*, 253, note 50).

13. Several different spellings are known, e.g. *jirid, jereed, çavgan, garid, cirit* (in Turkish).

14. Gülhan Benli, 'The Use of Courtyards and Open Areas in the Ottoman Period in İstanbul', in M. Özyavuz (ed.), *Environmental Sciences* (Istanbul: Florya Campus, 2013), 812; and Louis Mercier, *La Parure des cavaliers et l'insigne des preux* (París: Paul Geuthner, 1923), 403.

15. Ahsan, *Life Under the Abbasids*, 255.

16. Mez, *El renacimiento del Islam*, 487 (original sources included).

17. The cross-bow was a weapon popular among the Persians, being adopted by the Muslims by the mid seventh century (Ahsan, *Life Under the Abbasids*, 258).

18. Wrestling was very popular among all ranks of society, from the lower classes to the caliphs themselves. Besides, some caliphs did not limit themselves to watching the matches, but even joined in personally. For example, Caliph Amin took part in many matches, including one against a lion (with teeth and claws removed, we suppose). Facing lions seems to have been popular among caliphs in order to show their physical power, because apart from the previous episode by Amin, it is also attested that Caliph Mutadid entered a combat with a lion, though on this occasion he did not use wrestling (as Amin) but a sword to beat it, killing the feline with two strokes (Ahsan, *Life Under the Abbasids*, 261).

19. Animal fights were considered unlawful by the Sharia (because animals were hurt). See ibid., 261. In fact, as pointed out by Ahsan (ibid., 262), Caliph Muhtadi Billah (869–870), just after becoming caliph, 'banned all fighting between animals, ordering the beasts in the royal zoo to be killed immediately'. Yet, this measure did not last for long, because the court circle disliked such a severe decision. Muhtadi became unpopular (for measures like that), and as soon as he was assassinated animal fights were tolerated again.

20. Ahsan, *Life Under the Abbasids*, 243. About sport, see chapter 5 (202–38) and chapter 6 (243–72).

21. Alastair Northedge, 'The Racecourses at Samarra', *Bulletin of the School of Oriental and African Studies* 53 (1990), 48.

22. Ibid., 48, 52; Ahmad Ibn Hanbal, *Musnad* (Cairo: 1313), vol. II, 86, 91; and Franz Rosenthal, *Gambling in Islam* (Leiden: Brill, 1975), 97–9.
23. Northedge, 'The Racecourses at Samarra', 50.
24. Ibid., 49.
25. Ibid., 49.
26. Ibid., 51 y 53; al-Mas'udi, *Muruj*, VI, 348–9; Muhammad b. 'Abdus al-Jahshiyari (c. 920), *Kitab al-wuzara' wa 'l-kuttab* (redited Cairo: Mustafa al-Babi al-Halabi, 1938), 207–8.
27. Northedge, 'The Racecourses at Samarra', 50–1; and al-Jahshiyari, *Kitab al-wuzara'*, 207–8.
28. Northedge, 'The Racecourses at Samarra', 42 and following pages.
29. Ibid., 47.
30. Ibid., 51.
31. Ibid., 52.
32. Darab Dastur Peshotan Sanjana (c. 600). *Kârnâm î Artaakhshîr Pâpakân* (Bombay: The Education Society's Steam Press, 1896). See also Houchang E. Chehabi and Allen Guttmann, 'From Iran to All of Asia: The Origin and Diffusion of Polo', *The International Journal of the History of Sport* 19, nos 2–3 (2002), 385; and Darab Dastur Peshotan Sanjana, *The Kârnâm î Artaakhshîr Pâpakân* (Bombay: Education Society's Steam Press, 1896), 6–7.
33. Chehabi, 'From Iran to All of Asia', 385.
34. Ibid., 391.
35. Ibid., 391.
36. Chehabi, 'From Iran to All of Asia', 388; Ferdowsi, *The Epic of the Kings*, trans. Reuben Levy (London: Routledge & Kegan Paul, 1977), 97–8.
37. Chehabi, 'From Iran to All of Asia', 386, note 12; and Kai Ka'us ibn Iskandar, *A Mirror for Princes*, trans. Reuben Levy (London: Cresset Press, 1951), 86.
38. Chehabi, 'From Iran to All of Asia', 386.
39. Chehabi, 'From Iran to All of Asia', 386, note 15; Mowlana Jalâleddin Rumi, *Fihi ma fi hi*, in A.J. Arberry, *Discourses of Rumi* (London: John Murray, 1975), 146.
40. Chehabi, 'From Iran to All of Asia', 386.
41. Khaled Soufi, *Los Banu Yahwar en Córdoba 1031–1070 d.J.C.* (Córdoba: Real Academia de Córdoba, 1968), 106. 'Garid' in this source. The game of *djerid* was adopted by the peoples of the surrounding area, mostly during the times of the Anatolian Seljuks (1077–1307) (Abdullah Özen, Sebahattin Devecioglu, and Rahsan Ozen, 'Equestrian Games in Turkish History', *F. Ü. Sağ. Bil. Vet. Derg.* 26, no. 3 (2012), 201).
42. Benli, 'The Use of Courtyards', 812.
43. Joachim Gierlichs, 'Horse Games in Islamic Art', in A. Amendt (ed.), *Horse Games – Horse Sports: From Traditional Oriental Games to Modern and Olympic Sport* (Beirut: Arab Scientific Publishers, 2012), 54.
44. Ibrahim Yildiran and Tolga Sinoforoglu 'Revival of the *Djerid* Game in Turkey', in A. Amendt (ed.), *Horse Games – Horse Sports: From Traditional Oriental Games to Modern and Olympic Sport* (Beirut: Arab Scientific Publishers, 2012), 81.
45. Mez, *El renacimiento del Islam*, 484.
46. Emilio García-Gómez, 'Introducción a la España Musulmana', in E. Levi-Provençal (ed.), *España Musulmana hasta la caída del Califato de Córdoba (711–1031 de J.C.)*, vol. 4 of *Historia de España* (Pidal. Madrid: Espasa Calpe, 1954), IX–XXXVI.
47. Évariste Levi-Provençal, 'La sociedad andaluza', in R. Menéndez Pidal (ed.), *España musulmana. Instituciones y vida social e intelectual*, vol. 5 of *Historia de España* (Madrid: Espasa Calpe, 1965), 93–105.
48. María Jesús Viguera, 'Historia política', in Antonio Prieto Martín (ed.), *Andalucía Andalusí: del siglo VIII al XIII*, vol. 3 of *Historia de Andalucía* (Sevilla: Planeta, 2006), 45.
49. García-Gómez, 'Introducción a España musulmana', IX–XXXVI.
50. Henri Pérès, *Esplendor de Al-Ándalus* (Madrid: Hiperión, 1953), 23–8.
51. Levi-Provençal, 'La sociedad andaluza', 100.

52. Évariste Levi-Provençal, *España Musulmana hasta la caída del Califato de Córdoba (711–1031 de J.C.)*, in vol. 4, R. Menéndez Pidal (ed.), *Historia de España* (Madrid: Espasa Calpe, 1954), 39–44.

53. Levi-Provençal, 'La sociedad andaluza', 286 (polo and hunting) and 285 (falconry); and Pérès, *Esplendor de Al-Ándalus*, 347–8 (chess).

54. Fernando de la Granja, *Estudios de historia de Al Ándalus* (Madrid: Real Academia de la Historia, 1999), 254; and Antonio Arjona, *Historia de Córdoba en el califato omeya* (Córdoba: Almuzara, 2010), 46. Arjona explains how Muslims and Christians celebrated together the Christian festivities of New Year (*nayruz* in Arab), the birth of Jesus (*milad*), and the birth of John the Baptist (*mihrayān*, *ansara*), because the Muslims of Córdoba were descended in their majority from Christians and, consequently, they did not wish to give up celebrating those festivities.

55. Granja, *Estudios de historia*, 256, 267, 269, 270; Ahmad Al-Wansarisi, (c. 1480), *Al-Miyar*, edited in five volumes by Muhammad Hayyi (Rabat: Ministry of the Awqaf and Islamic Issues of Morocco, 1981), XI, 115–17; and Pérès, *Esplendor de Al-Ándalus*, 263.

56. Levi-Provençal, *España musulmana*, 286. See also Arié, *España Musulmana*, 316. Horse races really become important in Granada from the thirteenth century onwards.

57. Fragment in Pérès, *Esplendor de Al-Ándalus*, 348: 'My eyes can testify it, I've compared her [the crescent moon] to a curved stick on the point of hitting the ball'. See also Levi-Provençal, *España musulmana*, 286 and Mez, *El renacimiento del Islam*, 486.

58. Pérès, *Esplendor de Al-Ándalus*, 263.

59. Mez, *El renacimiento del Islam*, 484.

60. Isa Ibn Ahmad Al-Razi (c. 975), *Anales palatinos del Califa de Córdoba Al Hakam II* (edited and translated by Emilio García-Gómez (Madrid: Sociedad de estudios y publicaciones, 1967), 229–32.

61. Ibid., 23. See also Emilio Cabrera, 'Aproximación a la imagen de la Córdoba islámica', *Historia, Instituciones, Documentos* 25 (1998), 73–94 and Arjona, *Historia de Córdoba*, 75–6. According to Arjona, those exhibitions were performed on the day those riders received their pay, and consisted in intricate drills on horseback. The admiration of the caliph had started in the past, when he had fought the Hassaniyan Berbers in North Africa, and he admired them because of the skill and valour they showed riding their horses.

62. Al-Razi, *Anales palatinos de Alhakam II*, 264.

63. Abu al-Hasan 'Ali Ibn Bassam al-Santarini, (c. 1120). *Dajira*. (Reedited in Cairo: Matba'at Layna al-Ta'lif wa-l-taryama wa-l-Nasr, 1939), I-1, 140–7.

64. Ali Ibn Ahmad Ibn Hazm (c. 1023). *El collar de la paloma* (edited and translated by Emilio García-Gómez (Madrid: Alianza, 2007), 187.

65. José Miguel Puerta, 'La Alhambra de Granada: poder, arte y utopía', *Cuadernos de la Alhambra* 23 (1987), 74.

66. Abu Marwán Hayyán Ibn Khalaf Ibn Hayyan al-Qurtubi (c. 1030), *Al-Muqtabis* (edited in Beirut: Dar al-Kitab al-'Arabi, 1973), I, folio 174 vº; Levi-Provençal, *España musulmana*, 285; and Arié, *España Musulmana*, 312.

67. Arjona, *Historia de Córdoba*, 32.

68. Ibid.

69. Ahsan, *Life Under the Abbasids*, 207.

70. Levi-Provençal, 'La sociedad andaluza', 286.

71. Pérès, *Esplendor de Al-Ándalus*, 351.

72. Francisco Juez, 'La cetrería en la iconografía andalusí', *Anales de Historia del Arte* 7 (1997), 71; and Pérès, *Esplendor de Al-Ándalus*, 350.

73. Ahsan, *Life Under the Abbasids*, 216.

74. Évariste Levi-Provençal, *La Peninsule iberique au Moyen age d'après le Kitab al-Rawd al-mitar d'Ibn Abd al-Mun'im al-Himayari* (Leiden: E.J. Brill, 1938), 314.

75. Ibid., 314.

76. Arié, *España Musulmana*, 314. See also: Juez, 'Cetrería en iconografía andalusí', 72.

77. Ibid., 68; Arié, *España Musulmana*, 315.

78. Pero López de Ayala (1385), *Libro de la caza de las aves* (re-edited in Madrid: Castalia, 1980), chapter 42: '*e de los gavilanes en España los mejores, que yo sepa, e mayores e de mayor esfuerço son los que se crian en el pedroche, que es en termino de Cordova*'.

79. Mez, *El renacimiento del Islam*, 483, 484, 487.

80. Arié, *España Musulmana*, 316.

81. Soufi, *Banu Yahwar en Córdoba*, 113.

82. Ibn Jaldun, *K. al-'Ibar*, IV, 144, (in Pérès, *Esplendor de Al-Ándalus*, 247).

83. Mez, *El renacimiento del Islam*, 487.

84. Arjona, *Historia de Córdoba*, 36.

85. In Pérès, *Esplendor de Al-Ándalus*, 294.

86. Anonymous (c. 1150), *Libro del ajedrez, de sus problemas y sutilezas; de autor árabe desconocido*, vol. II, ed. Félix Pareja (Madrid: Publicaciones de las escuelas de estudios árabes de Madrid y Granada, 1935), vol. II, LXII.

87. Ibid., vol. II, XXI–XXV.

88. Ibid., vol. II, Li.

89. Reinhart P. Dozy, *Historia de los musulmanes de España* (Madrid: Turner, 1988), vol. 4, 136–9; Levi Provençal, 'España musulmana', 288; Pérès, *Esplendor de Al-Ándalus*, 347.

90. Anonymous, *Libro del ajedrez*, vol. II, LXXIII–LXXVIII.

91. Ibid., vol. II, LXXIII.

92. A little wooden horse replica (Ahsan, *Life Under the Abbasids*, 274), a stick horse, a hobby horse (Pérès, *Esplendor de Al-Ándalus*, 347), and a skirted hobby horse (Max Harris, 'From Iraq to the English Morris: The Early History of the Skirted Hobbyhorse', *Medieval English Theatre* 25 (2003), 73).

93. Ahsan, *Life Under the Abbasids*, 274.

94. Harris, 'From Iraq to', 73.

95. Pérès, *Esplendor de Al-Ándalus*, 347.

96. Soufi, *Banu Yahwar en Córdoba*, 117. The captain's name was Muhammad Ibn Martin. Harris, 'From Iraq to', 77 also refers to this episode. Both Pérès and Harris believe that in this episode a skirted hobby horse was used in the game-dance. See also Pérès, *Esplendor de Al-Ándalus*, 347.

97. Évariste Levi-Provençal, *La civilización árabe en España* (Madrid: Espasa Calpe, 1982), 116.

98. Arié, *España Musulmana*, 320.

99. Fragments from poems by Ibn Zaydun: 'And these pleasant evenings at Malik reservoir (*musannāt Mālik*), where I interchanged my cup with my friends or I gave myself over to swimming' (in Pérès, *Esplendor de Al-Ándalus*, 136) ... 'they drank in the inns built beside the bank and they gave themselves over to the pleasure of swimming or rowing' (ibid., 138).

100. Fragment of a poem by Ibn al-Labbaba: 'Sirens are seen then flying with black wings like those of ravens, whereas other boats are a same number of gyrfalcons [*šawdaq*]' (fragment in ibid., 352).

101. María Jesús Viguera, 'Sociedad', in *Andalucía Andalusí: del siglo VIII al XIII*, vol. 3 of *Historia de Andalucía* (directed by Antonio Prieto Martín. Sevilla: Planeta, 2006), 91.

103. Juan Carlos Fernández Truán, 'El deporte en Sefarad durante la Edad Media', *Revista do História do Esporte* 1, no. 1 (2008), 1–36.

104. Levi-Provençal, *Civilización árabe en España*, 65.

105. Ibid., 67–72.

106. Levi-Provençal, *España musulmana*, 279. According to him, there would be around 300 baths in the Córdoba of Abd-ar-Rahman III and around 600 in that of Almanzor.

107. Antonio Collantes, 'Las realidades económicas y sociales; el mundo urbano', in M. González (ed.), *El nacimiento de Andalucía*, vol. 4 of *Historia de Andalucía* (Sevilla: Planeta, 2006), 49.

108. Miguel Ángel Ladero, 'Sobre la génesis medieval de la identidad andaluza', in M. González (ed.) *El nacimiento de Andalucía*, vol. 4 of *Historia de Andalucía* (Sevilla: Planeta, 2006), 158–9.

109. Joaquín Centeno, *Los jurados de Córdoba, 1454–1579* (Córdoba: Universidad de Córdoba, 2000), 91.

110. Ibid., 98.

111. Ibid., 93.
112. Levi-Provençal, *Civilización árabe en España*, 125. Levi-Provençal describes the men from the kingdoms of Castile and Aragon as individuals marked by the Reconquest, with a high (often exacerbated) warlike spirit.
113. Centeno, *Los jurados de Córdoba*, 92.
114. Document kept at the archive of the cathedral of Córdoba: A.- acc, caj. T, n.457, per. 284×136 mm. B.- BCC, ms.125, fol.110rv. Copy of c. 1318. REG.-GCN, Catálogo, p.250, n. 293. CIT.-CVV, t. 258, fol.44v. (about la *collazión* de San Pedro de Córdoba en la Corredera): 'do bofordan ... Facta carta tres días del mes de agosto era M.CCC e diez e seys annos'; See also Manuel Nieto, *Islam y cristianismo* (Córdoba: Monte de Piedad y Caja de Ahorros de Córdoba, 1984), 238.
115. Document kept at the archive of the cathedral of Córdoba: A.- acc,caj. T, n-393, per.407×175 mm. B.- BCC, ms.125, 96 rv. Copy of c.1328, REG.-GCN, Catálogo, p. 247, n. 256: '... Facta carta veynte e tres días del mes de abril en era de mil e tresientos e ueynte e un anno'; See also nieto, *Islam y cristianismo*, 238.
116. The original manuscript of the *Descriptio Cordubae* is kept at the archive of the cathedral of Salamanca, Biblioteca del Colegio Trilingüe, signatura Est.4, Caj.8, núm. 18.
117. Jerónimo Sánchez (c. 1481), *Descriptio Cordubae* (ed. Manuel Nieto in *Córdoba en el siglo XV*. Córdoba: Diputación provincial de Córdoba, 1973), folio 50 and 51.
118. Christine Mazzoli-Guintard, 'Andalucía urbana: ciudades en al-Ándalus', in M.J. Viguera-Molins (ed.), *Andalucía en al-Ándalus*, vol. 3 of *Historia de Andalucía* (Sevilla: Planeta, 2006), 185.
119. The occasion was the wedding of Henry to Juana of Portugal. The wedding was held in Córdoba, but the couple quickly moved to Seville, where the tournament was held (Pedro Barrantes (1857), *Ilustraciones de la Casa de Niebla* (Reprint, Cádiz: Universidad de Cádiz, 1998), 370).
120. The occasion was the festivities to say farewell to their daughter Isabel, who was to leave for Portugal to marry Prince Alfonso, heir to the Portuguese throne (Hernando de Pulgar (c. 1492), *Crónica de la vida de los señores reyes católicos* (edited by Juan de Mata Carriazo), (Madrid: Espasa-Calpe, 1943), 369).
121. Document of the Archivo Provincial de Córdoba, Oficio 18, cuaderno 28, sin foliar, 4 de abril 1496. APCO.- Oficio 14, n. 15–536. 24 de febrero de 1481.
122. Anonymous (c.1476). *Libro de hacienda del Convento de la Purísima Concepción de Córdoba* (kept at Archivo General del Obispado de Córdoba), Fol.183v.
123. Document caj. D, n 84 of the archive of the cathedral of Córdoba.
124. Document caj, L, n.517, perg.- 735×535.mm. Copy of 1516. Archive of the cathedral of Córdoba.
125. The goshawk was used in the north of Spain (where there were many woods) because it was smaller than the falcon, so it flew better among trees, with the added advantage that the goshawk hunts on the ground (the falcon does not hunt on the ground, only in the air).
126. Don Juan Manuel (c. 1325). *El libro de la caza* (edited by José María Castro) (Barcelona: Instituto Antonio de Nebrija, 1945), VIII: 'la caça de los falcones altaneros vino a Castiella después que el sancto rey don Ferrando, que ganó Alendeluzía, casó con la reina doña Beatriz, que en ante d'esto dizen que non matavan la garça con falcones, sinon con açores'. That wedding was celebrated in 1219. See also Juez, 'Cetrería en iconografía andalusí', 72.
127. Don Juan Manuel, *Libro de la caza*, 235: 'Todo hombre que robe un azor fuera de su percha o que esté cazando, debe pagar C sueldos de multa, si es mudado pagará C sueldos por cada muda. Si roba un halcón, la multa será de L sueldos, y, si el halcón es mudado, pagará L sueldos más por cada muda'.
128. Asunción López-Dapena, *Cuentas y gastos (1292–1294) del rey D. Sancho IV el Bravo (1284–1295)* (Córdoba: Monte de Piedad y Caja de Ahorros de Córdoba, 1984), 219.
129. José Manuel de Bernardo, *Textos histórico-geográficos de Córdoba y su provincia* (Córdoba: Diputación Provincial de Córdoba, 1988), 294.

130. María Luisa Rodrigo, 'Deporte, juego y espectáculo en la España medieval: Aragón, siglos XIII–XV', *Estudios del Hombre* 23 (2007), 37–88, especially page 50.
131. Amelia García-Valdecasas and R. Beltrán, 'La maurofilia como ideal caballeresco en la literatura cronística del XIV y XV', *Epos: Revista de filología* 5 (1989), 131.

Disclosure statement

No potential conflict of interest was reported by the authors.

Art Works as Sources for Sport History Research: The Example of 'Sports Allegory/The Crowning of the Athletes' by Charles Louis Frédy de Coubertin

Natalia Camps Y Wilant

ABSTRACT

Sport historians rarely use works of art as sources for their research. The main challenge they face is the difficulty to draw information and insights from the paintings that lie beyond what is apparent at first glance. This paper introduces the art historical methodology of iconological analysis that is of benefit to sport historians. This three-step approach is a tool for interpreting art works and contextualizing them with relevant biographical and societal information that influenced the artist's life and work. The art work analyzed in this paper is the painting 'Sports Allegory/The Crowning of the Athletes' by Pierre de Coubertin's father, the artist Charles Louis Frédy de Coubertin (1822–1908). This painting was chosen because of its relevance and importance to Olympic history. Up to now this piece has not been critically analyzed in sport history, and hence hardly any documentation on it can be found.

Introduction

Among many others a visitor to the Musée d`Orsay will enjoy paintings such as Maurice Denis' 'Badminton' (1900), Gustave Caillebotte's 'Sailboats at Argenteuil' (around 1888) and Edgar Degas' 'The Parade' (between 1866 and 1868). The paintings have in common that they depict sports and physical activities. Art historical monographs about the painters mention sport-related topics in their works only *en-passant*. A recent example is the exhibition 'Degas – Klassik und Experiment'.[1] Next to Degas' famous ballet dancers are shown seven works depicting horse race scenes. The corresponding sport historical background is briefly explained by the German art historian Alexander Eiling:

> Sport coming from England had already established itself in the late 18th century in France, but only began to play a greater role with the opening of the racetracks of Chantilly (1824), Versailles (1836) and especially Longchamps (1857). Before Napoleon III had given the order to construct a tribune on the foundations of the monastery of Longchamps in the Bois de Boulogne, which was only about ten kilometers from the center of Paris. Since then the finer society went on a pilgrimage to the city gates to watch the races in the local Hippodrome and to participate at related events, which were organized by the elitist Jockey Club.[2]

What about art works in sport history research? The German sport historians Norbert Gissel, Michael Krüger and Hans Langenfeld list art works, statues, drawings and paintings among the sources for research in sport history.[3] However only few examples can be found. One is the work by Allen Guttmann.[4] In *Sport and American Art – From Benjamin West to Andy Warhol*, he describes how artists documented 400 years of sports development in the United States in their works. Gigliola Gori frequently refers to paintings in her research. Such as in her early work *Gli Etruschi e lo Sport* (1986) and more recently in *Female Bodies and Italian Fascism: Submissive Woman and Strong Mothers* (2004) or 'The Amazing Participation of Female Teams in Rowing Contests Organized by the Serenissima Republic of Venice', where paintings helped to reconstruct the history of female rowers in Venice.[5] A third example is the research by Roland Renson and Herman Smulders, in which they used art works to illustrate the development of physical activity games in Belgium, as for example in the project *Bruegel Revisited*, which was realized in 1979.[6] Concentrating on representations of boxing, the French historians Christian Vivier and Jean-Francois Loudcher, documented its historical development in their work published in 2007. Whereas the Polish Agata Grabowska explained in her presentation held in 2001, how Polish artists represented sports and physical activities.[7]

In all these examples the researchers acknowledge that art works provide detailed accounts of different times and therefore information, which is exploitable for their research. This 'academic value' of art works was also recognized by Wray Vamplew:

> Most academic sport historians generally prefer text ... What is required for sport historians is that they step outside the archive room and into the exhibition galleries, to add another dimension to their work. Sports museums can help us change by complimenting our literary text approach by emphasizing the visual, a component often neglected in the world of sports history scholarship ... [W]orks of art [could detail] impressions of sport from one person's view ...[8]

If art works are such profitable sources for historians, then why are they not used more often for their research? There are many reasons for the insufficient use of artworks as sources for sport historical research. The Swiss art historian Jean-Christoph Ammann observed some general reactions for situations in which people encounter art works, among them confusion and lack of knowledge.[9] Illustrative examples are the paintings and sculptures of the so called *Futurists*.[10] By using artistic means, for example changing colours and perspectives, artists present a reality which may be quite different from the reality we know and experience.

The representation of a changed reality is the main reason, because it is difficult to 'read and decode the information' which is presented by the artist. To overcome the reasons for the reluctant use of artworks in sport historical research, appropriate research methods are needed. This need was already postulated by Vamplew: 'As professionals, sport historians certainly need education to broaden their methodology both in teaching and research'.[11]

This paper explains how an art historical method can be used to enrich sport history research. The example is the international accepted *iconology* developed by the German art historian Erwin Panofsky in 1955.[12] The reason for choosing this method is its gradual approach towards the information within an art work through a set of analytical steps.

In this paper *iconology* is applied to the painting 'Sports Allegory/The Crowning of the Athletes' by Charles Louis Frédy de Coubertin. In the first step key elements of the painting are identified and their representational patterns are compared to art historical traditions.

Then it continues with a focus on the artist, the search for (additional) evidence he left and information on how the artist 'acted' in different contexts. The results of the analytical steps or findings help to explain the elements in the painting, to decode the message(s) and to gain an understanding of the artist's intention.

State of Research

The Artist and the Painting

The example used in this paper is the painting 'Sports Allegory/The Crowning of the Athletes'. The painter is Charles Louis Frédy de Coubertin (1822–1908), father of Pierre de Coubertin and a successful nineteenth-century painter. The painting is signed and dated to 1896 on the lower right corner and belongs to the collection of the Olympic Museum in Lausanne (Switzerland). The following sections take a closer look at the publications about the painting and the artist.

The Painting in Sport Historical Publications

The inventories of the Olympic Museum in Lausanne have some information about the painting. The first inventory, dated around 1953, lists the painting without title. In the second inventory from 1970, it is entitled 'Sports Allegory/The Crowning of the Athletes' ('Allégorie aux sports/Couronnement des Athlètes').[13] Under this title it is noted that it forms part of the recent exhibition of the Olympic Museum.

The earliest publication addressing the painting was the article 'Theories of Beauty and Modern Sport' by the Canadian Douglas Brown in 1997. He stated that Charles de Coubertin was inspired by an article written by his son, Pierre, when thinking about a title for his painting.[14] It was the article 'Le rétablissement des Jeux Olympiques' in the *Revue de Paris* in June 1894.[15] Accordingly, Brown entitled the painting 'Reintroduction of the Olympic Games – Allegory of Sports'. Although Brown brought the painting into the academic discourse, sport historians neither claimed a detailed description nor further sources as evidence. Also the contraction in the use of the titles has not been addressed yet.

Brown's work influenced later authors, such as the Austrian historian Erwin Niedermann or the American historian Lia Paradis.[16] Surprisingly both authors follow Brown's argumentation in an uncritical manner providing no evidence either.

The most recent examples are two exhibition catalogues. When it was exhibited outside the Olympic museum, the curators of these exhibitions adapted the title according to Brown's article. Norbert Müller and Christian Wacker refer to the painting as 'Reintroduction of the Olympic Games – Allegory of Sports' in the accompanying catalogue for the exhibition 'Pierre de Coubertin et les arts' which took place in Cologne in 2007/2008. Research uncovered that the exhibition had been conceptualized as a road show and that the painting was exhibited in several Olympic and/or sports museums in Europe as 'Reintroduction of the Olympic Games – Allegory of Sports'. It was exhibited in Warsaw (Poland) in 2004 and in 2009, in Cologne (Germany) between 2007 and 2008, in Paris (France) in 2009, and in Hattingen (Germany) in 2010.[17] Here the painting was part of an exhibition dedicated to heroes. The authors of the sport related part of the corresponding catalogue Robert Laube and Uwe Wick adopted the same title.[18]

Next to written sources, there is visual evidence in Olympic history research. First, there are 'printed reproductions' of Charles' painting 'Sports Allegory/The Crowning of the Athletes'. From 1901 until 1914 Pierre de Coubertin used a reproduction of his father's painting as covers for his *Revue Olympic*, a magazine, in which Coubertin wrote about his Olympic ideas and informed about the activities of the International Olympic Committee.[19] Recent publications about the modern Olympic Games use reproductions of this painting, too. Examples are a special issue of the *Journal of Olympic History* published in 2009 and the book *The International Olympic Committee: One Hundred Years, 1894–1994* by the Swiss Raymond Gafner from 1994.[20] So far sport historians did not find any explanation why Pierre used his father's painting for his journal. Even authors who did extensive biographical research about Pierre de Coubertin's life owe an answer to this question.[21] Second, there are photographs of the 'Sports Allegory/The Crowning of the Athletes'. One example shows a photograph of the artist in his studio with the painting on an easel next to him from 1898.[22] The second, recently discovered example shows the painting in Pierre de Coubertin's private museum in Mon Repos.[23] This finding proves Laube and Wick's statement right that the painting decorated Pierre de Coubertin's office during his lifetime.[24]

The examples emphasize the contradiction between the recent title 'Sports Allegory/The Crowning of the Athletes' and the title used in academic discourse – 'Reintroduction of the Olympic Games – Allegory of Sports'. This paper uses the recent title, because the inventories of the Olympic Museum are older than Brown's findings.

The Painting in Art Historical Publications

Charles de Coubertin does not appear in literature about French artists of the nineteenth century, neither does his *oeuvre*. Consequently, no published information about the painting was found. Fortunately, some information about the artist could be found. Sources which confirm his success are two articles in the issue of 1861 and 1870 in the *Gazette des Beaux-Arts*, an international leading art magazine published in France.[25] Additionally in the book by the French Louis Jourdan Charles de Coubertin is listed among the participants of the Salon 1859.[26] The *Salon* with its full title being *Salon de Peinture, Gravure, Sculpture et d' Architecture des Artistes Vivantes* was the most important artistic event in Paris for 90 years.[27]

These examples allow the drawing of two conclusions. First, they complement Müller and Wacker's argument of Charles' artistic success.[28] And second the available evidence for Charles de Coubertin's success illustrates that the artist has been wrongfully dismissed. The following sections pinpoint the missed information.

Methodological Approach to the Analysis of a Painting

As the information about the painting is scarce, the idea is to see if the information within the painting can be decoded. Therefore an interdisciplinary approach is applied. Art history research provides a helpful tool for 'decoding' the information in art works – the iconology; developed by the art historian Erwin Panofsky.[29]

The systematic analytical approach enables the interpretation of pieces of art by considering different types of information, like for example biographical, societal and historical information. To avoid misunderstandings concerning the result of the interpretation, it is crucial to emphasize that an iconological analysis does not lead to the only interpretation of

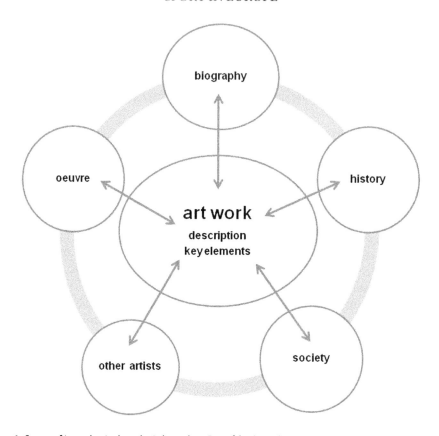

Figure 1. Steps of iconological analysis based on Panofsky (1955).

an art work. The results depend on the sources used. To understand the artist's intentions it is recommended to search for all biographical information available which can be included in the iconological analysis, enabling a decoding of the 'message'. Written statements by the artists about his or her art works, like correspondence of diary notes, serve as examples.[30]

The illustration above was developed to show the steps of the iconological analysis and to make Panofsky's theoretical approach more comprehensible (Figure 1).

The first step of the iconological analysis, represented in the centre of the illustration, is a description of the painting. By answering the question 'What can be seen?' all elements are denominated.

For 'Allegory of Sports/The Crowning of the Athletes' a condensed description of the main characteristics reads as follows: In the centre of the painting there are pedestal stairs, around which three groups of persons are positioned. In the middle, on the pedestal stairs there is a group of three persons. A female, the only one in the painting, wears a helmet and armour. A man kneels at her feet and bows his head to receive a wreath from the woman's hand. Above them a figure dressed in a pink cape is floating in the air. A second man stands aside and observes the scenery. At the foot of the stairs another man watches the scene leaning on a horse. On the right side of the painting, in the front, there is a group of 12 persons all dressed in tunics. In the background there are the ruins of a temple. On the left side in the front, two men are arriving in a boat. On the shore a group of three men on bicycles are arriving. In the background sailboats are cruising on a river in front of a skyline. The upper part of the painting is unusual as it ends in a semicircular arch. In each top corner there is a letter band, with a name written on it.

A standard description according to the iconological method comprises a description of the colour palette and the working techniques, like the brush strokes. As the purpose of this paper is the introduction of the iconography, the painting is not considered in relation to all these topics. Only some elements are chosen as examples. Doing the iconological analysis with all elements of the 'Allegory of Sports/The Crowning of the Athletes' would lead far beyond an introduction.

The second step within the analytical approach, called key elements in the graph, takes into consideration how things are positioned in the painting and how they are represented. In the analysis they are compared to traditional 'representational patterns' known in art history. In this context the topic chosen by an artist to convey his message is crucial, too.

This paragraph describes two key elements of the 'Allegory of Sports/The Crowning of the Athletes'. First, the cities of Paris and Athens. They are identified by the letter bands at each top corner of the painting and emphasized a second time by the architectural elements of the Eiffel tower and the ruins of the temple of the Erechteion. Second, the persons in the painting. On the left side the athletes can be easily identified by their sports equipment. This paper focuses on rugby, fencing and polo. For the persons on the right side their antique garments give a hint. Müller and Wacker describe them as 'representatives of the Greek people', and Laube and Wick describe them as 'citizens of ancient Athens'.[31] More difficult is the identification of the person between the goddess Athena and the rugby player in the centre of the painting. Laube and Wick assume that it is the god Apollo.[32] A comparison to representations of the God Apollo in art history allows a verification of the assumption. The first example is a Roman fresco in the Domus Aurea in Rome and entitled 'Science and Art' (20 b. Chr.). The painting the 'Apotheoses of Federico Zuccari' (1598) by the Italian artist Federico Zuccari is the second example.[33] Both examples represent the God Apollo in a pink cape. Charles de Coubertin's use of the 'representational pattern' of the pink cape confirms Laube and Wick's assumption. Also Müller and Wacker refer to 'compositional elements' in the 'Sports Allegory – Crowning of the Athletes', too. Focusing on the grouping of people and the pedestal stairs, Müller and Wacker draw parallels to the painting the 'Apotheosis of Homer' by the French painter Dominique Ingres.[34] Although the authors compare de Coubertin's painting to works of other artists, they fail to indicate the sources properly. Additionally Laube and Wick point out the anachronistic mix of architectural elements and figures.[35] An art historical example provides evidence. The Italian artist Raffael (1483–1520) used the compositional aspect of grouping persons in his work 'The School of Athens' (1511).[36] Charles de Coubertin's art teacher, François-Édouard Picot (1786–1868), used this compositional element as well as for example in his work 'L' Etude et le Génie dévoilent l'antique Egypte à la Grèce' (1827).[37]

Concerning the question why Charles de Coubertin used an allegorical topic for his painting, two assumptions can be made. The first purpose might have been to summarize complexity. Indeed, the 'Sports Allegory/The Crowning of the Athletes' shows a mixture of ruins and athletes and implies a contradiction between antique elements (the ruins) and modern elements (the athletes). By using the artistic mean of allegory Charles de Coubertin 'bridged' this contraction and 'summarized' many ideas. The explanation of the German Art historian Harald Olbrich backs up the artist's intention:

[an allegory] depicts abstract terms, ideas and theoretical coherences by transferring them into a person ... often special attributes, even explanatory texts are needed ... the personification is extended into fictitious plots (for which antique Greek mythology, history, literature as well as the bible serve as guidelines) ... an allusion to historical events.[38]

The second purpose might have been to conform to society's taste at that time. According to the Lebanese art historian, Andrée Sfeir-Semler, allegorical paintings were highly estimated in Paris society at the end of the nineteenth century.[39] As a *Salon* painter, Charles de Coubertin was familiar with the 'rules of the game'.

The first two steps of the iconological analysis allowed key elements (persons and buildings) to be 'identified'. It can be stated that Charles de Coubertin used traditional 'presentational patterns' and 'compositional elements'. He was a confident artist capable of playing with these standards to more fully portray his unique vision. The allegorical frame enabled him to comply with certain purposes. These findings allow continuation with the next step of *iconology*.

The Painting in Relation to Biographical Information

The third iconological step analyzes the painting according to different contexts, represented by the outer circles in the illustration. The purpose here is to search in the artist's background for information which helps to explain the elements in the painting. Therefore different contexts are considered. This section looks for explanations concerning the 'compositional elements', namely the athletes/sports and the cities of Paris and Rome.

At first Charles de Coubertin's knowledge about the paintings by Raffael and Ingres is considered. According to Müller and Wacker he was a student with Edouard Picot. The classical education for artists consisted in attending classes at the Louvre and studying paintings of the 'old masters'.[40] Therefore the assumption concerning Ingres painting can be verified. As to Raffael's painting, evidence was found, too. The first source is the book by Pietro Amato in which he explains that Pope Pius IX commissioned a work to Charles de Coubertin.[41] The second source, a sketchbook from 1852, confirms the stay in Rome as Charles drew sights of the city.[42] It has to be added that Charles de Coubertin used the 'composition and representational patterns' of these 'masters' in later works, like for example in 'Le Départ des Missionnaires' (1868).[43] Concerning the 'compositional elements', it is important to mention that evidence was found which allows a comparison with his painting to the work of a contemporary artist. The book cover of *L'Exposition de Paris 1889* has striking similarities with the painting 'Sports Allegory/The Crowning of the Athletes'.[44] The French painter Luigi Loir (1845–1916) used the same 'compositional element' as Charles de Coubertin, for example by dividing the painting into an antique and a modern part.[45] In terms of architectural elements, Luigi Loir used a temple and the skyline of Paris. Figures in antique and modern clothes are present in Loir's painting, too. The main difference is that Luigi Loir used a mirrored perspective compared to Charles de Coubertin's painting.

Unfortunately, concerning the athletes/sports no sources like for example sketches or written sources were found.[46] About the artist's relation to sports and physical activities, not much is known either. According to the descendant Jacques de Navacelle, de Coubertin was not participating in any sport. But still, his 'Sports Allegory/The Crowning of the Athletes' conveys an understanding for the interaction between anatomy, movement and perspectives.

Concerning Paris and Athens, little information was found. The Coubertin family owned a mansion in Paris in the Saint Germain-Luxembourg district.[47] But there is no evidence for any visits to Greece or Athens. His sketchbooks document journeys to other destinations.[48]

As the examples demonstrate, information about Charles de Coubertin is scarce. To overcome the information deficiency, this paper sets its focus to another family member – his son, Pierre de Coubertin. The idea here is to analyze his writings concerning information about his father and to find explanations for elements in the painting.

The first document consulted is Pierre de Coubertin's autobiography *Memoires de jeunesse*, published by Patrick Clastres. About his father Pierre de Coubertin wrote: 'Student of Picot, he had the courage to follow the lessons regularly'.[49] Then there is information in relation to physical activities. According to Pierre, the Coubertin family kept horses in Mirville. 'The soldiers walked about in the park and settled in the empty stables, without concern for the horses that had been hidden there'.[50] It can be assumed that all family members were involved in horseback riding. Consequently, Jacques de Navacelle's statement can be doubted. The second source consists of articles about sport which Pierre de Coubertin wrote for different magazines. The chosen examples illustrate analogies between the 'Sports Allegory/The Crowning of the Athletes' and the articles' contents.

The first example was published in the *Revue de Paris* on 15 June 1894 and was entitled 'Le Rétablissement des Jeux Olympiques'. Therein, Pierre de Coubertin wrote: 'The ancient amateur was fighting for a branch of wild olive'.[51] His father translated the information from the text into the coronation act, in which the goddess Athena puts an olive tree wreath on the head of the rugby player. The text continues explaining the development of different sports from the United States to England and other European countries, as for example rowing and cycling. The fencer in the 'Sports Allegory/The Crowning of the Athletes', standing above all other athletes and witnessing the coronation act, is 'explained' as follows:

> Fencing is there to prove that it is not impossible to achieve the sporting ideal in an almost absolute manner; often a fencer, does not even receive a medal as a token of his victory: we would say that the 'coup de bouton' which ends the attack is the highest award that can be awarded in itself, the only thing a hand holding the sword can accept.[52]

The results of this part of the analysis establish a relation between the 'Sports Allegory/ The Crowning of the Athletes' and the artist's background.

Although information scarcity concerning Charles de Coubertin exists, examples were found which explain links between the painting and the artist's background. However, due to the scarcity of other aspects, for example *œuvre*, 'other artists' and 'society' are not elaborated further. Here additional research is necessary. The approach to use Pierre de Coubertin's writings enables the analysis of the painting's key elements in relation to the context of Olympic history.

The Painting in Relation to Olympic History

The facts that the 'Sports Allegory/The Crowning of the Athletes' belonged to Pierre de Coubertin and was painted by his father are reasons to link it to Olympic history. This section now explores if there are further reasons. It is commonly known that Athens was the host city of the first modern Olympic Games in 1896, while Paris hosted them four years later. This section takes a closer look at the roles these cities played during the first years of Olympic history.

As early as 1894 Paris and Athens were sites for events related to Olympic history. Pierre de Coubertin organized the 'Congrès International Athlétique de Paris' in Paris in June. His book *Une campagne de vingt-et-un ans* gives a good account of it.[53] The 1894 congress provides facts that link to the 'Sports Allegory/The Crowning of the Athletes'. According to the programme the 'Hymne to Apollo' was performed – another analogy between the painting and an event in Olympic history.

During 1894 Pierre de Coubertin also travelled to Athens and gave a speech at the *Parnassos society* there.[54] In the text two important paragraphs about Athens, Pierre de Coubertin wrote:

> The city of Pallas Athena in her white marble dress was totally 'tailored' to the task of capital; it was a wonderful setting for the Olympic Games.[55]

In this sentence there are two elements which Charles de Coubertin composed into his painting: the Goddess Athena and the 'white marble' of the Erechteion. Then there is additional information concerning the choice of the host cities:

> I tried to calculate the financial gain the constant holding of the games in Greece would bring ... So I came very soon to conclude that the determination of the resurrected Olympics in Greece alone would mean the death of my work. I decided to fight with all their might against this intention.[56]

According to Konstantinos Georgiadis, Pierre de Coubertin would have liked to reintroduce the Olympic Games in Paris in relation to the 1900 World Fair.[57]

Elements in the painting do link to the 1900 Olympic Games, as described in the first step of the iconological analysis.[58] A closer look at the history of the Eiffel tower enables the relation of this site to an event in early Olympic history. The construction was assembled for the 1889 World Fair, the same year in which Pierre de Coubertin organized the 'Congrès International pour la propagation des exercises physiques dans l'éducation'.[59] There, school competitions in fencing, horse riding and athletics were part of the congress programme.[60] This means that sport competitions did not only take place during the 1900 World Fair, but also during the World Fair of 1889. Consequently, Charles de Coubertin represented two events in Olympic history by the Eiffel tower: the 1900 Olympic Games and the 1889 congress. Evidence therefore are Charles de Coubertin's familiarity with his son's articles and the similarities with the work of Luigi Loir mentioned previously.

Additional evidence was found in the documentation about the Olympic Games. One example is the first volume of the 1896 official report written by the Greek authors Spyridon Lambros and Nicolaus Politis.[61] All the pages are decorated with watermarks consisting of floral elements. Some of the floral elements appear in the 'Allegory of Sports/The Crowning of the Athletes', like the palm tree wrapping around the letter band. In this context another remark has to be added. Concerning the olive branch, Pierre de Coubertin mentioned it in his article for the *Revue de Paris*, described above already:

> It is this universal youth the representatives of whom should come together from time to time in the most peaceful battlefield, the field of play. Every four years, the twentieth century will see his children gather together sequentially near major capitals of the world for a struggle of strength and a play for the symbolic branch. Oh! no doubt there are many obstacles to overcome to get there.[62]

A second observation about the official report is that it was published in French and Greek. Is it a coincidence that the painting is composed in two parts, as well? This observation remains an assumption, because no evidence was found at this point in time. It is sure that Charles de Coubertin 'used' the inspirations from the first volume only, as the second part of the official reports was published in 1897, one year after the painting was finished.

The 'results' of this part of the analysis prove links between the 'Sports Allegory/The Crowning of the Athletes' and events in early years of Olympic history.

The Painting in Relation to Sport History

The previous two sections explained the biographical and Olympic historical contexts, now the paper focuses on sport history. Therefore, the sports in the painting, represented by the athletes, are compared to the sports of the first modern Olympic Games in 1896. Quickly discrepancies stand out. The painting depicts rowers, cyclists, a polo player, a fencer, a rugby player, and sailors, or better said, sail boats. The official report of the Olympic Games in Athens in 1896 allows identification of those which were Olympic. These were: athletics, fencing, weight lifting, cycling, lawn tennis, shooting, gymnastics, wrestling and swimming.[63] The report informed that sailing and rowing competitions were cancelled due to the lack of nominations and bad weather conditions.[64] Rugby and Polo were not part of the Olympic programme at that time. They became Olympic in 1900.[65] Based on the comparison it can be stated that only two of the sports represented in the painting formed part of the 'Olympic' programme of 1896 – cycling and fencing.

This paper attempts to explain the representation of the non-Olympic sports in the painting. The first example is polo, a respective equestrian sport. The sources consulted therefore were 'early' Olympic history documents as well as Pierre de Coubertin's writings. Albert Krayer published handwritten notes from a working group of the 1894 Olympic congress which list polo as well as sailing, rowing and fencing.[66] The competitions which appear in the official proceedings of this congress were different:

> 5. Organize, if possible, the following competitions at the Olympic Games: athletics, different ball sports, ice skating, fencing, boxing, wrestling, equestrian sport, shooting, gymnastics and cycling.[67]

Although after a visit to Athens in 1895 Pierre de Coubertin complained '[that] the great arena of the riding school was not particularly maintained, yet conveniently located', he was upset, that equestrian sports was not included in the programme.[68] Still the invitation letter for the 1896 Olympic Games addresses this issue:

> Attached was the program of the Games, as I had designed and implemented in the meeting at the Zappeion, however with the exception of the competitions in equestrian sports. Their reason therefore I did never ever get to know.[69]

But finally in the *Bulletin du Comité International des Jeux Olympiques* Pierre de Coubertin informed the IOC members about the infeasibility of the equestrian sports competitions due to transportation problems with the horses and insufficient sports facilities.[70]

The choice of competitions for the Olympic Games Programme might have also been influenced by the foundation of the French National Olympic Committee, too. Its members were representatives of different sports associations and sports clubs like, for example, fencing, gymnastics, polo, sailing, shooting and cycling. Strikingly, all these competitions appeared in the hand-written list of 1894.[71]

Among Pierre de Coubertin's writings some articles were found, which might serve as a third influence factor. In relation to polo, an article entitled 'Equitation' was published in 1890.[72] Three years later he published a second article about polo.[73] According to Jean-Luc Chartier and the *Fédération de Polo Française,* polo was a popular sport in France at the end of the nineteenth century.[74] The first polo matches were played in Dièppe in 1880. In this context the local proximity between the chateaux Mirville of the Coubertin family and Dièppe has to be mentioned. Evidence that local proximity influenced Charles de Coubertin gives the polo pony in the 'Sports Allegory/The Crowning of the Athletes', described before. The painter put a special emphasis on it by positioning it in the centre and by using the so-called 'gazing technique'. The pony looks directly into the beholder's eyes. This technique was commonly used among artists to emphasize special individuals or animals in their works. Charles de Coubertin used this technique in other works, too. An example is the 'Le Départ des Missionnaires', where the young Pierre is the only person looking at the beholder. Unfortunately, up to now there is no supporting evidence upon which this observation could be elaborated further.

The second non-Olympic sport is rugby. In contrast to polo, rugby was not mentioned in the sources of the Olympic Congress of 1894. A possible explanation for the decision to include rugby in the painting might have been personal preferences and the involvement of some family members in this sport. According to the French historian Jean Durry, Pierre de Coubertin took part in a rugby match as a referee in 1892.[75] There are sources which back up this observation. In his book *Une campagne* Baron de Coubertin described the development of rugby:

> In Paris new things lose their appeal fast, for that reason the games were hardly observed there. In the province this was still brand new and you could hear the strangest remarks about the boys ... wrestling in a tangle playing rugby.[76]

According to sport history sources, rugby was a popular sport in France in the nineteenth century. For example, the *Le Havre Athletic Club* had a rugby section already in 1872.[77] It has to be stressed that rugby and football were both played; during a certain time even a mixture of both.[78] About football Pierre de Coubertin wrote: 'The football season was wonderful. Finally, we did not have to play in the small patch of grass at the upper lake in the Bois de Boulogne anymore'.[79] Another description of a football match is the article 'L' Athlètisme, son role et son histoire' published in 1891.[80] In a later issue of the same magazine Pierre de Coubertin published an article about cycling entitled 'En bicyclette'.[81] Another magazine was found in which he wrote again about football – *La Revue de la Prytanéenne.*[82] Considering the fact that he started writing around 1887, this is supposed to be the earliest article about football of Pierre de Coubertin.

The third analytical step leads to the following findings: at this stage of the research Charles de Coubertin's biographical information does not enable an explanation for all elements in the 'Sports Allegory/The Crowning of the Athletes'. Instead, links to his son Pierre de Coubertin are identified. First, the events in early Olympic history and their settings. Second, the choice of sport competitions for the 1896 Olympic Games. The painting depicts all competitions Pierre de Coubertin wished to include in his Olympic programme. The non-Olympic sport depicted in the painting stand for the preparation of grounds and introduction of different modern sports. For example the athletes representing the modern sports are all depicted in movement. The movement symbolizes the introduction of modern sports as a process. The article examples prove a personal interest and involvement of Pierre de Coubertin in these modern sports.

For Charles de Coubertin the 'Sports Allegory – The Crowning of the Athletes' was a perfect way to convey his son's 'abstract' and sometimes contradictory ideas. With all the explanations, derived from the steps of the iconological analysis in mind, the reasons why Charles had chosen an allegorical representation becomes clearer. On the one hand it allows a bridge to be formed between the contradiction between Olympic and non-Olympic sport competitions. And on the other hand it met the taste of society. A quotation from the article of 1894 picks up vividly the aspect of taste again. Therein Pierre de Coubertin wrote: 'only the idea, adapted to the needs and tastes of the century, can resurge'.[83] A necessity to which Charles as well as Pierre de Coubertin paid attention to.

Conclusion

This paper has exemplified how the findings of an art historical analysis enrich sport historical research. The method described in this paper was Erwin Panofsky's iconological analysis.

For each analytical step of the 'Sports Allegory/The Crowning of the Athletes' by Charles Louis Frédy de Coubertin examples were found which explained the elements of the painting. All these findings then contributed to the 'decoding' of the painting's information. The artist's personal background as well as his son's background enabled the reader to build an understanding for the painting's 'message'.

Although the scarcity of information about Charles de Coubertin appeared to limit the analysis at first, it drew the attention to Pierre de Coubertin. Very soon the importance of his writings became clear, because they provide 'explanations' for the existing links between the development of Olympic history and its analogies in the painting. In this context it is important to recall Olbrich's claim (mentioned previously) concerning 'explanatory texts'. Without the articles many of the elements in the painting could not have been 'decoded'.

The findings of the iconological analysis illustrate how Charles de Coubertin used his son's writings as inspirational sources and 'translated' their messages on canvas. Taking into account that influences do have an impact in both directions a new question is raised: Are there any artistic influences from the father visible in Pierre de Coubertin's concept for the Olympic Games? A major field to elaborate this question further are the Olympic Art Competitions. This has to be addressed in future research. Another question concerning influences is whether or not Charles de Coubertin had an impact on later artists. An example is the Polish artist André Slom (1844–1909), who designed the Olympic diploma for the Olympic congress, which took place in Brussels on 9 June 1905. Slom's compositions show the architectural elements of the Eiffel tower and the Acropolis combined with a fencer, a runner and a polo player.[84] An iconological analysis would allow additional parallels to be elaborated further.

But the paper also makes clear that an important future research topic is the person Charles de Coubertin. The aim of the research would be to find 'explanations' for the open questions of the iconological analysis. For example concerning the origins of the 'Sports Allegory/The Crowning of the Athletes': Did Pierre de Coubertin commission the painting to his father? Or was it a present from Charles de Coubertin to his son? Further it is important to consider the painting in relation to Charles de Coubertin's oeuvre. For example, are there other sport-related paintings created by him? And last it is important to search for additional evidence from the artist such as written sources.

According to Jacques de Navacelle, personal documents of Charles de Coubertin are kept in different family archives of the descendants.[85] In 2014 he and his father gave documents to the *Fondation Nationale de Sciences Politiques* in Paris. These will be made accessible to the public in the near future.[86] It is hoped that further evidence about the artist will be found which will enhance understanding about Charles de Coubertin's intentions and the message he wanted to convey through his painting.

How important these private archives and the documents therein are, proves the most recent discovery of this research. Gilles de Navacelle owns an album which was compiled by Charles de Coubertin.[87] This 'authorship' is one reason which makes the document important. But more important is the information in the album. Therein is a photograph of the 'Sports Allegory – The Crowning of the Athletes' to which Charles de Coubertin annotated the words 'Jeux Olympiques' and '1896'. Therefore, the photograph is a proof for the title given by the artist. This discovery allows the introduction of the 'correct' title into Olympic history research and solves the (by historians undiscovered) title contradiction which existed up to now. It makes it also necessary to change the paper's title: Art works as source for sport historical research: The example of 'Jeux Olympiques' by Charles Louis Frédy de Coubertin. Future research has to revisit Pierre de Coubertin's articles in the light of the 'correct' title.

Notes

1. Alexander Eiling (ed.), *Degas – Klassik und Experiment* [Degas – Classicism and Experiment] (München: Hirmer, 2014).
2. Ibid., 216. The German text: 'Der aus England kommende Sport hatte sich bereits im ausgehenden 18. Jahrhundert in Frankreich etabliert, begann aber erst mit den Eröffnungen der Rennbahnen von Chantilly (1824), Versailles (1836) und vor allem Longchamps (1857) eine größere Rolle zu spielen. Kaiser Napoléon III. hatte zuvor den Neubau einer Tribühne auf den Fundamenten des Klosters Longchamps im Bois de Boulogne in Auftrag gegeben, die nur knapp zehn Kilometer vom Pariser Zentrum entfernt lag. Seither pilgerte die feinere Gesellschaft vor die Tore der Stadt, um sich die Rennen im dortigen Hippodrom anzusehen und an den vom elitären Jockey Club veranstalteten Begleitveranstaltungen teilzunehmen'. All translations in this paper are done by the author, unless indicated otherwise. Eiling refers to the work of Kimberle Jones, 'A Day at the Races: A Brief History of Horse Racing in France', in Jean Sutherland (ed.), *Degas at the Races* (New Haven, CT: Yale University Press, 1998), 208–23.
3. N. Gissel, M. Krüger, and H. Langenfeld, 'Grundlagen und Methoden Sporthistorischer Forschung [Foundations and Methods in Sport History Research]', in M. Krüger and H. Langenfeld (eds), *Handbuch Sportgeschichte* (Schorndorf: Hofmann, 2010), 48.
4. Allen Guttmann, *Sports and American Art from Benjamin West to Andy Warhol* (Amherst: University of Massachusetts Press, 2011).
5. Gigliola Gori, *Gli Etruski e lo sport* (Urbino: QuattroVent, 1986); Gigliola Gori, *Female Bodies and the Italian Fascism: Submissive Women and Strong Mothers* (London: Routledge, 2004); and Gigliola Gori, 'Sporting Events Organized in Venice: Male Boating and the Amazing Case of Women's Rowing Contests', *The International Journal of the History of Sport* 32, no. 4 (2015), 584–96.
6. R. Renson and H. Smulders, 'Bruegel Revisited: Research and Development of the Flemish Folk Games File' (NASSH Proceedings, Austin, 1979).
7. Ch. Vivier and J.-F. Loudcher, 'Utilisation de la représentation picturale en histoire du sport: quelques images de combats de boxe historiques comme examples', in Manfred Lämmer,

Everlyn Mertin, and Tierry Terret (eds), *New Aspects of Sport History* (Sankt Augustin: Academia, 2007), 357–62; and Anna Maria Grabowska, 'Sport in the Arts in the Framework of the Collection of the Museum of Sport and Tourism in Warsaw', in Agnieszka Majkowska, Tomasz Kosek, and Iwona Grys (eds), *Memory and Beauty* (Warsaw: MSiT, 2002), 177–84.

8. Wray Vamplew, 'Facts and Artifacts: Sports Historians and Sports Museums', *Journal of Sport History* 25, no. 2 (1998), 276.

9. Jean-Christoph Ammann, *Bei Näherer Betrachtung – Zeitgenössische Kunst Verstehen und Deuten* (Frankfurt am Main: Westend, 2008).

10. An artistic movement, whose founder was the Italian artist Filippo Tommaso Marinetti. It started with the publication of his 'Futuristic Manifest' in *Le Figaro* in 1909 and ended with his death 1944. The most famous painters of the Futurism were Umberto Boccioni and Giacomo Balla.

11. Vamplew, 'Facts and Artifacts', 276.

12. Erwin Panofsky, *Meaning in the Visual Arts* (New York: Doubleday, 1955).

13. Information based on the visit of the author to the Olympic Museum in Lausanne on 4 September 2014. As well as on email correspondence between the author and Stéphanie Knecht, Document Information Officer of the Olympic Museum in Lausanne, from 23 September 2014 and 2 October 2014. For the details see inventory list no. 34 and inventory list no. 65.

14. Douglas Brown, 'Theories of Beauty and Modern Sport: Pierre de Coubertin's Aesthetic Imperative for the Modern Olympic Movement 1894–1914' (PhD diss., University of Western Ontario, 1997), 208.

15. Pierre de Coubertin, 'Le Rétablissement des Jeux Olympiques', *Revue de Paris*, no. 3 (1894), 184, http://gallica.bnf.fr/ark:/12148/bpt6k207971w/f845.image (accessed 5 September 2014).

16. Erwin Niedermann, *Antike und Moderne Olympische Spiele – Ein historisch kritischer Vergleich* (Wien, 2000), 61, http://www.sport.uni-mainz.de/müller/29.php (accessed September 5, 2014); and Lia Paradis, 'Manly Displays: Exhibitions and the Revival of the Olympic Games', *The International Journal of the History of Sport* 27, nos 16–18 (2010), 2719.

17. N. Müller and Ch. Wacker (eds), *Pierre de Coubertin et les arts* - Pierre de Coubertin and the arts (Lausanne: Comité International Pierre de Coubertin, 2008). The exhibition catalogue does not mention the other exhibition places. See also the following websites: http://decoubertin.info/ (accessed 21 April 2013), www.muzeumsportu.waw.pl/ (accessed 15 April 2013) and http://www.lwl.org/pressemitteilungen/mitteilung.php?urlID=2209 (accessed 4 April 2013).

18. R. Laube and U. Wick, 'V. Medaillen, Medien, Macht und Markt – Sporthelden', in LWL-Industriemuseum (ed.), *Helden – Von der Sehnsucht nach dem Besonderen* (Essen: Klartext, 2010), 238.

19. Ibid., 238. Müller and Wacker, *Pierre de Coubertin et les arts*, 58; and Brown, 'Theories of Beauty', 31. Historians do not know why Pierre de Coubertin used his father´s painting: No evidence concerning this question was found up to now.

20. Raymond Gafner, *The International Olympic Committee: One Hundred Years, 1894–1994 – Volume I* (Lausanne: International Olympic Committee, 1994).

21. Marie-Thérèse Eyquem, *Pierre de Coubertin: L'épopée olympique* (Paris: Calmann-Lévy, 1968); Louis Callebat, *Pierre de Coubertin* (Paris: Fayard, 1988); Patrick Clastres, *Mémoires de jeunesse – Pierre de Coubertin* (Paris: Nouveau Monde, 2008); Daniel Bermond, *Pierre de Coubertin* (Paris: Perrin, 2008); and Yves-Pierre Boulongne, 'Pierre de Coubertin, His Roots and the Congress in Le Havre in 1897', *Olympic Review* 17, no. XXVI (1997), 49–51.

22. Geoffroy de Navacelle, *Pierre de Coubertin – sa vie par l´image* (Zürich: Weidmann, 1986), 28. The same photograph was found by the author in the archives of *Château de Coubertin* during a visit on 2 April 2015.

23. Photograph found by the author in the private collection of Jacques de Navacelle during a visit to *Château Mirville* on 17 June 2014. La baroness de Coubertin gave her husband´s photograph to the International Olympic Committee (IOC) after his death.

24. Laube and Wick, 'Medaillen, Macht', 238.

25. Leon Lagrange, 'Salon de 1861', *Gazette des Beaux-Arts* 6 (1861), 340; Bureau de la Gazette des Beaux-Arts, *Annuaire Publié par la Gazette des Beaux-Arts – Ouvrage Contenant tous les Renseignements Indispensables aux Artistes et aux Amateurs* (Paris: 1870), 18, http://gallica.bnf.fr/ark:/12148/bpt6k6207923z/f28.image (accessed 5 September 2014).

26. Louis Jourdan, *Les Peintres Français: Salon de 1859* (Paris: Librarie Nouvelle, 1859), http://gallica.bnf.fr/ark:/12148/bpt6k6216880m.r=Jourdan%2C%20Dominique (accessed 7 September 2014).

27. Gérard-Georges Lemaire, *Histoire du Salon de Peinture* (Paris: Klincksieck, 2004); and Andrée Sfeir-Semler, *Die Maler am Pariser Salon 1791–1880* (Frankfurt am: Campus, 1992).

28. Müller and Wacker, *Coubertin et les arts*, 33.

29. Vamplew, 'Facts and Artifacts', 276.

30. An example are the letters Vincent van Gogh wrote to his brother, Theo. For additional reading see Fritz Erpel (ed.), *Van Gogh – sämtliche Briefe* (Bornheim-Merten: Lamuv, 1985).

31. Müller and Wacker, *Coubertin et les arts*, 58; and Laube and Wick, 'Medaillen, Macht', 238.

32. Ibid., 238.

33. Frederico Zuccari painted it in 1598. For more information about the artist see Davide Tontis and Sara Bartolucci, *Sacro e profano alla maniera degli Zuccari. Taddeo, Federico e Giovampietro Zuccari. Una dinastia di artisti Vadesi* [Sacred and Profane - The Manner of the Zuccaris. Taddeo, Federico and Giovampietro. A dynasty of Vadesian Artists] (Sant' Angelo in Vado: Editrice Tipolitografia Vadese, 2010). For more information about the fresco see Gianfilippo Carettoni, *Das Haus des Augustus auf dem Palatin* (Mainz: Zabern, 1983).

34. Müller and Wacker, *Coubertin et les arts*, 58. Jean Auguste Dominique Ingres (1780–1867) created the painting in 1827. It is part of the collection of the Louvre INV 5417. See Lawrence Gowing, *Die Gemäldesammlung des Louvre* [The Painting Collection of the Louvre] (Köln: DuMont, 1987), 625.

35. Laube and Wick, 'Medaillen, Macht', 238.

36. This painting was commissioned by Pope Julian II. around 1511. It is a fresco in the *Stanze di Raffael* of the Vatican Museum in Rome visited by the author 31 October 2013.

37. The painting belongs to the collection of the Louvre. See http://cartelfr.louvre.fr/cartelfr/visite?srv=car_not_frame&idNotice=15750 (accessed 6 April 2014); Bibliothèque Nationale de France, *Receuil. Portraits d´artistes et des compositeurs* (Paris, 1875), 6, http://gallica.bnf.fr/ark:/12148/btv1b8438630k/f6.item (accessed 14 February 2015).

38. Harald Olbrich, *Lexikon der Kunst* (München: DTV, 1996), 108–9.

39. Sfeir-Semler, *Die Maler*, 302.

40. Renate Prochno, *Konkurrenz und ihre Gesichter in der Kunst – Wettbewerb, Kreativität und ihre Wirkungen* (Berlin: Akademie, 2006), 174.

41. Pietro Amato, *Charles Louis Frédy de Coubertin – Il Corteo Pontificio di Pio IX 1959* (Città del Vaticano: Edizioni Musei Vaticani, 2011), 9.

42. The author consulted the sketchbook (no. 10) during a visit to *Château Mirville* on 17 June 2014. It is one out of 10 sketchbooks, which belong to the private collection of Jacques de Navacelle.

43. Today it is in the *Chapelle des Missiones Etrangères* in the rue du Bac, Paris.

44. Cornette de Saint Cyr, *Gustave Eiffel, la Tour Eiffel, les Expositions Universelles: livres, photos, affiches, objects; vent publique aux enchères*; lundi 26 juin 2006, Tour Eiffel, Salle Gustave Eiffel [Gustave Eiffel, the Eiffel Tower, the World Fairs: Books, Photographs, Posters, Objects; Public Auction] (Paris: La Tour Eiffel Société, 2006), 85.

45. For more information see Noë Willer, *Luigi Loir (1845–1916) – peintre de la Belle Epoque à la publicité: catalogue raisonné* [Luigi Loir - Advertising a painter of the Belle Epoque] (Carmel: Classic Art Gallery & Nebosja Calic, 2005).

46. The sketchbooks analyzed by the author during a visit to Mirville on 17 June 2014 did not include any preparatory sketches for the painting.

47. The address was 20, rue Oudinot. See Bermond, *Pierre de Coubertin*, 28. Navacelle *Vie Par l'Image*, 14. P. Clastres, 'Scolarité et pré-ralliement. Pierre de Coubertin auditeur de l'École libre des sciences politiques (mars 1884-juin 1886) [Education and pre-rally. Pierre

de Coubertin student at the Free School for Political Sciencies (March 1884-June 1886)]', in Stephan Wassong (ed.), *Internationale Einflüsse auf die Wiedereinführung der Olympischen Spiele durch Pierre de Coubertin* (Kassel: Agon, 2005), 107; and Comte Maurice de Madre, 'Physiognomie intime du Baron de Coubertin [Intimate Physiognomy of Baron de Coubertin]', *Revue Olympique* 47 (1971), 414.

48. Today it is in the *Chapelle des Missiones Etrangères* in the rue du Bac, Paris.

49. Patrick Clastres, *Mémoires de jeunesse* [Youth memories] (Paris: Nouveau Monde, 2008).

50. Ibid., 54. The original French text: 'Les soldats errèrent dans le parc et s´établirent dans les écuries vides, sans se préoccuper des chevaux quón avait cachés dans une étable'.

51. Pierre de Coubertin, 'Le Rétablissement des Jeux Olympiques [The Reintrduction of the Olympic Games]', *La Revue de Paris*, 15 June 1894, 178. The French text: 'L'amateur antique luttait pour un simple rameau d´olivier sauvage'.

52. Ibid., 178.

53. Pierre de Coubertin, *Einundzwanzig Jahre Sport-Kamgagne (1887–1908)* [A 21 Year Campaign] (Ratingen: Aloys Henn, 1974), 34–41. Interestingly, Pierre de Coubertin also explained the fact, that the 1984 congress was the result of an earlier event. Because of the experience of the congress 'Physical Exercises in Ancient Times, in the Middle Ages and in Modern Times' held in November in 1892, he felt that it was mandatory to explain his ideas to the audience.

54. Pierre de Coubertin, 'Jeux Olympiques. Discours à Athènes (16 nov.1894)', *Le Messager d´Athens*, no. 39 (1894), 287–8 and no. 42 (1894), 306–9; Norbert Müller, *Pierre de Coubertin, 1863–1937. Olympism. Selected Writings* (Lausanne: International Olympic Committee, 2000), 365; Brown, 'Theories of Beauty', 203; and Coubertin, *Einundzwanzig Jahre*, 92.

55. Ibid., 91. The German text: 'Die Stadt der Pallas Athene in ihrem weißen Marmorkleid war ganz und gar auf die Aufgabe einer Hauptstadt zugeschnitten'; es war ein würdevoller Rahmen für die Olympischen Spiele'.

56. Ibid., 102. The German text: 'Ich versuchte den finanziellen zu errechnen, den die ständige Abhaltung der Spiele in Griechenland bringen würde ... So kam ich sehr bald zu dem Schluß, daß die Festlegung der wiedererstandenen Olympiade auf Griechenland allein den Tod meines Werkes bedeuten würde. Ich beschloß also, mit allen Kräften gegen diese Absicht anzukämpfen'.

57. Konstantinos Georgiadis, *Die Ideengeschichtlichen Grundlagen der Erneuerung der Olympischen Spiele im 19. Jahrhundert* [The Foundations of the History of Ideas concerning the Renewal of the Olympic Games in the Nineteenth Century] (Kassel: Agon, 2000), 121; and Coubertin, *Einundzwanzig Jahre*, 110.

58. For more information about the 1900 Olympic Games see A. Cartier, 'Mythes et réalités olympiques: les jeux de 1900' [Olympic Myths and Facts: The 1900 Games] (PhD diss., University of Paris, 2010).

59. Pierre de Coubertin, 'Congrès des Exercices Physiques. Compte rendu des séances et concours [Proceedings]' (Paris: Publications des Annales Economiques, 1889).

60. Pierre de Coubertin, 'Rapport. Présenté à l'Assemblée Générale du Comité de Propagation des Exercices physiques tenue à la Sorbonne le 15 janvier 1890 [Report]', *La Revue Athlétique* 15, no. 1 (1890), 44.

61. S.P. Lambros and N.G. Politis, *Die Olympischen Spiele 776 v. Chr.- 1896 n. Chr. - Erster Theil - Die Olympischen Spiele im Altertum* (Athens, 1896), http://library.la84.org/6ic/OfficialReports/1896/1896part1.pdf (accessed 4 April 2014).

62. Coubertin, 'Le Rétablissement des Jeux Olympiques', 184. The French text: 'C´est cette jeunesse universelle dont il s´agit de grouper périodiquement les représentants sur le plus pacifique champs de bataille. le champ de jeu. De quatre ans en quatre ans, le vingtième siècle verrait ainsi ses enfants se réunir successivement près des grandes capitales du monde pour y lutter de force et d' adresser et s´y disputer le rameau symbolique. Oh! sans doute il y a beaucoup d' obstacles à franchir pour en arriver là'.

63. P. de Coubertin et al., *The Olympic Games B.C. 776 – A.D. 1896 – Second Part – The Olympic Games in 1986* (Athens, 1897), http://library.la84.org/6oic/OfficialReports/1896/1896part2.pdf (accessed 4 April 2014). The Official Report of the Olympic Games of 1896 was published

in two volumes. The first volume, published in 1896, starts with the history of the ancient Olympic Games, their starting point and the most important events over the centuries. It continues with a fictive description of the former sport facilities. The description is based on the fragments of buildings which were found during excavation works in Athens. The second volume about the sport competitions was published in 1897.

64. Wolfgang Decker, *Die Wiederbelebung der Olympischen Spiele* [The Revival of the Olympic Games] (Mainz: Rutzen, 2008), 140.

65. Rupert Kaiser, *Olympia-Almanach. Geschichten, Zahlen, Bilder* [Olympic Almanac. Stories, numbers, photographs] (Kassel: Agon, 2004).

66. Albert Krayer, 'IOC-Präsident Vikelas und Generalsekretär Coubertin, der Schöpfer der modernen Olympischen Bewegung [The IOC President Vikelas and the Secretary General Coubertin, Creator of the Modern Olympic Movement]', in Karl Lennartz (ed.), *Die Olympischen Spiele 1896 in Athen* [The 1896 Olympic Games in Athens] (Kassel: Agon, 1996), 43.

67. Georgiadis, *Ideengeschichtliche Grundlagen*, 125.

68. Coubertin, *Einundzwanzig Jahre*, 91–2. The German text: 'die große Bahn der Reitschule war zwar nicht besonders gepflegt, aber günstig gelegen'.

69. Ibid., 98.

70. Decker, *Die Wiederbelebung*, 140; and Georgiadis, *Ideengeschichtliche Grundlagen*, 227.

71. Coubertin, *Einundzwanzig Jahre,* 98.

72. Pierre de Coubertin, 'Equitation', *Les Sports Athlètiques* 32, no. 32 (1890), 1, 4; Pierre de Coubertin, 'L´equitation populaire', *Excelsior*, no. 1616 (1915), 3; and Pierre de Coubertin, 'A cheval', *Excelsior*, no. 1630 (1915), 3.

73. Pierre de Coubertin, 'A travers l´athlétisme: le polo', *Journal des Débats Politiques et Littéraires*, no. 105 (1893), 1, http://gallica.bnf.fr/ark:/12148/bpt6k466272p/f1.zoom.langDE (accessed 23 March 2015).

74. Visit of the author to the Deauville International Polo Club on 14 June 2014. For more information see Jean-Luc Chartier, *Cent Ans de Polo en France* (Paris: Polo Club Edition, 1992); Additional reading: Horace Laffaye, *Polo in Argentina: A History* (Jefferson: McFarland, 2014); Horace Laffaye, *Polo in Britain* (Jefferson: McFarland, 2012); Horace Laffaye and Dennis Amato, *Polo in the United States: A History* (Jefferson: McFarland, 2011); and Herbert Spencer, *A Century of Polo* (Cirencester: World Polo Associates, 1994).

75. Jean Durry, *Pierre de Coubertin – The Visionary* (Paris: Comité Francais Pierre de Coubertin, 1996), 31, 81.

76. Coubertin, *Einundzwanzig Jahre*, 61. The German text: 'In Paris verliert das Neue schnell seinen Reiz und so werden die Spiele dort auch kaum noch beachtet. In der Provinz war dies jedoch alles noch ganz neu und man konnte die seltsamsten Bemerkungen hören über die Jungen ... [die] beim Rugby in einem Knäuel miteinander rangen'.

77. Boulongne, 'Pierre de Coubertin, his roots and the Congress in Le Havre in 1897', *Olympic Review* 17, no. XXVI (1997), 50.

78. For detailed information see J.-Y. Guillain and P. Porte, *La planète est rugby – regards croisés sur l'ovalie* [The Planet is Rugby - Intersecting Looks on Rugby] (Anglet: Atlantica, 2007); Jean-Pierre Bodis, *Histoire mondiale du rugby – dimensions économiques et sociales* [Rugby´s World History - Social and Economic Dimensions] (Toulouse: Privat, 1987); Jean-Pierre Callède, 'L'origine d'un sport, le contenu d'une tactique, à propos du livre de Saint-Chaffray et Dedet: Football (Rugby), 1895 [The Origin of a Sport, the content of tactics, about the book by Saint-Chaffray and Dedet: Football (Rugby), 1895]', in Georges Vigarello (ed.), *Anthologie commentée des textes historiques de l'éducation physique et du sport* [Anthology of Historical Texts on Physical Education and Sport - Commented Edition] (Paris: EPS, 2001), 233–7; and Robert Lubar, 'Running with the Ball – Robert Delaunay, Pierre de Coubertin and Rugby Football in France', in Patricia Berman and Gertje Utley (ed.), *A Fine Regard – Essays in Honor of Kirk Varnedoe* (Hampshire: Ashgate, 2008), 134–53.

79. Coubertin, *Einundzwanzig Jahre*, 59. The German text: 'Die Fußballsaison war herrlich. Endlich mussten wir nicht mehr auf dem kleinen Rasenstück im oberen See im Bois de

Boulogne spielen.' There is a painting by Charles de Coubertin entitled 'Ball Game in the Bois de Boulogne' (1892) which might be related to these texts. Further research is needed to clarify this.

80. Pierre de Coubertin, 'L'Athlètisme, son role et son histoire [Athletism, its Role and its History]', *Revue Athlètique*, no. 4 (1891), 206.

81. Pierre de Coubertin, 'En Bicyclette [By Bycicle]', *Revue Athlètique*, no. 75 (1891), 1–2. For more information about cyclism see Louis Baudry de Saunier, *Le cyclisme, théoretique et pratique* (Paris: Libraierie Illustre, 1892).

82. Pierre de Coubertin, 'Les excercises physiques. Disours au Prytanée de la Flèche', *La Revue de la Prytannée. Organ des anciens élèves de la Flèche*, no. 7 (1889), 572.

83. Coubertin, 'Le Rétablissement', 184. The French text: 'l'idée seul peut revivre, approriée aux besoins et aux goûts du siècle.'

84. Coubertin, *Einundzwanzig Jahre*, 135. The full family name of the artist was Slomszynski. There is a contradiction with the description of the Olympic Museum though: 'La création du diplôme olympique avait été décidée en 1901. Créé par André Slom (1844–1909), il représente l'acropole d'Athènes vue à travers l'une des arches de la Tour Eiffel et au premier plan des athlètes s'exercent à la boxe, l'escrime et la lutte'. See website of the IOC (accessed 23 October 2014).

85. Information given by Jacques de Navacelle to the author during a visit to *Château Mirville* on 17 June 2014.

86. Information confirmed by email from Florence Carpentier, member of the research team at the University of Rouen, on 15 September 2014. The *Foundation the Sciences Politiques* in Paris is analyzing these documents at the moment. The author requested access.

87. The author was allowed to consult this album from the collection of Gilles de Navacelle during a visit to the *Fondation de Coubertin* at *Domain de Coubertin* on 2 April 2015. The leather-bound album with iron fittings carries a 'C' on the cover and has no pagination. According to the author´s pagination the photograph is on page 63.

Disclosure statement

No potential conflict of interest was reported by the author.

Salvador López Gómez: Apostle of Gymnastics in Spain

Gonzalo Ramírez-Macías (iD) and José P. Sanchís Ramírez

ABSTRACT

Salvador López Gómez was a great exponent of gymnastics in Spain in the nineteenth and the twentieth century. His role as a teacher, a writer and even as a law developer who promoted gymnastics deserves a detailed study. For that reason, through primary sources of this era and, specially, papers from López Gómez himself, this paper depicts his long professional career, his conception of gymnastics and the constant efforts, not always properly rewarded, that he made for its social respect and acknowledgement during that time.

Introduction

The historical period that includes the nineteenth and the beginning of the twentieth century was very complex for Spanish gymnastics. There were many factors that influenced it. At the political level, the War of Independence, the dramatic political changes (First Republic, Restoration and Second Republic) and the loss of the last colonies were all worthy of note. Socially, the population increased in a largely rural society, which very slowly and, only in some areas (mainly Catalonia and the Basque Country), incorporated the industrial revolution. Economically, Spain experienced several periods of crisis, from the 1860s until the early twentieth century, which mainly affected the common people and the petty bourgeoisie. Regarding health, medical services were very poor, and there was an increase in infectious diseases and mortality. These factors were to influence, remarkably, the future of this discipline; which began to be gradually more recognized for its hygienic worth by the Regenerationist Movement.[1]

In general terms, we can affirm that, in a period in which gymnastics developed in most parts of Europe (Germany, Sweden or France), Spain experienced some movements that determined a peculiar gymnastic development which featured, above all, in the political sphere, with highly progressive actions together with others that were fully reactionary.

Bearing that in mind, we could highlight, as an example, the early inclusion in 1847 of the subject named gymnastics, thanks to the Study Plan of Pastor Díaz, Minister of Commerce, Education and Public Works.[2] However, this did not last long for gymnastics lovers because in 1849, the minister, when amending the Secondary Education study plan, eliminated the recently established gymnastics.[3] Hence, in the nineteenth century, there were five progressive regulations and four which limited or simply eliminated this subject in the study plans.[4]

The example above shows clearly what could be and was not in the case of gymnastics in Spain. The most paradigmatic case is that of Francisco de Paula Amorós y Ondeano (1770–1848), from Valencia and the father of gymnastics in France. It is possible that, if he had not been expatriated because of his fondness for France and had got the necessary support, we could be referring to a diverging gymnastics reality regarding the slow and winding path that this discipline had to go through in the Spanish context.[5]

According to Pastor Pradillo, gymnastics was in a pre-scientific state in Spain.[6] In order to understand the devious evolution that gymnastics had in Spain during this period, the situation requires some deep research about such facts as: the objectives pursued, the influences received, the way it was accepted by citizens, the reasons why these regulatory movements took place and, above all, the characters who were pioneers in the introduction and development of this discipline in the lives of Spanish people at that time.

In this field, we find Salvador López Gómez, a famous gymnastics teacher who fought all his life to promote this subject within Spanish society, not only in the practical sphere, but also in the theoretical and political one. He always looked for the highest recognition and respect towards gymnastics. This promoter, as it should be in the agitated Spain of the nineteenth and the beginning of the twentieth century, was supported and rejected but he never ceased in his idea of defending and spreading the practice of gymnastics as a healthy and necessary activity in a person's comprehensive training. In fact, he is recognized as one of the apostles of gymnastics by Torrabadella. This author named 'apostles' to a group of gymnastics teachers, 12 men and one woman, who stood out for their tenacity in spreading the benefits of gymnastics. He also vindicated the academic and professional rights of these professionals.[7]

To become familiar with Salvador López Gómez will improve our understanding of the situation of gymnastics in Spain in the nineteenth and the beginning of the twentieth century, especially that which was practiced in Southern cities, since Seville was the city where he mainly worked as a teacher. Regarding this, it must be pointed out that the South of Spain was characterized as being especially disadvantaged, far from the airs of social, industrial and economic progress that permeated Europe and that, partly, was noticed in some other more developed areas such as Madrid, Catalonia or Basque Country.[8] Thus, it is possible to say that Sevilla was the main town in the rural South of Spain. However, the city had a major university, schools and a bourgeoisie concerned with its city. This bourgeoisie wanted Seville to resemble and become one of the most important Spanish cities.

This situation of underdevelopment, as it should be, also affected gymnastics.[9] There were few professionals who developed their practice in Southern cities. Most of them, such as the well-known Francisco Aguilera y Becerril, José María Aparici y Biedma, and Francisco Pedregal o José María Martínez Bernabéu, worked in the capital Madrid, and some close cities such as Segovia or Guadalajara.[10]

This brings to prominence even more the figure of Salvador López Gómez. Indeed, he is not unknown, since some researchers have studied him,[11] but this paper deals with his life and works, as a way to know deeply not only this relevant person but as a way of progressing in the knowledge of Spanish gymnastics, especially the form practiced in the South. The sources, mostly used in this research, were primary sources and the methodological line

Figure 1. Image of Salvador López Gómez. Source: Book cover of S. López Gómez, *El Gimnasio* (Sevilla: Imprenta de Baldaraque, 1873).

used to access them was the consultation of several documentary collections centres,[12] and different computerized datebases.[13]

Salvador López Gómez: Background and Professional Career

Emilio Salvador López Gómez was born in Seville in 1852.[14] Apart from studying Baccalaureate, he studied to become a public accountant, a title that he never used although this appeared in some guides to his academic training.[15] His true passion was studying and practicing gymnastics.

This discipline was introduced in Seville by the Frenchman Víctor Venitien. As in other Spanish cities by that time, this way of doing physical exercises and their justification regarding citizens' health could be soon noted in Sevillian society. In 1840, Venitien opened a gymnastics school in the old abbey of Jerónimos monks. Also here, in 1839, was settled the *Colegio Sevillano de Buena Vista* ('Buena Vista Elementary Gym') directed by Francisco Alejandro Fernel.[16] Some years later, in 1860, he appeared as a gymnastics teacher in the *Colegio de primera clase San Fernando* ('San Fernando Elementary School'),[17] and only five years later, not only was the first Sevillian gym opened, named *Gimnasio Elemental* ('Elementary Gym') but he was also recognized as being the instigator of this discipline in this part of Spain, as reflected on some pages of the *Guía de Sevilla* ('Seville Guide'), published by Gómez Zarzuela: 'GIMNASIO ELEMENTAL. Placed in "calle de Tarifa n° 1". Under the direction of Don José García Barraca ... the gym which was directed by Mr. Víctor Venitien, the true importer of gymnastics in the southern part of Iberian Peninsula'.[18]

As it appears in the previous quotation, José García Barraca, second director of the referred gym, was also important for gymnastics in this city. López Gómez was his disciple and there he met Méndez Bejarano, who stated:

> Although he was five years older than me, he was my English and Gymnastics classmates, in the 'salón de Barraca', placed in 'calle de Tarifa' number one. All my advantage in English over him was recovered, and even more, in Gymnastics. I remember this with some envy since nowadays, old and weak, I understand the value of feeling strong over speaking English.[19]

The enthusiasm that López Gómez felt towards gymnastics made him open his first gym when he was only 21 years old, specifically in 1874. He named it *Centro de Educación Físico, Profiláctico y Terapéutico* ('Physical, Prophylactic and Therapeutic School'), since one of his main goals in this discipline was giving it scientific rigour that made it be socially recognized, basically aligning gymnastics to medicine, as this was a fully recognized science by the scientific community and by citizens.[20]

This passionate condition made him study in the *Escuela Central de Profesores y Profesoras de Gimnástica* ('Gymnastics' Teachers Central School') and he was one of the 87 persons (71 men and 16 women) who received this degree.[21] Nevertheless, his training was not limited to the knowledge that he got from this institution since from his years prior to his admission he knew the works of expert teachers and he had contact with some of them, mainly in the neighbouring France, as can be noticed in the following reference:

> Now, approaching 1849, the future of gymnastics was already based and, even better, some well-known people, among other, the lieutenant colonel d'Argy, Laisné current gymnastics inspector and our friends the hard-working Mr. Triat, and honourable Mr. Paz, forerunner and first President of the 'Unión de las Sociedades gimnásticas francesas' [French Gymnastic Societies Union].[22]

From his beginnings as a teacher, López Gómez always tried to reach important goals and it seems that he was duly recognized because many people were interested in his figure and knowledge. In fact, this emerging teacher was the honorary director of many gyms in Spain: 'From October 1874, he was awarded with the position of honorary director of gyms in Cádiz, Alicante, Badajoz, Barcelona, Coruña, Cuenca, Valencia, Sabadell, Alcoy, Bilbao y Oporto (Portugal)'.[23]

This fame and recognition went beyond gymnastics and was noted in society. Thus, in this year, he was proposed by Real Camara's doctor as gymnastic teacher of Montpensier's dukes. He was so notorious that, as Méndez Bejarano indicates (Figure 1):

> When I was a child, all young boys stopped at the bookshop window to look at the portrait of Salvador López, naked from the waist up, stamped in the cover of his first gymnastics books. His powerful muscles, his excellent thoracic development and his strong arms seemed to be stolen from Hércules Farnesio, were admired by Sevillian youngsters.[24]

In 1877, there was an advertisement in the newspaper *El Universal* which referred to the gym of Medicine School, that was the transformation from the one founded by López Gómez three years before and that, when affiliated to the medical school, followed its way: 'Great gym in the Surgery and Medicine School by Mr. Salvador López Gómez. Provincial Gyms Director. Teacher through public contest in the main schools of the capital city'.[25] This is not a trivial fact since this teacher achieved the association that gymnastics was openly related to the medical world. This, as it has been emphasized above, was one of his objectives: a higher recognition and more respect towards gymnastics.

A year later, because of the Universal Exhibition, he visited Paris and that enabled him to know *in situ* some of the most prestigious French gyms. One of them was paradoxically directed by a Spanish man, Vicente López Tamayo. Both teachers had met in Madrid, when López Tamayo directed the so-called gym *Gimnasio Vignolles*, one of the first ones to be opened in Spain.[26]

López Tamayo truly believed in Amorós' ideas and, desperate because of Spain's delay in many aspects (including gymnastics, obviously), decided to move to Paris, where he achieved his best accomplishments.[27] The fluent relationship among them is not only proved by the fact that López Tamayo was appointed as honorary director of the gyms in the province of Seville,[28] but for the description that López Gómez makes of his visit to Paris:

> … in charge of our special friend and correspondent, Mr. Vicente López, current chief teacher of Heiser Gym in Paris, set in rue Martyurs, whose gym we could satisfactorily visit in our stay in the neighbouring republic, in 1878 because of [the] Paris Universal Exhibition.[29]

In his stay in Paris, he also visited the gym run by Eugène Paz, a pupil from one of Amorós' classmates, specifically *Hippolyte Triat*.[30] In this visit, he was pleasingly surprised when observing that: 'In our visit, in 1878 to the gym "Gimnasio Paz" in Paris, there was, subsidized by the Town Hall, a night training session exclusive for workers'.[31]

In 1879, López Gómez was still a teacher in the Medicine School gym, but his fame and prestige had expanded because of his increased knowledge, relationships and new machines. Additionally, by that time, he was a teacher in the private schools of San Pelayo and San Ramón in Seville. These schools offered gymnastic lessons within their complementary instruction.

Next year, in 1880, he visited France again in order to be enriched by its gymnastic advances. Back to Spain, and in the line that was initiated by Amorós with his public shows, he organized an event during the Seville Spring Festival.[32] His purpose was to make gymnastics known and he organized again a similar event some years later, in 1888.

On 12 August 1880, López Gómez won a battle that he had started years ago when he wanted to teach gymnastics in Seville School. This position was held, from its beginning, by García Barraca and he had to accept this position in Málaga: 'Positions held … On 12th August 1880 he was appointed Gymnastics teacher in Málaga School'.[33] After some years working in Málaga, in 1884 he received another award since after being proposed by a group of representatives in Seville, he was responsible for teaching gymnastics in Seville Hospice.[34] This recognition does not refer to holding this position since it was more important to be a teacher at Málaga School, but to the institutional conviction that gymnastics should be a subject in the training of children living in that hospice.

But if all previous appointments were important steps in López Gómez's life, the most important one, because of its spreading effect, was his appointment as a gymnastics teacher at the Education School in Seville. There he could teach and transmit students their love towards this healthy activity, fundamental for children's future life.

> Education School Gym. Agreed by 'Excelentísima Diputación provincial' the construction of a gym here, and appointing Mr. Salvador López Gómez as his teacher on 30 June 1886. He taught there from 1886 to 1887, working exclusively with students from this school and some others appointed by the Director.[35]

In 1887, his appointment as teacher in this School was confirmed by the *Dirección General de Instrucción Pública* (Public Education General Direction). A year later, he was appointed by the same institution as a member of the tribunal of free examination in the *Escuela Central de Gimnástica* (Gymnastics Central School), where he had studied. This is shown in a personal file that can be found in its General Archive:

> Public Education General Direction appointed him as a member of the tribunal of free examination in the 'Escuela Central de Gimnasia' [Gymnastics Central School], because of his role as gymnastics teacher in Seville School and of the publication of two Physical Education works that were awarded by several 'friend societies' all over Spain and in some pedagogical and literary exhibitions.[36]

In the previous document from 1916, he appears as a Seville School teacher. Nonetheless, chronologically, this would not take place until 1893. With this, López Gómez reached one of his biggest ambitions. His appointment was published with a Crown Order on 24 January 1893,[37] taking possession of this position on 9 March of the same year,[38] and a year later he participated in the entrance examination and became a permanent teacher in that School:

> Public Education General Direction, Section 2°. To the Public Education General Director, Madrid 15 June 1894. Mr. President: By virtue of the public tender and proposal of Public Education Board; The King of Spain and the Queen has appointed Mr. Salvador López Gómez as permanent gymnastics teacher at Seville School with a yearly salary of two thousand pesetas. To Seville University Dean and to the School Director.[39]

This made him depart his position as gymnastics teacher at Education School, as both positions were not compatible, but, as Ávila states, this was not a sudden decision that he could luckily reconsider.[40] One academic year later, based on the fact that according to the Seville School Director, that incompatibility was not true since the Crown Order of 27 May 1984 requested that he return to the position that he had left vacant. This request was accepted by the Seville University Dean.[41]

Therefore, in 1895, he was teaching gymnastics in the two most important academic institutions in Seville, the Secondary School and the Education School. He did so in the coming years and until his retirement with the private teaching of this subject. This gives us an idea of the recognition that this teacher had and of his extensive job regarding the development of the practice of gymnastics among citizens.

His recognition was such that, in 1899, he taught subjects traditionally linked to the medical sphere, something quite remarkable since it is not frequent that a teacher with gymnastic training teaches a subject related to the medical sphere:

> On 17 February 1899, and by virtue of a Crown Order 27 January, he explained, at Seville School, notions of Physiology and Hygiene, as it is specified in the Royal 8th in the fourth article of the Crown Decree 13 September 1898.[42]

This teacher kept on with his job within the gymnastics world during the first quarter of the twentieth century. He was well settled in some reference locations (a teacher in Secondary School and in Education School) and he was considered as a great expert in this subject in the national sphere. His last merit, one more in his broad curriculum, is his appointment as a member of the Childhood Protection Committee from 1913.[43]

The long professional career of López Gómez ended on 28 March 1922, when he was 70 years old. That day the Crown Order 22 March was published and his retirement was effective.[44] Until this moment, he had worked more than 48 years in the teaching of gymnastics and it is estimated that he trained more than 30,000 students in nearly these five decades as a teacher. The words from his contemporary Méndez Bejarano exemplify the social relevance that this illustrious gymnastics teacher had:

On 26 March 1922, it has been published in the Gazette the decree that retires, currently in good health, the Dean of Physical Education teachers in Spain. He has been awarded with fourteen prizes in contests and exhibitions because of his works and more than thirty thousand, one hundred and twenty-five students have attended his gym, according to this gym's records.[45]

Emilio Salvador López Gómez died in Seville on Sunday, 16 February 1936, before being 84 years old and, as Ávila indicates, on the same day that Spanish general elections were held and the 'Frente Popular' (Popular Front) won. These were the last months of the second Republic.[46]

Promoter and Critic of Laws Regarding Gymnastics

In the nineteenth century, as already mentioned, there were even five progressive laws regarding gymnastics and there were four which limited or simply eliminated this subject in study plans.

Within these regulatory variations, it can be stated that López Gómez's influence was relevant in the regulatory initiative that culminated in the Decree 3 June 1873 establishing a new Plan which intended to reorganize secondary education that, as will explained below, included teaching hygienic gymnastics.[47]

By chance, the Sevillian representative De Gabriel wanted to register their children in a Medicine School gym directed by López Gómez and he took advantage of this moment to remark on the importance of this subject in the training of Spanish youngsters. It seems that the persuasive endowments of this gymnastics teacher were fruitful in the initial stage of this project:

> … that one of the emerging patricians, to whom we dedicate this humble work, attended our premises in Seville's Medicine School to trust the training of his children and there … we dared, in fear, to communicate what our criterion regarding Physical Education was, the way that Spain was similar to other nations concerning this important subject and the urgent need for the government to leave the empiricism governing by that time. At this point, Mr. De Gabriel asked us how to achieve our intended purpose. Very easy, my honourable friend: Submitting the Courts a draft bill, declaring official and compulsory teaching Hygienic Gymnastics in our beloved nation.[48]

The defence of this law proposal had to be assumed by Manuel Becerra, as he had been appointed Málaga's civil governor. The proposal text was brief but enormously clear in its objective, as it appears in the diary of Court sessions:

> LAW PROPOSAL. Article 1 – Teaching Hygienic Gymnastics is official, fixing, gradually and within a short deadline, established by Development Ministry, lessons in secondary schools and education schools. Article 2 – These lessons' attendance will be compulsory for those pupils of the schools in the previous article. Article 3 – Baccalaureate degree could not be achieved if gymnastics had not been studied for a year and, from now on, three years. Article 4 – The Minister of Development will dictate the appropriate measures to enforce the current law.[49]

This proposal was signed by representatives De Gabriel, Becerra, Carvajal, Domínguez, Conde y Luque, Loring y and the Marquess of El Arenal.

After this proposal, the Minister of Development Eduardo Chao, by means of Decree 3 June 1873,[50] specifically in its second article, considered hygienic gymnastics as a subject, but not a compulsory one. Unfortunately, shortly after Joaquín Gil Berges was appointed as Minister of Development, his first measure was a new Decree suspending the one previously passed by Chao only a few months ago.

It was not until 1893 that gymnastics appeared again in the curriculum. In this year, the Minister Segismundo Moret signed a Crown Order, on 10 September, in which hygienic gymnastics lessons became compulsory from the academic year 1893–1894.[51] One year after, there was a new study plan for the Baccalaureate, promoted by Minister Groizard in the Decree 16 September 1894,[52] which, in order to harmonize purely mental and physical education, among other changes, proposed the substitution of the word gymnastics by the term physical education.

López Gómez, as a gymnastics professional who was committed with this discipline, openly criticized the rulers who, until this moment, had forgotten the official protection of these beneficial practices for citizens' health. Specifically, this can be read in the prologue of his book *Manual de ejercicios Gimnásticos para los Institutos y Escuelas Normales*:

> One feels sorrow and grief when you worry about humankind's sake. Society is governed by physiological poverty and this seems to be the compulsory heritage of future generations. As little as we reflect on this, we can regret the indifference shown by the public powers as well as corporations and humans. They all ignore physical education, above all in childhood and adulthood, and this is very important and necessary in these dangerous life stages.[53]

However, in the prologue, he keeps on thanking those who have made an effort to drive Physical Education far from the legal abyss where it was because of what was referred above.

> Thanks to the effort and energetic enthusiasm of Excellencies Mr. Fernando de Gabriel, Mr. Manuel Becerra, Mr. Germán Gamazo, Mr. José L. Albareda, Mr. Carlos Navarro Rodrigo, Mr. Julián Calleja, Mr. Aureliano Linares Rivas, and lately the Ministers of Development, Mr. Moret and Groizard, and the estimated Sr. D. Eduardo Vincenti, Physical Education will not be a dead letter as it has been until now … Today, through the last Crown Order 10th September 1893, Physical Education will go parallel to intellectual culture, this is a skillful way to balance energies.[54]

The above explained ideas reflect the level of political information of teacher López Gómez in the regulatory future in which gymnastics lived. From his privileged position as a teacher, he initially fostered one of the progressive laws for this discipline although it was little in force. This fact made him, now from his position as a respected and prolific author of gymnastics books, denounce the situation of regulatory abandonment that Spain lived in. Nevertheless, he fairly recognized the effort of those who tried to promote it in a period, as it has been said, that was marked by continuous regulatory changes.

Prolific Author and Speaker

The same year when he opened his first gym, in 1873, he began with his prolific dedication as an author with the publication of *El Gimnasio*.[55] The prologue was made by Francisco de Molina and it is dedicated to the Deputation of Seville.

As a clear example of this author's concern about this work's scientific rigour and, hence, gymnastics, this information appears in the acknowledgements:

> It is a pleasure for me to announce, for those who favour me with the purchase of this Treaty, that my special friend Mr. Carlos de Voisins, Medicine and Surgery teacher, has helped me since this book is related to the important theories that can be considered as new (it would not be regarded as such without them).[56]

The book has a chapter dealing with preliminary notions, a brief anatomical human study and then, its next sections deal with gymnastic machines and their usefulness. Thus,

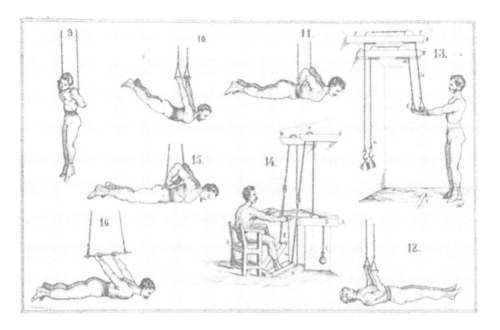

Figure 2. Gymnastic exercises and machines used by López Gómez, namely rings, gymnastic pulley machine, trapeze and pulleys. Source: S. López Gómez, *El Gimnasio* (Sevilla: Imprenta de Baldaraque, 1873), 241.

there are chapters regarding parallel bars, rings, pulleys and their different ways (gymnastic pulley machine, Vignolles' machine, Picheri's system, neupmo-dynamic machine), climbing frames, vaulting bucks, platforms, bars, octogon, ropes, poles and so on (Figure 2).

In 1881, he published his second work, *Breve Reseña Histórica de la Gimnástica en Europa*. It contains 39 pages in which he reviews gymnastics in the main European countries. It remarks that the Spanish situation is argued in just six pages. In this book's cover, his professional biography (until that moment) can be read and this indicates the impact that the works had at a national and international level:

> Royal Dukes of Montpensier's teacher, director of the province gyms in Seville and Málaga. Teacher, forerunner of official gymnastics project in Spain. Collaborator in some sport national and foreign newspapers, author of 'El Gimnasio', the first and only of this type published in this city, awarded with medals in Paris, Sevilla, Cádiz and Pontevedra's universal exhibitions. Honorary Director of the first gyms in Madrid, Barcelona, Valencia, Cádiz, Córdoba, Coruña y Bilbao, former honorary member of 'Centro Gimnocológico Barcelonés' and correspondent of 'Gran Gimnasio Heiser' from, teacher in the first class schools of this capital city: Espíritu Santo, San Ramón, San Lorenzo, San Pelagio y San Hilario.[57]

Because of the importance he achieved, the monthly magazine *El Gimnasta Español* (which published 12 numbers for 1892) included his bibliography. Even this magazine characterized him as one of the most renowned teachers of gymnastics.[58]

Some years later, he published several articles in the magazine *Ilustración Gimnástica* (1886–1887), created by Felipe Serrate Martinez.[59] In 1892,[60] he published 'Higiene de la Gimnástica',[61] which entered the competition called up by the *Sociedad Española de Higiene* ('Hygiene Spanish Society') and was awarded with an honourable mention.

On 20 October 1892 he gave a speech in the Ateneo entitled 'La Gimnástica como uno de los tratamientos de la escoliosis',[62] at which many people attended. Next year,[63] he published a small book entitled *Hidroterapia. Su historia y aparatos portátiles más usuales*.[64] Its content, after a historical review on this subject, focuses on the benefits that water exercise have for someone's health.

In 1894, he published *Manual de ejercicios gimnásticos para uso de los Institutos y Escuelas Normales*. This 200-page book, mainly didactic, is based on the contents of his first work (*El Gimnasio*), but with a clear methodological approach so as to be used as a teaching manual in schools at that time. According to Torrebadella, in this book he demonstrates a significant knowledge of foreign sources.[65] However, its attempt to cover all the contents to be dealt with in gymnastics make it be a scattered work which contains information about gymnastic exercises, machines, games, fencing, dumbbells and so on.

That year, as part of his job as a teacher in the secondary school, he published the 'Programa razonado de Teoría y Práctica de la Gimnástica'.[66] This programme consists of seven chapters made up of lessons, which are 86 in total. The topics of the chapters are to be highlighted since they convey a clear idea of this subject's approach and content. Hence, the first one refers to gymnastics history, the second one to mechanics, the third one is anatomy, the fourth one physiology; the fifth one, which is the most extensive, on exercise; the sixth one deals with the usefulness and importance of physical exercises, and last, the seventh one, is focused on gymnastic equipment, machines and instruments.

López Gómez, even without respite, presented in 1895 another work: 'Educación Física de las niñas',[67] that, according to the author, was aimed at answering girl school's needs, whose facilities were usually poor for physical exercise and games, provoking inactivity. This year, the magazine *La Regeneración Física* (1895–1897) appeared. López Gómez was a founding member and shareholder of this magazine, and he even became a contributor.[68]

In the remaining years of the nineteenth century, he wrote two works. In 1897, *La Gimnástica en España; su historia y legislación*, in which he makes an overview on the history and regulations of Spanish gymnastics, but with extensive references to the European context.[69] Apart from this, there is a speech from 1899, in the General Meeting of Spanish Gymnastics Federation, with the title 'Unificación de la enseñanza de la Gimnástica por un solo método',[70] that would be published that year and which refers to the importance of gymnastics, noting that to be respected as an educative and scientific discipline, it must unify its method and be based on a scientific perspective, in which medicine must have a dominating position, overcoming those positions based on experience and acrobatics.

He was invited to the second and fourth General Meeting, giving speeches, whose titles were: 'Manera de armonizar la Educación Física con la intelectual y la moral durante todo el periodo educativo, desenvolviendo la educación integral' and 'Modernos derroteros de la Gimnástica'.[71] In both texts, he emphasizes the idea of basing gymnastics on science and the importance that this discipline has not only in a person's physical development, but in the intellectual and moral one.

At the beginning of the twentieth century, when he was older than 50, López Gómez continued writing some monographs and newspaper articles. Indeed, in 1902 he published his second important article: 'Algunas consideraciones sobre la obesidad y su tratamiento',[72] in which the author proposes some specific physical exercises to lose weight to counter what he calls 'nutrition vices'.

Some years later, he published a small book *Atlas de ejercicios gimnásticos higiénicos*, made of some charts of easy physical exercises, specifically devised and illustrated for students in these schools.[73] This job would be published again in 1914 under the name *Atlas de ejercicios de cultura física*.[74]

Within the framework of the first Education General Meeting held in 1910, López Gómez presents a work named '¿Debe subsistir la enseñanza de la Gimnástica?', in which he defends vehemently gyms and education's social need of teaching gymnastics as a fundamental part not only of a person's welfare but of comprehensive education.[75]

Also in another specialized sphere, the National Meeting for Child Protection and Homelessness Repression, we find the publication: 'La cultura física en sus relaciones con la higiene de la infancia', a speech in which he gathers different theories on the importance of gymnastics as hygienic practice, especially recommended in childhood.[76]

Two years later, he published *Curso teórico práctico de Educación Física*, made up of two volumes. He changed the term used for this discipline and he will not use again the term 'gymnastics', but, in accordance with the times, the modern concept of physical education. With this work, López Gómez wanted this discipline to be considered as 'public utility' and to be compulsory at schools. With this goal, he wrote a request to Education and Arts Minister on 14 April 1917:

> … while teaching in those schools he had published a work on Physical Education and I would like you to give the appropriate commands to inform Education Ministry in case it is necessary to declare it useful to be read at schools.[77]

This claim was denied in a devastating report given by Medicine Royal Academy. Here, are some compelling paragraphs:

> The work entitled 'Curso teórico-práctico de Educación Física', is made of a small volume, whose printing is average, its paper of low quality and with some images which are not properly correct or carefully done … It is obvious that it is not a book of elementary study; but a mere summary whose only goal is to give an idea of what Physical Education is and what its aims are; but it is so brief, and it lacks explanation, that this study can just be regarded as a subject index[78].

In spite of this setback, López Gómez kept on working and a year later, in the 'VI Congreso de la Asociación Española para el progreso de las Ciencias', he published 'La Educación Física en la mujer'. In this presentation, the author foregrounds the importance of gymnastics practice in women in order to keep a balanced body and, accordingly, according to López Gómez and to the prevailing thought by that time: '… complies with the physiological goals that nature itself imposes, because of the interesting purpose that must be accomplished here, since it is well proved that healthy, vigorous and strong mothers usually have strong, powerful and virile children'.[79]

His last book was *Pro Educación Física*.[80] In this work, López Gómez emphasized again, with ideas previously pointed out, the importance of physical education in society of that time, the need to make it a habit in citizens' everyday life (as a subject at school and as a frequent practice in gyms) and the scientific basis of this discipline.

The year he retired, being 70 years old, he published a brief 10-page booklet titled *Las colonias escolares desde el punto de vista higiénico, educativo y social*.[81] In this text, he points out the need of childhood protection, the importance of physical education in infant training because of its hygienic and educative value and, consequently, he proposes that these new educative experiences, named school camps, use this educative mean: physical education.

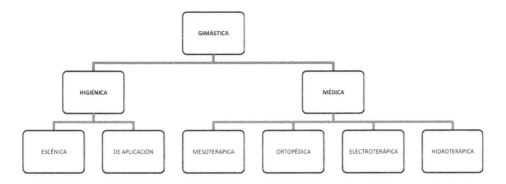

Figure 3. Gymnastics classification according to López Gómez. Source: Chart made from his work, S. López Gómez, *Manual de ejercicios gimnásticos para los Institutos y Escuelas Normales* (Sevilla: Imprenta de Gironés y Orduña, 1894).

Last, when he was already retired, he published a vast number of articles in the magazine *Pro-Infantia*, probably due to the fact that he was a member of the 'Junta de Protección de la Infancia' (Infant Protection Society) from 1913. Their contents are directly related to other previous publications. The total number of articles that he published in this magazine from 1924 until 1931 is 16.[82] We should highlight that he made these publications when he was between 72 and 79 years old. This gives us an idea of his productivity as an author and also of his commitment and professionalism with the discipline to which he dedicated his life.

Gymnastics Teacher

López Gómez was a man ahead of his time in all the aspects regarding physical practices, thanks not only to his training but to some trips to France. He knew methods, machines, exercises, games and even sports which came from France. This would be a fundamental source in his idea of gymnastics, but not the only one since, as it has been already pointed out, he attempted to bring gymnastics closer to medicine, as this was a fully recognized subject by the scientific community and citizens.[83]

In order to understand his idea of gymnastics, we should begin stating that even he himself admitted this term's ambiguity because of its three senses: for some people it implies fight, struggle and rivalry, for others it implies a superhuman effort and for a reduced group, just some deliberate and methodical exercises.

Taking into account this conceptual and processing ambiguity, the implementation of gymnastics admits that it has provoked opposed results. On the one hand, it has been praised by doctors, philosophers and educators but, on the other hand, it is conceived in some gyms according to some principles, which are far from the essential medical, philosophical and educative precepts.

Bearing this in mind, he claims that the most accurate concept of this term is the one given by Colonel Lieutenant Amorós: 'Reasoned science of our movements, our relationships with our senses, our intelligence, feelings and customs'.[84]

From this definition, and with the clear purpose of providing this discipline with seriousness and scientific recognition, López Gómez himself gives his own definition: 'Set of deliberate movements, wisely and perfectly calculated, reasoned, ordered and systematic whose goal is the improvement and balance of all body forces'.[85]

Once gymnastics are defined, he takes a classification already cited by other authors, who differentiate between hygienic gymnastics (which had a corrective character and whose aim was to prevent disease) and medical gymnastics (whose objective was to contribute to the cure of diseases).[86] The first one, López Gómez says, is subdivided into Scenic and Applied. For the second one, the division is based on the different therapeutic applications that it has: Message Therapy, Electrotherapy, Orthopaedics and Hydrotherapy (Figure 3).[87]

For López Gómez, gymnastics' fundamental component, in all its categories, was physical exercises. He makes a deep bibliographical review of contemporary authors on these and, from it, he proposes his own classification: (1) Elementary or free exercises: those in which different parts of the body are moved without needing any machines at all. These are divided into: head, upper limbs, trunk, lower limbs and general body movement exercises. Within this last group, he studies gymnastics running, that he curiously defines: 'Running is just a hasty March alternated with jumps';[88] (2) Mixed exercises: those in which some machines or material is needed in order to move someone's body.

All in all, López Gómez understands gymnastics from a useful and healthy sense, both preventive and therapeutic. This is pointed out in the following clear paragraph:

> He embraces the practice of all the exercises which, appropriately done, make people strengthen and able to resist different life hardships, getting used to overcome difficulties and be successful no matter how many obstacles there are. This is also a fundamental part of many illnesses' therapies.[89]

Also, we must point out, due to the importance in his efforts for using gymnastic machines, the idea that he has of mechanics. He follows D'Alembert's principles: inertia, complex movement and balance power. Accordingly, mechanics is defined as the science which studies balance and human body movements and keeps on making a division into two categories: static and dynamic mechanics.[90] The first one has to do with balanced postures, whereas the second one is related to movements.

This concept of mechanics, together with Amorós' influence, was crucial in his interest towards the usage of gymnastic equipment, which he called machines.[91] He differentiated two categories of machines: constant and mobile. The first ones were 'objects aimed at fixed exercises' and the second ones aimed at 'objects aimed at easy exercises'.[92]

Within constant machines, according to some writings,[93] the most used ones were: parallel bars (simple, ortophaedic and triple), rings (separated 43 or 45 centimetres approximately and with a height of 2.15 metres), pommel horse (from Amorós' 'Manual de Educación Física y Moral'), gymnastic pulley machine, trapeze, Vignolles' machine and pulleys. López Gómez comments accordingly on gymnastic pulley machines:

> The gymnastic pulley machine has a roller of average dimensions hung on the roof and a rope which goes through a cleft. In one of its ends, there is a hook to hang on it the different weights that are used in diverse exercise. From the other side, there are two ropes that end in a cylindrical stick similar to the one in a trapeze or in a small stick similar to a triangle.[94]

Also, within mobile machines, he makes a distinction among ropes, poles (as pole vaults), climbing ropes, trampolines, bats, short dumbbells (a metal bar whose ends are linked to metal balls of different weights), big dumbbells (the same as the previous ones but with large weights) and long dumbbells (with a metal bar whose length varies between a metre and a metre and a half).

Furthermore, as a complement of his gymnastic proposal, López Gómez turns to sports, making brief descriptions of the ones which were more popular by that time and that he used in his lessons. Among them, horse riding is found and it is defined, in a peculiar way, as an activity based on mixed exercises, neither passive nor active ones.[95] He claims that its effects are healthy if it is practiced sensibly and that tone, energy, balance apart from other moral and leisure ones are among its benefits.[96]

Similarly, he writes on swimming, which he defends. In his works, there is an extensive historical review of this sport activity, mainly focused on the classical period in which it was already used as military training.[97] It is defined, according to Dr Ronquillo's work written in Barcelona in 1876 as: 'The most perfect of all active exercises, the art of sustaining and advancing in the water, executing some rhythmic exercises that we should learn'.[98]

He distinguishes among two swimming varieties, the sport one and hydratia, a term that from the nineteenth century is equivalent to hydrotherapy, which dates back to the seventeenth century.

Another sport that he deals with in some chapters is fencing, that he defines as an art and says that some people regard it as a science.[99] Despite describing some fencing exercises, he recognizes, in a hidden way, that he is not specialized in it. In the book *El Gimnasio*, the four pages dedicated to it are from an article taken, literally, according to his description: 'To the benevolence of our special friend M. Tirso de Arregui, *Caballero Teniente Mayor del Reino y de la Real Orden americana de Isabel la Católica*, we owe him the following copied lines'.[100]

In this line, he also admits that he knows most exercises of this kind thanks to Carbonell brothers, who visited Seville to teach in the 'Círculo de Labradores':

> For the description of fencing exercises, we follow the one from our special friends Mr. Carbonell brothers, which is the best one known, as we could see in the hall of arms of Seville's 'Círculo de Labradores', where they were established as teachers for some years.[101]

Through fencing, we could notice his interest in the therapeutic and rehabilitative aspects of these exercises. He said about fencing that medicine uses it in order to correct lack of balance or side body weaknesses, making people exercise those weak sides.

Last, in his vast works he dedicated, although briefly and with less knowledge, attention to croquet, lawn tennis, bowling and football. In this last case, because of the descriptions that he makes of its rules in his work *Manual de Ejercicios Gimnásticos para uso de Institutos y Escuelas Normales*, his knowledge was biased and rudimentary since in its description there are some elements already disappeared with the unification of rules that took place in 1863. Nonetheless, López Gómez, as a gymnastics teacher, made his students in the secondary school play football in 1895, when this sport was barely practiced. Hence, there is a specific reference in a Sevillian newspaper in 1895.[102]

Conclusions

The figure of López Gómez as a teacher, prolific writer and speaker, law developer and critic make him one of the most relevant figures in Spanish gymnastics in the nineteenth and twentieth centuries.[103] In fact, this is proved by the high number of gyms all over Spain that recognized him as honorary director or the large number of books and articles that he published in his life.[104] As a result, he was given a striking name that was reflected in this article's title: apostle of gymnastics in Spain.

Regarding this, it is to be pointed out that his professional career was developed in a remarkably hostile context. Even though there are some remnants of the growing development of gymnastics in Europe, this was only perceived in the largest cities as Madrid or Barcelona since the underdeveloped and rural South was far from those modernity flares.

It is true that he did not develop his own method but his enormous job as an author shows the knowledge that he had from the different nineteenth century gymnastic trends and even those of the emerging sports. In any case, he always had the gymnastics from his admired Amorós as a model, although he was informed of the latest news and innovations that emerged in this discipline. Actually, he was acquainted with the newest material and machines, which he introduced in the sphere of Sevillian gymnastics for the first time.

His ultimate purpose was to make gymnastics, which was considered as a fundamental discipline not only in physical but in intellectual and moral personal training, be respected and acknowledged by society at that time. In order to achieve this, there were two objectives: on the one hand, trying to bring gymnastics closer to medicine since he thought that gymnastics should be more scientific and medicine was the right science in which they could support, and; on the other hand, achieving this through the discipline's legal acknowledgement so that its practice was spread not only at schools but to the everyday life of citizens in gyms. To that end, apart from criticizing the laws which went against this, he tried unsuccessfully to make gymnastics regarded as 'publicly useful'. Nevertheless, this setback cannot obscure his professional career but, on the contrary, it must be an example of his commitment and passion towards this discipline. This is the last point of the paper since its outcome cannot be other than López Gómez's acknowledgement as a passionate gymnastics person who, with his huge professional effort, made this discipline become more popular, respected and practiced.

Notes

1. As Tuñon de Lara shows in his book, the Regenerationist Movement wanted to modernize all spheres of social and political life. See M. Tuñón de Lara, *La España del siglo XX* (Barcelona: Laia, 1974), 15–6.
2. Crown Decree, 8 July 1847. Gaceta de Madrid, 12 July 1847.
3. Crown Order, 14 August 1849. Gaceta de Madrid, 16 August 1849.
4. J.P. Sanchís Ramírez, *La actividad gimnástica y deportiva en Sevilla durante el siglo XIX* (Sevilla: Diputación de Sevilla, 2010), 231–5.
5. Fernández Sirvent, *Francisco Amorós y los inicios de la Educación Física moderna. Biografía de un funcionario al servicio de España y Francia* (Alicante: Servicio de Publicaciones de la Universidad de Alicante, 2005), 309–15.
6. J.L. Pastor Pradillo, *Manuales escolares y libros de texto de Educación Física en los estudios de Magisterio (1883–1978)* (Alcalá de Henares: Servicio de Publicaciones de la Universidad de Alcalá, 2005), 31.
7. X. Torrebadella Flix, 'Los apóstoles de la Educación Física. Trece semblanzas profesionales en la Educación Física española contemporánea', *Revista Española de Educación Física*, 406 (2014), 58.
8. J. Castro Prieto, *Orígenes del fútbol sevillano. La olvidada memoria británica* (Madrid: Punto Rojo, 2012), 14.
9. In fact, as X. Torrebadella Flix, J. Olivera Betrán and M. Martínez Bou show in 'Origen e institucionalización del asociacionismo gimnástico-deportivo en España en el siglo XIX (1882–1900)', *Apunts. Educación Física y Deportes* 119 (2015), 7–54, there were 34 gymnastics associations in Spain during the nineteenth century, out of which only two were located in

the south of the Iberian Peninsula (Badajoz and Cádiz). X. Torrebadella Flix and J. Olivera Betrán also show in 'The Birth of the Sports Press in Spain Within the Regenerationist Context of the Late Nineteenth Century', *The International Journal of the History of Sport* 30, no. 18 (2013), 2164–96, this reality, because there were no magazines related to gymnastics in southern Spain.

10. J.L. Hernández Vázquez, 'Los aparatos de Amorós y su influencia en la gimnástica española del siglo XIX', in T. González Aja and J.L. Hernández Vázquez (eds), *Seminario Francisco Amorós su obra entre dos culturas* (Madrid: Excmo, Cabildo Insular de Gran Canaria, 1990), 35.

11. A. Ávila Fernández, 'Salvador López Gómez y la conformación de la gimnasia como disciplina académica durante el siglo XIX: Postulados teórico-prácticos', in *XI Coloquio de la Historia de la Educación. La acreditación de saberes y competencias. Perspectiva histórica* (Oviedo: Universidad de Oviedo, 2001), 39–47; A. Ávila Fernández, 'La importancia y necesidad de la gimnasia según el pensamientos educativo de Emilio Salvador López Gómez', in *I Jornadas Andaluzas de Historia del Deporte* (Sevilla: Departamento Educación Física y Deporte de la Universidad de Sevilla, 2008), 3–21; and Herrera García, 'Emilio Salvador López Gómez'.

12. Documentary collection centres: Archives (Archivo del Casino Militar de Sevilla, Archivo de la Diputación Provincial de Sevilla, Archivo General de la Administración, Archivo General de Andalucía, Archivo Histórico Provincial de Sevilla, Archivo Histórico de Protocolo de Sevilla, Archivo Histórico de la Universidad de Sevilla, Archivo del Instituto de Enseñanza Secundaria y Bachillerato 'San Isidoro' de Sevilla, Archivo Municipal de Sevilla, Archivo de la Sociedad Económica de Amigos del País de Sevilla); Libraries (Biblioteca de la antigua Real Sociedad de Medicina, Biblioteca del Ateneo de Sevilla, Biblioteca Municipal de Sevilla, Biblioteca de la Escuela de Magisterio de Sevilla, Fondo Antiguo, Biblioteca del Instituto Nacional de Educación Física de Madrid, Biblioteca Nacional, Biblioteca Central de la Universidad de Sevilla); Newspaper libraries (Hemeroteca Municipal de Sevilla, Hemeroteca Nacional, Hemeroteca del Instituto Andaluz del Deporte).

13. Computerized datebases (Google Scholar, Red de Bibliotecas Universitarias Españolas, Catálogo Colectivo del Patrimonio Bibliográfico Español, Catálogo de Bibliotecas Públicas del Estado, Fondo de las bibliotecas perteneciente al Consejo Superior de Investigaciones Científicas, Catálogo Colectivo del Fondo Antiguo en Lengua Española en materia de actividad física y deporte).

14. A. Herrera García, 'Emilio Salvador López y Gómez, Catedrático de Gimnástica'. *Hespérides: Anuario de investigaciones* 15 (2007), 66.

15. Ávila Fernández, 'La importancia y la necesidad', 7. Sanchís Ramírez, *La actividad gimnástica y deportiva en Sevilla,* 246.

16. X. Torrebadella Flix, 'Victor Venitien, un gimnasiarca discípulo de Amorós en Sevilla (1839–1861). Notas para completar la historia de la Educación Física española', *Arte y Movimiento* 9 (2013), 25.

17. V. Morillas Alonso, *Guía general de Sevilla y su provincia* (Sevilla: Imprenta y litografía de la Revista Mercantil, 1860), 83.

18. Ibid., 206.

19. M. Méndez Bejarano, *Diccionario de escritores, maestros y oradores naturales de Sevilla y su actual provincia* (Sevilla: Tipografía Gironés, 1922), 406.

20. Ávila Fernández, 'Salvador López y la conformación', 44.

21. This is the commonly accepted number of graduates, but Martínez Navarro raises it to 97 (80 men and 17 women) in 'Datos para la historia de una iniciativa fallida'. A. Martínez Navarro, 'Datos para la historia de una iniciativa fallida: la Escuela Central de Gimnástica', *Historia de la Educación,* 14 (2013), 147.

22. S. López Gómez, *Breve reseña histórica de la gimnástica en Europa* (Sevilla: Imprenta de Juan Moyano, 1821), 21.

23. *Revista La Educación Física*, 1919, 25.

24. Méndez Bejarano, *Diccionario de escritores, maestros y oradores*, 405.

25. *El Universal*, 16 January 1877, 37.

26. A. Ávila Fernández, *Moverse es vivir. Emilio Salvador López Gómez (1852–1936). La gimnasia en Sevilla* (Sevilla: Diputación de Sevilla, 2014), 242.
27. R. Fernández Sirvent, 'Memoria y olvido de Francisco Amorós y su método educativo gimnástico y moral'. *RICYDE Revista Internacional de Ciencias del Deporte* 6 (2007), 42.
28. Ávila Fernández, *Moverse es vivir*, 55.
29. López Gómez, *Breve reseña histórica*, 34.
30. Fernández Sirvent, 'Memoria y olvido', 32.
31. S. López Gómez, *Curso Teórico-Práctico de la Educación Física* (Sevilla: Imprenta Eulogio de las Heras, 1916), 65.
32. F. Collantes de Terán Delorme, *Crónicas de la Feria (1847–1916)* (Sevilla: Ayuntamiento. Servicio de Publicaciones, 1981), 111.
33. *Revista La Educación Física*, 1919, 25.
34. Ibid.
35. A. Ávila Fernández, *Historia de la Escuela Normal de Maestros de Sevilla en la Segunda Mitad del Siglo XIX* (Sevilla: Alfar, 1986), 230.
36. 'Standing committee of Public Instruction Ministry's report, dismissing Salvador López's request to appear in the secondary teachers' general scale', Salvador López Gómez's personal file, Signatura 5766, Archivo General de la Administración.
37. 'Release from Public Instruction's General Direction informing Salvador López Gómez of his appointment as gymnastics teacher in the secondary school of Seville, with annual wages of 2000 pesetas, Legajo 5766–7, Archivo General de la Administración.
38. 'Literary University of Sevilly in which the Seville University Chancellor communicates Public Instruction's General Director that the headmaster of Seville Institute sent a him a letter informing that the current 9th March (1893), D. Emilio Salvador López Gómez took office as Gymnastics teacher', Legajo 5766–7, Archivo General de la Administración.
39. Salvador López Gómez's personal file, Signatura 5766, Archivo General de la Administración.
40. Ávila Fernández, *Moverse es vivir*, 60.
41. 'Report from 13th June 1984 for Public Instruction General Director made by Province Institute of Secondary Education of Seville', Legajo 661, Archivo Histórico de la Universidad de Sevilla.
42. *Revista La Educación Física*, 1919, 25.
43. Legajo 5766–7, Archivo General de la Administración.
44. Crown Order, 22 March 1922. Gaceta de Madrid, 28 March 1922.
45. Méndez Bejarano, *Diccionario de escritores, maestros y oradores*, 406.
46. Ávila Fernández, *Moverse es vivir*, 37–8.
47. *Colección Legislativa de España*, Tomo 110 (Madrid: Imprenta Ministerio de Gracia y Justicia, 1960), 1443–54.
48. López Gómez, *Breve reseña histórica*, 36.
49. P. Alcántara García, *Teoría y Práctica de la Educación y la Enseñanza* (Madrid: Gras y Compañía Editores, 1882), 90.
50. *Colección Legislativa de España*, 1443–54.
51. Crown Order, 10 September 1893. Gaceta de Madrid, 11 September 1893.
52. Decree, 16 September 1894. Gaceta de Madrid, 16 September 1894.
53. S. López Gómez, *Manual de ejercicios gimnásticos para los Institutos y Escuelas Normales* (Sevilla: Imprenta de Gironés y Orduña, 1894), 6.
54. Ibid., 9.
55. López Gómez wrote many books, unpublished typescripts, magazine articles and conference papers. Due to the scope of this paper, we will focus on the books, since they are his most relevant publications, dedicating less importance to unpublished typescripts, conference papers and articles (quoting only the most relevant).
56. S. López Gómez, *El Gimnasio* (Sevilla: Imprenta de Baldaraque, 1873), 3.
57. López Gómez, *Breve reseña histórica de la gimnástica en Europa*, cover page.
58. X. Torrebadella Flix, 'Las primeras revistas profesionales y científicas de la Educación física española (1882–1936)', *Apunts. Educación Física y Deportes* 109 (2012), 14.

59. Ibid.
60. Two years before, he published 'Importancia y necesidad de la gimnástica. Concepto de esta parte de la Educación Física en las escuelas públicas', which has not yet been discovered.
61. S. López Gómez, 'Higiene de la gimnástica', unpublished typescripts, Sevilla, 1892.
62. This conference paper text, consisting of 17 pages, was published in several numbers of the biweekly magazine *Los Deportes* (1897–1910). In fact, this was his first great article.
63. In 1893, he published another work 'Catálogo descriptivo de aparatos. Proyecto de Gimnasia Higiénica Municipal', which has not yet been discovered.
64. S. López Gómez, 'Hidroterapia. Su historia y aparatos portátiles más usuales', Unpublished manuscript, Sevilla, 1893.
65. X. Torrebadella Flix, 'Crítica a la bibliografía gimnástica de la Educación Física publicada en España (1801–1939)', *Anales de Documentación* 16, no. 1 (2013), 8.
66. S. López Gómez, *Programa razonado de Teoría y Práctica de la Gimnástica. Lecciones explicadas* (Sevilla: Imprenta de Díaz y Carballo, 1894).
67. S. López Gómez, 'Educación Física para niñas', unpublished manuscript, Sevilla, 1895.
68. Torrebadella Flix, 'Las primeras revistas', 15–6.
69. S. López Gómez, 'La Gimnástica en España. Su historia y legislación', unpublished typescripts, Sevilla, 1897.
70. Although X. Torrebadella Flix indicated in *Repertorio bibliográfico inédito de la educación física y el deporte en España (1800–1939)* (Madrid: Fundación Universitaria Española, 2011) that he has not found this publication, we have located a copy of this book in 'Archivo Histórico de la Universidad de Sevilla'. See S. López Gómez, *Unificación de la enseñanza de la Gimnástica por un solo método* (Sevilla: Imprenta El Mercantil, 1899).
71. S. López Gómez, *Manera de armonizar la Educación Física con la intelectual y la moral durante todo el periodo educativo, desenvolviendo la educación integral* (Sevilla: Imprenta El Mercantil, 1900); S. López Gómez, *Modernos derroteros de la Gimnástica* (Sevilla: Imprenta de Francisco de P. Díaz, 1902).
72. This article, consisting of 17 pages, appeared in several numbers (published between 29 June and 31 August 1902) of the biweekly magazine *Los Deportes*.
73. S. López Gómez, *Atlas de ejercicios gimnásticos higiénicos* (Sevilla: Escuelas Profesionales de Artes y Oficios, 1906).
74. S. López Gómez, *Atlas de ejercicios de cultura física* (Sevilla: Establecimiento tipográfico Francisco Díaz, 1914).
75. S. López Gómez, *¿Debe subsistir la enseñanza de la Gimnástica?* (Sevilla: Imprenta Eulogio de las Heras, 1910).
76. S. López Gómez, *La cultura física en sus relaciones con la higiene de la infancia* (Sevilla: Imprenta del Asilo de los Huérfanos del Santo Corazón de Jesús, 1914).
77. Salvador López Gómez's personal file, Signatura 5766, Archivo General de la Administración.
78. Ibid.
79. S. López Gómez, *La Educación Física en la mujer* (Sevilla: Imprenta La Exposición, 1917), 6.
80. S. López Gómez, 'Pro Educación Física', unpublished typescripts, Sevilla, 1918.
81. S. López Gómez, 'Las colonias escolares desde el punto de vista higiénico, educativo y social', unpublished typescripts, Sevilla, 1922.
82. The referenced articles can be viewed in Ávila Fernández *Moverse es vivir*, 544–5.
83. According to Pastor Pradillo lack of knowledge of the early teachers tried to compensate with knowledge from other areas, such as medicine. See J.L. Pastor Pradillo, *Gimnástica. De la inopia conceptual a la utopía metodológica* (Madrid: Librería deportiva Esteban Sanz, S.L., 2003), 139.
84. López Gómez, *Manual de ejercicios gimnásticos para los Institutos y Escuelas Normales*, 12.
85. Ibid.
86. A. Ávila Fernández, 'Influencia de la educación física (gimnástica) en la higiene infantil como fuente de salud: estudio analítico a través de la bibliografía pedagógica de Emilio Salvador López Gómez', in P. Dávila y L.M. Naya (ed.), *La infancia en la historia: espacios y representaciones*, vol. 1 (San Sebastián: Erein, 2005), 510.

87. Ibid., 48.
88. Ibid., 46.
89. Ibid., 13.
90. Ibid., 35.
91. López Gómez, *El Gimnasio*, 98.
92. Ibid., 99.
93. His two works in which he deeply explains the notion of machine and its types are: López Gómez, *El Gimnasio*, and López Gómez, *Manual de ejercicios gimnásticos para los Institutos y Escuelas Normales*.
94. López Gómez, *El Gimnasio*, 92.
95. López Gómez, *Manual de ejercicios gimnásticos para los Institutos y Escuelas Normales*, 187.
96. Ibid., 188.
97. Ibid., 185.
98. Ibid., 173.
99. Ibid., 180.
100. López Gómez, *El Gimnasio*, 189.
101. López Gómez, *Manual de ejercicios gimnásticos para los Institutos y Escuelas Normales*, 143.
102. *Diario el Noticiero Sevillano* 321 (1895), 23.
103. We agree with Miguel Ortega because he says that López Gómez boasted a great leadership within gymnastics at his time, which was manifested in his work as a teacher, author and promoter of laws. Indeed, he was a great propagandist of gymnastics during the last third of the nineteenth century and during the first third of the twentieth century. See A. Miguel Ortega, 'Don Emilio Salvador López Gómez. Iniciador y propagandista de la formación del profesorado de Educación Física en España' (PhD diss., Universidad de Burgos, 2015).
104. In fact, Torrebadella Flix and Olivera Betrán presented a selection of 100 books from the bibliographic repertoire of physical education and sport, which included three of López Gómez´s books: *El Gimnasio, Breve reseña histórica de la gimnástica en Europa* and *Manual de ejercicios gimnásticos para los Institutos y Escuelas Normales*. See X. Torrebadella Flix and J. Olivera Betrán, 'Las cien obras clave del repertorio bibliográfico español de la Educación Física y el deporte en su proceso de legitimación e institucionalización (1807–1938)', *Revista General de Información y Documentación* 22 (2012), 119–68.

Disclosure statement

No potential conflict of interest was reported by the authors.

ORCID

Gonzalo Ramírez-Macías http://orcid.org/0000-0002-3749-6658

Sport Versus Bullfighting: The New Civilizing Sensitivity of Regenerationism and its Effect on the Leisure Pursuits of the Spanish at the Beginning of the Twentieth Century

Antonio Rivero Herraiz and Raúl Sánchez-García

ABSTRACT

This article analyzes the influence of the new civilizing sensitivity of the Spanish regenerationists in the introduction of sport, in place of bullfighting, during the first third of the twentieth century. Following the colonial collapse of the late nineteenth century and the subsequent demoralization of the country, the regenerationists saw in physical education and sport a way to reform the broken Spanish population. Sport had arrived in Spain in the mid-nineteenth century by way of the aristocracy and would then spread to the urban middle classes, imbued with the reformist sense of the regenerationists. It came in the form of amateur sport, with values of modernity and a civilizing sensitivity which were diametrically opposed to activities such as bullfighting that had such great support from the Spanish public. Amongst the urban middle classes, sport developed as a kind of amateur practice, used for the formation of a more civilized character and the expression of individuality; on the contrary, amongst the working classes, sport spread primarily in its professional form, by way of mass spectator sports (football and boxing), representing a civilizing spurt in severing the link between entertainment and death which was central to bullfighting.

Introduction

After the demise and loss of its colonies in 1898, Spain entered into a deep process of demoralization, which went as far as to question the very essence of the nation, and the Spanish as a 'race'. Faced with this state of affairs, the Regenerationist movement, with its principal advocate Joaquín Costa at the forefront, tried to improve the conditions of a demoralized population. One of the main weapons in their arsenal to achieve the *regeneration* of the nation was sport.[1] Although English-style sporting activities had been present since the mid-nineteenth century, thanks to the upper-classes identifying the British aristocracy as a symbol of status and class, sporting practice began to spread to the urban middle classes, a group imbued with the sense of reform that drove regenerationism[2].

Sporting activity saw itself enlivened by a new sense of competition, guided by *fair play* and regulated accordingly to the typical mind-set of the century. Sport was considered a symbol of European modernity in contrast to the dominant physical culture of Spain, a culture linked to *casticismo* [authentic traditional customs],[3] and whose most obvious example was bullfighting, considered at that time to be a 'national *fiesta*'.[4] We are informed by way of *castizo* [authentic traditional] practices – originating in certain literary, cultural and ideological attitudes – that since the eighteenth century, traditional Spanish customs directly contrasted enlightened or 'Gallicized' stances. Between the end of the nineteenth and the first third of the twentieth century, we could cite as examples of such customs: bullfighting festivals, flamenco, zarzuela [a type of operetta], sainete [a type of comic sketch] and so on; all of which held great prestige in popular urban culture.

Curiously enough, bull-related activities had formed a part of what had hitherto been encompassed by the term 'sport' since the medieval period in Spain. According to various authors,[5] the word 'sport' appears in Castillian (coming from the Provençal *deport*) to denote a series of courtly leisure activities, some of which included hunting, jousting, juegos de cañas (a game that consisted of rows formed by men on horseback throwing wooden canes at each other and blocking them with shields) and even bullfighting. As asserted by Ramírez Macías, bullfighting was a sport that was extremely characteristic of Spain in the Golden Age (sixteenth–seventeenth centuries).[6] However, this medieval-style 'sport' underwent a series of very significant semantic changes during the nineteenth century, owing on one hand to different European gymnastics schools, and on the other to English *sport*. English sporting activities had arrived in Spain in the mid-nineteenth century. By this point, bullfighting had achieved a certain status of autonomy in its development and had come to be considered as the 'national *fiesta*'. Nevertheless, even by the mid-1800s, we still find contemporary dictionaries including bull-related activities in the translation of the word *sport*. In 1852, the *Sociedad gimnástica-tauromáquica* (Gymnastic Bullfighting Society) was founded in Barcelona, as an example of a sporting association.[7] In fact, it is interesting that the first uses of the revived Castillian word *deporte* (which would end up coming into fashion in its use as the word *sport* in the 1920s) appear in the bullfighting reports of Mariano de Cávia in 1887 and 1888 as a translation of the English word *sport*.[8] However, we do not find this link between bullfighting and the terms *sport* or *deporte* in any dictionary of the 1890s.[9] It was in this decade that the regenerationists drew contrast in their speeches between what was meant by English *sport* and bullfighting,[10] displaying a new sensitivity with a higher degree of 'civilization' in the sense that Norbert Elias uses this term. To better understand this specific use, we will pause briefly to look at the analysis which Elias carried out on the Civilizing Process in relation to the pacification and systemization of leisure and sport.[11] Based on the analysis of empirical data on European books of manners, Elias draws the conclusion that a long process of pacification took place after the series of hegemonic battles which gave rise to modern-day nation states.[12] This pacification brought with it a refinement of manners, an increase in self-control with regard to the spontaneity of emotional display and a lowering of the threshold of repugnance in the face of violence, as much in committing it as in witnessing it. The civilizing process has a lot to do with the emergence of modern sport. In eighteenth-century England, characterized by a period of peace, there emerged simultaneously processes such as participation in Parliament and the commencement of sporting activities. The same forces at work in one field were also at work in the other. The decision to conduct the resolution of conflict in a peaceful manner existed as much in the area of politics as it did in the area of leisure (for example, the practice of boxing would come to replace duels to the death with sword and pistol), forming what Elias would call a 'civilizing spurt', which in the case of sport came in two waves: one in the eighteenth century in country sports such as horse racing, fox hunting, cricket or boxing; and another in the nineteenth century, pertaining to the systemization of ball games (e.g. football and rugby) in public schools. In sporting practice itself we also see this civilizing tendency; as time goes by, as much in its regulation as in the reaction of the players and spectators, people become more sensitive towards the violent actions and verbal abuse in the game.

In England, there was continuity and integration between the two successive waves of sportization; in contrast to this, in Spain the first wave showed an autochthonous development (with examples of popular games, bullfighting and fencing, even if in the case of fencing there was an element of exchange and influence between various European countries). This demonstrated continuity in some cases, and discontinuity in others, with the arrival of the second wave, which came from English sport. We find an example of continuity in the case of the forms of Basque *pelota* [ball game], which as well as being a popular sport in major towns and in the middle of rural northern Spain (the Basque Country, Navarra and some parts of Castile and León), also cropped up in other places.[13] *Pelota* continued to be the most widespread game in the Basque-Navarre region, in spite of the fact that even there its popularity was dropping in the face of the spread of English sports. As an example of discontinuity, we find the case of bullfighting; it continued to develop, but only on the sidelines of the sporting movement, even clashing with it on the spectrum of tradition/ modernity, barbarism/civilization.

For the analysis of the values linked to both sport and bullfighting, a search was carried out in the vaults of the Newspaper and Periodicals Library of Madrid as well as in the National Library, for references and articles published in Spanish magazines and newspapers between 1898 and 1936 related to the sporting phenomenon; more specifically *Gran Vida*, Madrid (1910–1935) and *Heraldo Deportivo*, Madrid (1915–1936). The project was concluded with a study of the body of work produced by the *Regenerationist* ideology, analyzing the leading publications of Joaquín Costa and his followers, such as the educational methods of the *Institución Libre de Enseñanza* (the Free Educational Institution) linked, in particular, to the subject of sport.

In the following section, we will briefly deal with the degree of civilization in bullfighting in the second half of the nineteenth century; next, we will demonstrate the opposing evaluation that the regenerationists made on the topic of bullfighting and sport; we will see how the regenerationist influence on sport touched different groups of the Spanish population in different ways; and we will finish by drawing some conclusions about the studies presented.

The Degree of Civilization in Bullfighting in the Second Half of the Nineteenth Century

Bull-related activities in Spain, originating in the Middle Ages, had undergone a lengthy civilizing process.[14] They went from being a noble pursuit, like activities such as bull-spearing, to developing into bullfighting on foot as mass entertainment, which according to Cossío 'didn't have its own form until the end of the eighteenth century'[15] but had achieved a spectacular social presence by the second half of the nineteenth century, and one that was in the ascendancy. The growth of specialized magazines and newspapers on bullfighting over this period accounts for its increasing popularity.[16] According to Shubert, around 400 bullfights were held in the year of 1860, more than 700 in 1895, and over 800 in 1912.[17] Throughout the entire second half of the nineteenth century, bullfighting continued to display low standards of civilization when compared with the new leisure pursuits that came from England under the banner of 'sports'.

In 1836, the great matador Francisco Montes 'Paquiro' concluded his work *Tauromaquía completa* (A Complete Guide to Bullfighting) with a call for 'civilization', in the Eliasian sense: 'Banish that which is uncivil and bloodthirsty; enhance the enjoyment and combine skill and safety'.[18] We will now examine some of the reasons for which we regard the bullfighting with which the regenerationists were confronted at the end of the century as continuing to be uncivilized:

Jiménez Bajo documents that in the season of 1851 in Madrid, 165 bulls and 173 horses died as a result of bullfighting.[19] Giving figures for specific bullfights, the author uses examples of fights in 1850 and 1852 in which 30 horses died in each.[20] This pattern of each bull killing between two and three horses continued to be commonplace until the end of the century, as attested by the bullfighting reports of the time.[21] According to Shubert in the 1884 season, throughout the whole of Spain, 1244 bulls were fought and over 2000 horses died.[22] The horses did not wear any form of protection (the protective mantle was not introduced until 1927) and they ended up being ripped open and strewn across the bullring (Figure 1). In this sense, the description that Díaz-Cañabate gives of the level of civilization of the crowd at the end of the nineteenth century is very revealing:

> It cannot be refuted that bullfights back then were enormously cruel. 'Horses! Horses!' demanded the spectators, not content with the four or six or eight spike horses that died in each bullfight, ripped apart in the bullring. 'Goring!' screamed the crowd, eager to see blood spilled on the arena, in the very same Madrid that hosted circuses and cock fights on every corner.[23]

Figure 1. A cartoon about the widespread gory episodes of spike horses. Source: *La Lidia*, 11 August 1914, 8.

Speaking of the deaths of bullfighters, picadors and banderilleros [bull-fighting assistants] in the ring, de Bonifaz and de Roble show how the figures remained consistent (around 12 deaths per decade) in the 1850s, 1860s and 1870s, but climbed to 25 in 1880 and to 46 in 1890, rising even further at the turn of the twentieth century, arriving at the figure of 62 deaths between 1911 and 1920.[24] According to Shubert, this was due to the rise in both the number of bullfights and the number of fighters who entered the ring without the necessary training.[25]

They also continued to use, although less frequently, barbaric disciplines such as flaming barbs (to provoke the animal when it is docile); the *media luna* (a type of spear with a half-moon shaped blade on the end) used to hamstring the animal (to cut the tendons in the bulls' legs); or the dogs, to finish off the bulls that could not fight on. Nevertheless, the use of the dogs and the media luna to hamstring the animal rather declined in the mid-1800s and disappeared completely in the final quarter of the century.[26]

Regenerationism and Sport: A New Civilizing Sensitivity

The regenerationist movement and its ethical and political ideology was the most influential school of thought in Spanish political life during the first third of the twentieth century. The father and primary advocate of this movement was Joaquín Costa (1844–1911) with such influential works as *Reconstitución y Europeización de España* (The Reconstitution and Europeanization of Spain, 1899) and *Oligarquía y Caciquismo* (Ologarchy and Caciquism, 1901). Regenerationism demanded the general modernization of the nation and the structures of the state. Other renowned regenerationists were Lucas Mallada (*Los males de la patria y la futura revolución española* [The Ills of the Homeland and the Future Spanish Revolution], 1890), Ramiro de Maeztu (*Hacia otra España* [Toward Another Spain], 1899), Macías Picavéa (*El problema nacional* [The National Problem], 1899), Luis Morote (*La moral de la derrota* [The Moral of the Defeat], 1900), Rafael Altamira (*Psicología del pueblo español* [The Psychology of the Spanish People], 1901), etc. Regenerationism held sway over the intellectual life of the country (see the work of Ortega y Gasset) and it was warmly welcomed amongst the middle classes who were in favour of a modernized society.

The fact is that the regenerationist discourse was fundamental to the arguments of the first proponents of sport and physical culture.[27] Physical regeneration as an aim, and advances in hygiene and cultural habits as a by-product of practising sport would be, for its pioneers, the most obvious and beneficial consequences of the development of physical culture and education in Spain. The institutionalization of such ideas through school physical education served also a political-administrative interest in boosting the national productive capacity through the health improvement of its citizens.[28] There were three professional sectors which actively encouraged physical education and sport in our country: teachers, doctors and the military. All of these three groups, by way of specialized texts and articles – which they frequently published in daily and sporting newspapers – are the best testimony to the prevailing regenerationist theories and their relationship with physical education and sport.

In contrast to the advocates of bullfighting, who saw the national *fiesta* as a sign of the country's virility,[29] the regenerationists sought out sport as a means of development, confronting the *castizo* [traditional] culture that had both fostered and maintained the backwardness and degeneration of the country.

The first person to concern himself with talking about the importance of physical education as a basis for all regenerative activity was the self-same Joaquín Costa, in a speech that he gave on 13 November 1898 in the Agricultural Chambers of Alto Aragón. An institution bound to the regenerationist movement that was pivotal in the articulation of sporting values and programmes was the Institución Libre de Enseñanza (The Free Educational Institution) or ILE, which put their faith in the practice of games and sport as a pedagogical model and as a means of regeneration amongst the nation's youths, providing a huge amount of written output on the importance of these practices in their educational systems.[30] The Institution always made clear its preference for English educational styles, to which it attributed the sense of superiority and prestige which everything British enjoyed worldwide at this point in time. The archetype of the 'gentleman' was always at play amongst the institutionalists. This led them to employ outdoor games and sport as a means of education, for the physical and ethical improvement of the student body. Games were introduced in the Institution, replacing gymnastics, amongst other reasons because regeneration should not be limited to the physical, but should also include the perfection of morals and character:

> … in all ages and all nations the playing field has been and continues to be the most suitable place for a child to understand, practise and improve the notion of rights, of duty, of liberty, of authority, of subservience, of responsibility, of protection, of criticism and so many other social concepts of the utmost importance, that which in books doesn't hold any sort of appeal for a child.[31]

Texts about the importance of physical education and sport regularly appeared in specialist magazines of the time, linking backwardness and crisis with the poor health and limited physical abilities of the Spanish people. Physical and sporting activities inevitably led to a rapprochement with Nordic and Anglosaxon civilizations, held in such high esteem in a Spain in decline, still reeling from the 'Disaster of 98'.[32] To this effect, we can read in the *Heraldo Deportivo* in 1920 a piece by prominent educator and supporter of the sporting cause, Lorrenzo Luzuriaga, who viewed sport and physical exercise as prestigious social and cultural activities, progressive and inseparable from the study of technology, sciences and arts; he valued physical education and sporting practice as signs of cultural advancement, commenting as such in his thesis, which placed sport as a civilizing activity, a force for social modernization pertaining to the most developed populations and nation of the twentieth century.[33]

The regenerationist prestige was at its greatest in cities, amongst the middle classes who sympathized with their proposals and who were characterized by sharing with them a high level of education and a culture forged in the big city. These groups would make up the advance civilizing party who strongly disagreed with the bullfighting activities which were associated with a more conservative social structure. This sensibility against animal mistreatment in so-called animal sports was a characteristic feature of other European middle classes, especially acute in the British case.[34] As an example of this active social movement in England, the Stanford bull running (an activity close to current Spanish bull running) was fiercely opposed by these middle class groups at least since 1788, finally succeeding at banning the activity in 1840.[35] In Spain, bullfighting had been under extreme scrutiny from the regenerationists from day one. Joaquín Costa strongly criticized bullfighting on account of the harmful effects that it had on the spectators. In 'Los Pulmones del Español' (The Lungs of the Spanish), Costa criticized the moral state of a population engrossed in cruel pastimes:

> [W]e do not lack the lungs to insult the blood-stained horses, with more vigour, with more enthusiasm, not than the Romans, but than the very cannibals surrounding their prisoners who are pierced on the spit.[36]

In 'Un mal inveterado' (A deep-seated evil), Costa criticized bullfighting not only as a school of vice, but also for being an obstacle which prevented the integration of Spain on the stage of international modernity:

> Bullfighting is a deep-seated evil that is much more harmful to us than many people believe, and much more so than it at first appears; from the perversion of public feeling to disrepute abroad, there is a sinister series of steps that debase us.[37]

The works of Eugenio Noel, very much aligned with the hypotheses of Costa's regenerationism, show bullfighting as one of the principal causes of Spain's backwardness.[38] In chapter 23 of his 1913 work *Campaña antiflamenca* (Anti-flamenco Campaign), Noel compares the figures of the British adventurer Scott and the Spain bullfighter Dominguín as examples of national heroes, and laments his country's inability to take part in such scientific expeditions:

> Norwegians, Frenchmen and Englishmen have competed for these feats. We have competed with Bulls. I have in front of me a photograph of those heroes at the foot of Mount Erebus; compared with a photograph of Dominguín's funeral, at which the immense crowd is so tightly packed, I must confess that I'm ashamed not to be English. I do not understand how a wound from a bull's horn can put a man on a pedestal.[39]

We have already noted that the influence of the regenerationists made itself known during the first few decades of the twentieth century. Throughout these years, the attitude of some sportsmen and people partially involved in the promotion of physical activity was very clearly at odds with bullfighting. Their concern for rationally demonstrating how wrong and uncivilized the traditional *fiesta* was led them to carry out detailed studies on them, like the one that was published in 1931 in various issues of the *Heraldo Deportivo* by Dr Luis Lozano Rey, the professor of Natural Sciences of the Central University of Madrid. His study was divided into 13 chapters which give an impression of just how exhaustive it was: (1) The Bullfighting *fiesta* and its urgent and mandatory mellowing; (2) Bullfighting, as a *fiesta*; (3) Bullfighting, in its artistic aspect; (4) Bullfighting as showcase of cunning; (5) Bullfighting as an educational school; (6) Bulls, as a fertile source of physical and moral pain; (7) The process of the bullfight; (8) The crowd; (9) The bullfighting critics; (10) The professionals; (11) The profiteers of bullfighting; (12) Others involved; (13) A conciliatory formula. We will highlight one particular extract of this study:

> It is clear that bullfighting constitutes a show that, for various reasons – in particular its traditional nature – has such ingrained support in our country that it is considered, perhaps hyperbolically, as unrealistic to try and abolish it completely. However I believe it is what must be done, if only to weaken the bad reputation that Spain holds in other civilised countries; it is for this stigma that we are seen as a population on the edge of barbarism …
>
> And although it can be defended in certain, purely incidental ways, bullfighting is essentially barbaric, and in this sense it will not stand up to a calm and impartial analysis like the one that we are going to try to carry out, examining separately the *fiesta* itself and the elements that comprise it.[40]

The Spread of the Civilizing Sensitivity of Sport in Spanish Society

The ideas and the message of the regenerationists – that advocated practising physical activities and sport as a way of healing the physically and morally sick population – did not arrive in all the social sectors in the same way. The new civilizing sensitivity encountered many different obstacles. The development of the new phenomena of sport, which was quite clearly limited to cities, highlighted the evident duality that existed in Spain at the start of the twentieth century, between urban and rural life; a duality which, in many ways, and especially in the arena of sport, lasted for a large part of the twentieth century.[41] That is to say, the civilizing spurt that sport represented did not spread at the same time and in the same way throughout the land; nor did it spread the same throughout the entire population, what with the significant differences that existed between the social classes.[42] We must bear in mind that in Elias's analysis of the development of European societies, we see that civilizing spurts do not take place in all social groups simultaneously. As a matter of fact, in the subtitle of his most famous work *The Civilizing Process,*[43] the author mentions the fact that the changes that took place in the *habitus* (the structure of personality) related to the secular upper classes: the courtiers. Later on, such civilizing spurts would come to be democratized, spreading to the rest of the population. But this in itself would take time; for example, for this to happen they would need to create an education system at a national level, as well as introducing compulsory education. The analyses of social processes – the civilizing process being an example of such – which Elias carries out are always linked to another of his concepts, that of figuration, defined as chains of functional interdependence between people. In these figurations, we always find power dynamics between different social groups, whether dependent on class, gender, ethnicity, age and so on.

Therefore, when we talk about sport as a civilizing component of leisure in the Spanish society of the early twentieth century, we must take into consideration what the social figuration that made up leisure was at this point in time. To fully understand the relationship between bullfighting (a ritualistic endogenous tradition) and sport (a modern foreign practice), conceived as the opposition between 'two opposed mentalities that rivalled over the country's social, cultural and institutional space,'[44] we must anchor these symbolic struggles to specific social figurations, paying special attention to the dynamic relationship between social classes during that period. The sport and physical activity promoted by the regenerationists was essentially the English amateur model, which was linked to using sports in the formation of the character and the expression of individuality. This message made a strong impression on the new emerging urban middle classes – dedicated to liberal professions – and to the industrial bourgeoisie, both of whom were very much connected to reformist and modernizing stances, who contrasted this way of understanding sport (as a means of care, development and personal expression) with professional sports which were especially appealing to the working classes acting as spectators of large mass events. The professional model, whose leading players in the case of bullfighting were the promoters (the land-owning nobility and bourgeoisie) and the bullfighters (who came from the working classes), gave educational and formative values a backseat and prioritizes its own economic interests. The bullfighter was doubly rejected by the amateur sport model: he represented a pitiful educational school (demonstrating all the vices of barbarism) and his was a completely professional activity, a fact that had been well-established since the end of the eighteenth century. This double criticism of the bullfighter was very neatly summarized in the following article, published in the *Heraldo Deportivo*:

> In bullfighting, we can and should consider rural practices (and only for the performers, WITH THE EXCEPTION OF THE BULL AND THE HORSE) as sport; that is to say spearing cattle, on foot or on horseback, in the middle of the countryside, without wounding them, much less killing them.[45]

As a matter of fact, in the symbolic fight upheld by both blocs (professional and amateur) for the suitable definition of sport and other leisure activities, the criticism of the urban reformists was directed towards the weakest point of the rival bloc: the common people. The way to articulate this argument was to treat the masses (equated with the common people) as savages, as uncivilized people. As Maguire states, '… established groups almost invariably experience and present themselves as more civilized, while constructing outsiders as more barbaric'.[46] For the vast majority of bullfighting's critics, their biggest concern was not really for the welfare of the animal (although it is true that the Society for the Protection of Animals was founded in 1874 and its members were actively anti-bullfighting), but more for the moral corruption and backwardness it caused in its spectators. As asserted by Lozano Rey:

> Many cultured and learned people go to bullfights, but they are greatly outnumbered by spectators that, when it comes to learning and culture, leave a lot to be desired. All of them, in real life, behave normally, with the prudence that befits their class. But as soon as they get together inside the bullring, with the fuel that is provided by the mutual encouragement and guaranteed impunity, it becomes impossible to impose a code of conduct, or rules, or laws upon this congregated horde; each and every one is let loose and unleashes their passions, voicing them with the most expressive vocabulary that everyone craves, easily leading to fist-fights; and from all of this comes no small harvest/yield of outbursts/interjections, profanities, obscene sayings, insults aimed at the bullfighters, even sometimes towards the mother that raised them, and often directed towards the authorities that preside over the festival, the authorities which they defy and shame if, by the judgement of the *experts*, they do not correctly fulfil the tricky task of putting on the festival; the authorities that frequently find themselves being threatened by the throwing of bottles and other missiles, with the sole intention of cracking open the head of the matador that, by the doctors' judgement, hasn't fought well; when things do not come to an end with the sovereign crowds bursting onto the arena, ready to commit all kinds of abuse; or even with the outbreak of bitter arguments or violent clashes staged between groups of spectators, mainly because of differences of opinion with respect to the course of the fight or the matadors that take part in it. Vulgar expressions, violence, a lack of respect in the face of authority: these are the lessons that the bullfighting spectator habitually receives.[47]

But despite such criticism, bullfighting was far from disappearing. In the field of leisure, bullfighting had a long tradition of being linked to the well-established bloc comprised of both noble land-owners and also of common people. Such was its popularity amongst the Spanish people that the governmental prohibition of bullfighting in 1768, 1785, 1791 and 1805 had no effect. Proposals to ban bullfighting also passed through the Courts throughout the whole of the second half of the nineteenth century, but they never came into effect. In order to see the extent to which this national *fiesta* was ingrained in popular leisure pursuits, we can look at what happened in 1908 following the banning of the *capeas* [informal village bullfights]: in Cáceres the people, ignoring the ban, started the event, at which point the local governor called in the Civil Guard, creating a riot and resulting in various injuries, leaving three or four dead.[48]

It was from 1910 onwards that there began to change of emphasis in physical practices. English *sport*, in its most athletic forms, and as much in its individual forms as in its team sports, began to capture the attention of many fans and to be valued in the professional environments that, although stemming from different concepts and objectives, had so strongly encouraged the development of physical activity: doctors, the military and teachers. The result was the rise of English sports creating definitively, from the second decade of the century, the Spanish associative and federative system, on both a regional and national level.[49] The national sporting federations and institutions of today were formed from this base.

But if the change in the civilizing sensibility of the Regenerationists had spread straight away through the urban followers of the middle classes by means of amateur sport, the way in which this civilizing advance reached the working classes was by means of the offer of professional sports like football and boxing – two sports which, alongside bullfighting, came to share the reputation of being a true 'subculture of the masses' in the eyes of the popular classes in the 1920s.[50] In the summer of 1915, for example, a wrestling competition was held in a Madrid bullring. Commentaries on this very event appeared in the *Heraldo Deportivo* under the title of 'Wrestlers in the Bullring':

> What an enormous triumph it is that a display of physical culture has taken the place of the *spolarium* of Spanish horses and bulls … The day in which all of the bullrings in Spain are turned into athletics stadia, perhaps that will be the first day of the true regeneration of our people. Sadly, this day is still far off, but everything must start somewhere. We expect that one day, perhaps, the bull promoters will regret having let the herculean Greco-Roman champions take over the red-hot sand.[51]

The very essence of the regenerationist discourse, that for decades remained present in Spanish politics/political life, was made plain in these lines. The passion for football kept on growing, as is asserted in the article entitled 'The enormous football following and the success of our special issue', published in the magazine *Gran Vida* in 1924:

> Support for football continues to *crescendo*, in spite of a few taurophile writers who observe with unease how the support for sports in general, with football undoubtedly occupying first place, overshadows the *other* love. Evenings of 25,000 or more spectators are not uncommon in the Stadium, and recently there was a conflict on the racing track, during the championship race, which took place on the 10th of the tournament: in spite of the expansion of the stands – in such a way that today there is much more space than last year – they didn't come close to housing the immense crowd that amassed outside its walls; a crowd which fought so hard to get inside that it knocked down doors and any other obstacles in its path, causing the aforementioned conflict.[52]

Even if football and boxing could also be criticized for their professionalism, they without doubt represented a civilizing surge in comparison to bullfighting, steering clear of the death and gore that it epitomized (Figures 2 and 3). In the case of boxing, the following comparison that Ruiz Ferry draws with bullfighting is very revealing:

Figure 2. A big crowd attended the Spain versus Belgium match at San Mamés (Athletic Bilbao's Stadium). Source: *Heraldo Deportivo*, Madrid, no. 208, 25 February, 1921, 58.

Figure 3. A boxing championship held in the sports ground of the Real Sociedad Gimnástica Española.
Source: *Gran Vida*, no. 181, July, 1918, 201.

In boxing matches, the *Knock-out* is not essential to the outcome of the fight. Not long ago the *technical Knock-out* was discovered, an incredible subterfuge which replaces the voluntary k.o., which was entirely permitted within the rules of boxing. In bullfights it is rare that there are no horses killed, and it is rarer still that a bull leaves the ring alive; but if it does so, you can be sure that it leaves more dead than alive … only to die moments later.[53]

Conclusions

Sport in Spain in the first third of the twentieth century was another form of regeneration for a population who, without any confidence in its own forces after its loss of empire, found itself clinging to outdated traditions and customs that separated them from the cutting edge of European civilization. English-style sport represented a civilizing spurt with respect to other widespread and well-established leisure activities in Spain like bullfighting. The way in which sport spread amongst the population was not homogenous. The practice of sporting activities was extremely linked to the upper classes and later to the professional middle classes, who were the true heirs of the reforming policies propagated by regenerationist writers. In contrast, the working classes came into contact with sporting practice chiefly as spectators of large mass events. Sport, both as an amateur practice and a spectacle, implied a civilizing spurt in the area of leisure. If we compare this with bullfighting, mass spectator sports like football or boxing offered a distancing from death in the spectacle. However, bullfighting continued to have a huge following at this point in time; we have seen how within the complicated figuration of Spanish society, the influential capacity of this cultural and educational vanguard that the middle classes represented was limited when it came to influencing the sensitivities of the common people.

Norbert Elias's theory on leisure and sport in the civilizing process, based on indisputable evidence from the social history of England, could be applied in order to understand the importance of sport in Spain; although taking place in a different time and geographical place, the process was similar in so far as it represented a search for new ways and forms to live and to feel. In order to form a flawless account of the social history of contemporary Spain from the end of the nineteenth century, one would have to bear in mind the origins and the development of sport, as a social and cultural event of great importance; and one which in large cities – Madrid, Barcelona, Bilbao, etc. – started to forge a more European and less *castiza* [traditional] society, based on a regenerating and modernizing effort from its institutions and its way of life.

Notes

1. Antonio Rivero Herraiz, 'Los valores del regeneracionismo en la educación física española (1898–1936)', *REEFD*, no. 38 (April–June 2009), 11.
2. A. Rivero Herraiz and R. Sánchez-García, 'The British Influence in the Birth of Spanish Sport', *The International Journal of the History of Sport* 28, no. 13 (2010), 1788–809.
3. The Spanish adjective 'castizo' has a complex range of meanings, which makes it impossible to find an exact translation: traditional, typical to the country, authentic, pure, and sometimes with the more negative connotation of antiquated or outdated.
4. Antonio Rivero Herraiz, 'Los orígenes del deporte y la fiesta taurina', in AA.VV, *Sport and Violence* (Sevilla: Universidad Pablo de Olavide, 2006), 210–4.
5. Joan Corominas, *Diccionario crítico etimológico de la lengua castellana* III (Madrid: Gredos, 1956); Miguel Piernavieja, 'Depuerto, deporte, protohistoria de una palabra', *Citius, Altius,*

Fortius, no. 7 (1966), 5–190; Maximiano Trapero, *El campo semántico 'deporte'* (Tenerife: Confederación de las Cajas de Tenerife, 1979).

6. Gonzalo Ramírez Macías, 'Deporte espectáculo en España durante el Siglo de Oro', *Cultura, Ciencia y Deporte* 7, no. 3 (2007), 10.
7. X. Torrebadella Flix, J. Olivera Betrán, and M.M. Bou, 'Origen e institucionalización del asociacionismo gimnástico-deportivo en España en el siglo XIX (1822–1900)', *Apunts*, no. 119 (2015), 39.
8. J. Olivera Betrán and X. Torrebadella-Flix, 'Del sport al deporte: una discusión etimológica, semántica y conceptual en la lengua castellana', *Revista internacional de Medicina y Ciencias de la Actividad Física del Deporte* no. 57 (2015), 75.
9. Ibid.
10. Rivero Herraiz, 'Los orígenes del deporte y la fiesta taurina.'
11. N. Elias and E. Dunning, *Quest for Excitement: Sport and Leisure in the Civilising Process* (Oxford: Blackwell, 1986).
12. Norbert Elias, *The Civilizing Process: Sociogenetic and Psychogenetic Investigations* (Malden, MA: Blackwell Publishers, [1939] 2000).
13. As asserted by del Rivero: 'In this magazine, I have been constantly defending the advantages of promoting a *sport* which, like the game 'pelota', brings together, in my opinion, more benefits for physical education than all those imported from abroad put together … As we can see, *pelotarismo* [appreciation for 'pelota'] has not died, as is desired by some of those *sportsmen* who so enthusiastic about these *sports* that have foreign names …' (*Gran Vida*, no. 82 [1910], 76–7).
14. Raúl Sánchez-García, *Análisis sociológico de las actividades lúdicas caballerescas en la Edad Moderna española: el toreo a caballo en los siglos XVI y XVII*. Museo del Juego (Madrid: INEF, 2011).
15. José María de Cossío, *Los toros Vol 4. El Toreo* (Madrid: Espasa Calpe, 2007), 651.
16. Torrebadella-Flix and Olivera-Betrán, 'The Birth of the Sports Press in Spain Regenerationist Within the Context of the Late Nineteenth Century', *The International Journal of the History of Sport* 30, no. 18 (2013), 2170.
17. Adrian Shubert, *Death and Money in the Afternoon: A History of the Spanish Bullfight* (Oxford: Oxford University Press, 1999), 17.
18. Francisco Montes, *Tauromaquia completa* (Madrid: Egartorre, 1994).
19. Óscar Jiménez Bajo, *1851, historia de una temporada. Los toros a mediados del siglo XIX* (Madrid: Egartorre, 2002), 35–6.
20. Ibid., 44, 47.
21. José Altabella, *Crónicas taurinas. Antología* (Madrid: Taurus, 1965).
22. Shubert, *Death and Money in the Afternoon*, 41.
23. Antonio Díaz-Cañabate, 'Panorama del toreo hasta 1979', in J.M. de Cossío and A. Díaz-Cañabate. *Los toros Vol 5. La Historia* (Madrid. Espasa Calpe, 2007), 388.
24. J.J. de Bonifaz, and F.C.S. de Robles, *Víctimas de la fiesta* (Madrid: Espasa Calpe, 1991).
25. Shubert, *Death and Money in the Afternoon*, 63.
26. de Cossío, *Los toros Vol 4*, 462, 466.
27. Rivero Herraiz, 'Los valores del regeneracionismo en la educación física española.'
28. Torrebadella Flix, 'Regeneracionismo e impacto de la crisis de 1898 en la educación física y el deporte español.'
29. Shubert, *Death and Money in the Afternoon*, 90.
30. Antonio Rivero Herraiz, *Deporte y modernización. La actividad física como elemento de transformación social y cultural en España, 1910–1936* (Madrid: Consejería de Cultura y Deportes, 2003).
31. Ricardo Rubio, 'Juegos corporales en educación.' BILE (1894), 41.
32. The 'Disaster of 98' refers to the loss of the last Spanish colonies in America (Filipinas, Puerto Rico and Cuba) which heightened the moral and political crisis of the nation. The events were experienced as a verification of the diminished role played by Spain on international relations when compared to the glorious old days.

33. Rivero Herraiz, *Deporte y modernización*.
34. Keith Thomas, *Man and the Natural World* (London: Allen Lane, 1983), 159.
35. Shubert, *Death and Money in the Afternoon*, 13.
36. Cited in Paulo César Juárez, *Clásicos españoles contra toros y toreros* (Barcelona: La Tempestad, 2010), 168.
37. Cited in ibid., 169.
38. Jesús Vicente Herrero, 'El ideario costista en Eugenio Noel', *Anales de la Fundación Joaquín Costa*, no. 20 (2003), 5–24.
39. Cited in Juárez, *Clásicos españoles contra toros y toreros*, 178.
40. Luis Lozano Rey, 'Protección de animales y plantas', *Heraldo Deportivo*, no. 563, 5 January 1931, 16.
41. Rivero Herraiz, *Deporte y modernización*.
42. Rivero Herraiz and Sánchez García, 'The British Influence in the Birth of Spanish Sport'.
43. Elias, *The Civilizing Process*.
44. Torrebadella-Flix and Olivera-Betrán, 'The Birth of the Sports Press in Spain Regenerationist Within the Context of the Late Nineteenth Century', 2170.
45. *Heraldo Deportivo*, no. 748, 25 February 1936, 79.
46. Joseph Maguire, *Power and Global Sport: Zones of Prestige, Emulation and Resistance* (London: Routledge, 2007), 10.
47. *Heraldo Deportivo*, no. 563, 5 January 1931, 18–9.
48. Shubert, *Death and Money in the Afternoon*, 173.
49. Rivero Herraiz, *Deporte y modernización*, 154.
50. J.P. Fusi and J. Palafox, *España: 1808–1996. El desafío de la modernidad* (Madrid: Espasa-Calpe, 1997).
51. *Heraldo Deportivo*, no. 8, 5 August 1915, 8.
52. *Gran Vida*, no. 259, 1 December 1924, 9.
53. Ricardo Ruiz Ferry, 'A propósito de una fórmula conciliadora', *Heraldo Deportivo*, no. 566, 5 February 1931, 35–7.

Disclosure statement

No potential conflict of interest was reported by the authors.

Football with Friends? How the German Sporting Press Covered the German–Danish Sports Collaboration, 1939–1944

Christian Tolstrup Jensen

ABSTRACT
This paper concludes that a number of different discourses marked the coverage of Danish–German sports collaboration during the Second World War in German newspapers, sports magazines and newsreels. From the outbreak of the Second World War to the German occupation of Denmark on 9 April 1940, the discourses cover neutrality and friendship with Germany. After the invasion of Denmark, a discourse of Nordic sentiments became very important in the communications of the press, with Danish athletes portrayed as Nordic citizens, which some circles of German society could interpret as a euphemism for the Nazi idea of a strong Aryan Scandinavia. During the autumn of 1941, the rising strain on Germany's resources made the sports media a supplier of success. The discourse of a strong Germany replaced the previous discourses. As German–Danish sporting events ceased in 1942, Danish sport alone would still make occasional appearances in the German media until 1944, providing a German audience with entertainment and distraction.

Introduction

The comprehensive sports collaboration between Denmark and Germany in the course of the Second World War, as well as the policy that underpinned it, has been thoroughly investigated from the sides of both Germany and Denmark. But how the results (for example, of sports events) were disseminated to the German people through the German mass media has never previously been studied extensively – neither in a Danish setting nor from a broader European perspective. The aim of this paper was to describe how this dissemination changed drastically during the war as the situation on the front developed. Thus, it brings to light an early and prominent example of the political use of sports by state-controlled media platforms – a most relevant topic today in discussions about the relationship between sport and politics.

The prerequisite for this analysis is to connect the sports communication of the media with sports discourses in society, especially among leading German politicians. This is done by examining the sports discourses in various media and then relating them to the sports policy of the German Government. In this way, it becomes clear how and to what extent the German press supported official German sports policy in its collaboration with Denmark and its sports authorities.

Before turning to the analysis of the German–Danish sports collaboration in the German press during the war, the following sections outline the background of the collaboration and characterize the German press in Nazi Germany with a presentation of the study's empirical data and the research state in the field.

Danish–German Sports Collaboration from 1936 to 1943

In the inter-war period sporting relations between Denmark and Germany were stable with the 1936 Olympics as a highlight. When German forces attacked Poland on 1 September 1939 the Sports Confederation of Denmark (Dansk Idræts-Forbund [DIF]) had to make the first of several political decisions concerning its collaboration with German sports and this initiative turned out to be positive. The Danish sports confederation's commitment to a continuation of its collaboration with Germany set Denmark apart from other neutral states in Europe, and thus increased the interest of the German press in Danish sport even more. In Scandinavia, both Sweden and Norway followed the majority of neutral countries with their boycott of German sport after the outbreak of the war. The pool of Germany's opponents now consisted, apart from neutral Denmark, only of German allies such as Italy, Hungary and Romania.[1]

This particular Danish position lasted until the war reached Denmark with the German occupation of the country on 9 April 1940. At first, this made DIF stop all international sport until September 1940. Then international sport was resumed after political pressure from the German side and a steadily increasing wish from leading figures in the Danish sports federations. Sweden had already continued their collaboration with Germany in March 1940 after experiencing pressure from the German sports authorities.[2]

The continuation, eagerly supported by the Danish sporting media, sparked the most intensive period of German–Danish sports collaboration during the war. Since 1933, the media, with the exception of some of the leftist press, had promoted a very positive impression of the development of German sport and once again, in autumn 1940, looked forward to welcoming the German sports elite to Denmark.[3]

They were not to be disappointed as several friendly matches and other events over a broad spectrum of disciplines were arranged before the collaboration abruptly came to a halt in June 1941. At that time, the German occupying authorities in Denmark suspended the sports collaboration due to anti-German riots at a football match at the Danish national stadium between a Danish and an Austrian team, Admira.[4] The German Government prolonged the interruption shortly afterwards when its forces invaded the USSR on 22 June 1941. With this invasion the Second World War entered a new phase, and the German Government temporarily stopped all participation in international sports. The German army, the Wehrmacht, initially experienced many victories, but in the following winter from 1941 to 1942 it became clear that the Soviet Union could not be defeated as fast as the German General Headquarters had expected. Despite the pressure which this new front put on German resources, international sport was not at first brought to a halt. The German national handball and football teams played another two matches against Denmark in the autumn of 1941, with corresponding close coverage in the German media.

In the course of the winter from 1941 to 1942 the pressure on Germany only increased, and the collaboration with Denmark diminished in the German press before coming completely to a halt in January 1942, probably because of the riots during the summer mentioned above. Germany, however, continued to collaborate with other countries in staging sporting events (among them both neutral Sweden and Switzerland as well as German allies such as Romania and Hungary) until in February 1943 the German propaganda minister Joseph Goebbels declared total war, thereby putting an end to all international sport for German athletes.

The German Mass Media and Their Sports Coverage

The source material for the present study is comprised of a number of German newspapers, illustrated sports magazines and newsreels. The following section, with its description of the organization of German sports coverage by the various, now standardized media platforms, gives a context for the source material after the Nazi government brought the German press in line with their political desires from 1933 onwards (the so-called *Gleichschaltung*).

The Nazi government and its *Gleichschaltung* specifically changed the conditions for the sporting press in two ways: firstly, through the standardization, which also was affecting other parts of the German press; and secondly, as the illustrated sports magazines, which mainly covered only a few disciplines each, became a tool for the Nazis in their attempt to control and reorganize German sport.

The *Gleichschaltung* of the press meant, first of all, the creation of fewer and bigger publishers with the closure of smaller newspapers, mainly socialist and religious ones. The bigger publishers followed as the Nazi press exploited this and the party's own newspaper, the *Völkischer Beobachter*, became the most widely read newspaper during the war, followed by the renowned conservative and smaller newspaper *Frankfurter Zeitung*. The *Völkischer Beobachter* had a circulation of 310,000 in 1933, which increased to 982,000 in 1940,[5] before peaking in 1944 with a circulation of 1.4 million.[6]

The two papers' contents differed, however; and most relevant for this study is the fact that the sports coverage of the *Frankfurter Zeitung* was in general less extensive and less 'enthusiastic' than the material found in the *Völkischer Beobachter* and other openly nazified papers.[7]

The contents of the newspapers were centrally controlled. The German propaganda minister, Josef Goebbels, wanted a press which was 'polymorphous to look at … but monomorphous in its will'.[8] Research into the *Gleichschaltung* of the press demonstrates, however, that the Nazis never succeeded in imposing total control over the press.[9] Since the 1980s, the focus of the research has been on individual publications and most often their specific role in possible resistance against the Nazi party. It has led to a situation in which the best-explored part of the German war press is not the big party newspapers such as the *Völkischer Beobachter* but rather the *Frankfurter Zeitung* and the weekly *Das Reich*. The research on these publications focuses on whether – and, if so, to what extent – it was possible for the newspapers to put up resistance 'between the lines'. The trend also to conduct research with a focus on smaller publications is followed by the present paper, which includes the *Frankfurter Zeitung*, the *Völkischer Beobachter* and *Das Reich* as source material.

Besides newspapers, a number of other printed publications, the so-called general sporting press, were available for the sport-interested German. The most seminal monograph in the field of the general sporting press's conditions in Nazi Germany during the Second World War is the dissertation from 1976 by sociologist and communications researcher Siegfried Weischenberg. Even though it is focused on West Germany's sporting press in the post-war era, it offers a detailed account of the conditions in which the press operated during the war.[10] It is also the most recent work to have been published on this subject which is based directly on sources.

This branch of the sporting press covered a wide spectrum of disciplines. The following two figures show the sports coverage of Danish sport in the aforementioned newspapers, the sporting press, the general and the specialized magazines, and the newsreels (see Figures 1 and 2).

The national German sports authority's (*Nationalsozialistischer Reichsbund für Leibesübungen* – NSRL) own magazine *NS-Sport* (NS-S), published from 1939 onwards, became here an important organ for Nazi sports policy. The NS-S's reach, however, was limited compared with the far more accessible illustrated sports magazine *Reichssportblatt*. This magazine had been founded in 1934. Its extensive pictorial coverage and broad sports interest quickly provided the *Reichssportblatt* with a huge audience of 123,000 readers.[11]

Readers with a more focused interest in sport would consult the sports journals, which came in smaller circulations and covered only one or two disciplines.[12] Altogether, these publications had a print run of 3.1 million in 1934, of which the football magazine *Der Kicker* accounted for 25,000.[13] With the *Gleichschaltung* the number of journals was cut to only one per discipline, and at the same time the remaining journals were turned into the official mouthpiece, which further strengthened governmental control.[14]

They should therefore be considered official publications. Central sports journals were *Der Kicker*, *Handball*, *Box-Sport* and *Der Schwimmer*. On several occasions they all reported extensively on German–Danish matches or Danish sports alone. *Der Kicker* is also the only magazine to have been a subject for research. Claudia Kaiser, who carries out research in the field of comparative literary studies, has analyzed the magazine's coverage of German international matches during the war. She concludes that a nationalistic and strength-orientated rhetoric was present throughout the period.[15] The present paper, with its larger focus and broader empirical foundation, is able to put this conclusion into a larger perspective.

A recurring tendency in research into the Nazis' use of the mass media is their modern and effective use of the radio, which had proved well suited to reaching a large audience. However, there are no records available for the contents of German radio broadcasts during the war which would allow an inclusion of broadcasting in the empirical data in this study. A general search for the term 'sport' in the records of the German radio archives (*Deutsches Rundfunkarchiv*, Frankfurt a. M.) covering the years from 1939 to 1945 but only searching independent programmes (such as special broadcasts, not regular programmes) only yielded one result with Danish participation: an interview conducted by the Danish sports reporter, Gunnar 'Nu' Hansen, with the *Reichssportsführer*, Hans von Tschammer und Osten, the head of the German sports authority, in October 1940, which was subsequently broadcast by the German (and Danish) radio.[16] A German printed record of sporting reports from 1907 to 1945 in film and radio also only yielded results with regard to films.[17]

Of visual material depicting Danish–German sport during the Second World War (apart from photograph sequences), several clips from the newsreels were readily available. The study has drawn on all occurrences of Danish athletes in German cinema newsreels, first

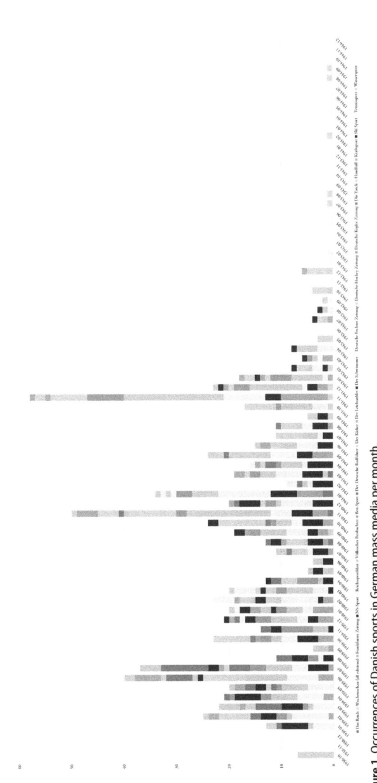

Figure 1. Occurrences of Danish sports in German mass media per month.

Notes: It is seen that the German press experienced several fluctuations in the course of the period coincident with the changing relations between Denmark and Germany and Germany's position in the war.

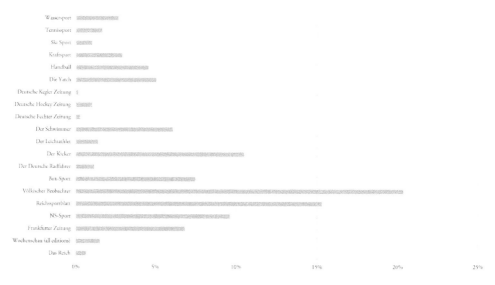

Figure 2. Relative distribution of occurrences of Danish sport in German mass media, October 1938–1944
(*n* = 791).

Notes: The main providers of news about Danish sports were the daily paper the *Völkischer Beobachter* together with the large illustrated sports magazine *Reichssportblatt*. These two publications also had the largest print runs. Looking at the specialized publications, swimming, football and boxing stand out as the most popular Danish sports in Germany. The listed publications and film productions fall into four categories: (1) News reels (Wochenschau – all editions), (2) Daily and weekly general newspapers and magazines: *Frankfurter Zeitung* (daily) *Völkischer Beobachter* (daily) and *Das Reich* (weekly), (3) general sports magazines: *Reichssportblatt* and *NS-Sport* and (4) specialized sports magazines, both a source of news of the sport as well as the official publication for respective associations (listed in the brackets): *Box Sport* (boxing), *Der Deutsche Radfahrer* (cycling), *Der Kicker* (football), *Der Leichtathelt* (athletics), *Der Schwimmer* (swimming), *Deutsche Fechter Zeitung* (fencing), *Deutsche Hockey Zeitung* (hockey), *Deutsche Kegler Zeitung* (bowling), *Die Yatch* (yachting), *Handball* (team handball), *Kraftsport* (wrestling), *Ski Sport* (skiing), *Tennissport* (tennis) and *Wassersport* (rowing).

and foremost the *Deutsche Wochenschau*. Like the press, the movie and newsreel branches of the media were also affected by the Nazi *Gleichschaltung* policy and carefully monitored by the propaganda ministry. The Danish athletes' participation on this media platform has been possible through the above-mentioned archive of sport in German radio and newsreels from 1907 to 1945, made by the German historians, Hans Joachim Teichler and Wolfgang Meyer-Ticheloven, and published as *Filme und Rundfunkreportagen als Dokumente der deutschen Sportgeschichte von 1907–1945*.

State of the Research

The authors and historians, Hans Joachim Teichler and Hajo Bernett, are essential contributors to the field of German sports history, especially concerning the Second World War. Their main interest has been in research on German sports policy seen from an international perspective, where Teichler's work *Internationale Sportpolitik im Dritten Reich* from 1991 is still of key importance for scholars studying international sport in the Nazi era. However, his research only took a sparing look at the propagation of the government's international sports policy to the German people, and his approach lacks a national angle. The present paper presents for the first time a broader analysis of this propagation, but other trends have also supplemented Teichler's and Bernett's research.

The predominant new field, concerning national sport at the lower levels, such as local teams or sports clubs, has recently been the subject of different projects.[18] Through one of these, historian Erik Eggers has argued against Weichensberg's view that the *Gleichschaltung* quickly took hold in the field of sport, which has to be viewed as a source of entertainment rather than propaganda. The latter proved difficult to stage in sport, at least before the war.[19] Football research has not been without its controversies. The results presented in 2005 in the official history of the German Football Federation (Deutscher Fußball-Bund [DFB]) during the war by Nils Havemann was heavily criticized by fellow historians for wrongfully exonerating the German football federation from willingly cooperating with the Nazi regime.[20]

Key to the Danish context is the book *Football with the Foe* written in 2008 by the Danish historian, Hans Bonde, which concludes that the positive attitude of the DIF towards the German occupying administration went far further than would have been necessary to support the official policy of collaboration.[21] The book also analyzes the uncritical sporting press in Denmark and its standpoint in relation to the collaboration, whose consequences are also discussed in the present paper as a supplement to the work of Hans Bonde.

The Peculiar Case of Denmark: From the Outbreak of War to Danish Occupation

When Germany set off the Second World War with its invasion of Poland on 1 September 1939, Denmark declared itself neutral. The Danish national sports federation, DIF, reasoned that neutrality meant abiding by the matches the federations had already agreed upon with their international counterparts. The decision, however, also had a political dimension as part of the general Danish consideration that good relations with Germany were critical for Denmark as a state.[22] In the German press and among athletes, the decision led to a new great interest in Denmark and Danish sport because of the decrease in available opponents as a consequence of the war and the unique Danish status as a neutral state still wanting to compete with German athletes.[23]

The decision was soon taken up by the German press, which in its entirety, from the highly political *NS-Sport* to *Der Kicker*, followed the Danish press and sport very closely. They now translated and printed Danish articles praising German sport and the continued collaboration between the two countries after the outbreak of war.[24]

In October 1939, *NS-Sport* commented on the DIF's decision in a long article which took stock of the sporting conditions in Europe. Referring to Denmark, it reported: 'In Denmark they still have national sport, and furthermore they also participate in international contests. They support it as much as possible'.[25]

A Handball Match in Leipzig in 1939

The best example of the exceptional status given to Danish sport after the outbreak of the Second World War is a handball match played in Leipzig on 8 October 1939. In particular, the German sports authority had put great effort into organizing the event. The press coverage was massive and striking, even in view of the fact that Danish sport was generally closely covered at this time. Not only the match itself was important but also the setting, especially in the host's (NSRL) own magazine, *NS-Sport*.

The German aim was firstly to establish a connection between sport on the one hand and peace, mutual recognition and understanding on the other. The newspapers saw a parallel between 1939 and the period after the First World War. At that time Denmark had been one of the first to revive its sporting connections with Germany, thus starting to normalize its relations with Germany. In 1939 the newspapers saw a similar development and, with it, a sign of normal everyday life and peace.[26] Denmark's neutral status was especially important and became the sign of an acceptance of Germany among other neutral countries, which was not certain in the same way as the continuing cooperation between Germany and its allies, Italy and Hungary. *Handball* wrote under the (misspelled) heading: 'Danskar! Hjertlig velkommen!' [Danes! A warm welcome!] that the match should be seen as part of Germany's effort to stand by the neutral countries. It signalled the German 'continuation of the international sports in service of the peaceful understanding of the peoples'.[27]

An ideological element with connotations of an idealized Denmark also marked the reports. The Danish team consisted, according to *Reichssportblatt*, of 'magnificent young men … who with open eyes and hearts experience, take in and reflect on such an international tour; here we will bring this educational process to fulfilment in the body'.[28]

The hosts did what they could to frame the match in an impressive way. As a prelude, NSRL had invited 1000 members for a sports appeal according to NSRL's own press organ. The appeal took the form of a speech by the Reichssportsführer, Tschammer und Osten, followed by a concert with Nazi songs on the programme.[29] The article on the event in *NS-Sport* said that these songs 'resounded' both in a following speech given by the German handball federation and in a speech by the Danish counterpart.[30] Subsequently, the songs were said to have appealed not only to the German audience but also to the Danish team members. This Nazi manifestation, therefore, emphasized the ties between German and Danish sporting ideals and athletes. It does not come as a surprise that *NS-Sport* was the only media to cover the appeal along with the match. The magazine was the official organ of the organizers, the German sports authority.

After the outbreak of war Danish sport became a political instrument in the German government's efforts to propagate an appearance of peaceableness among the German people. The German press and German sport, supported by the propaganda ministry, downplayed the war and publicized the sports collaboration with Denmark as exemplifying Germany's good relations with its neighbours.

Intermezzo: Negotiations, Summer 1940

These close relations lasted until the German occupation of Denmark on 9 April 1940. After the prompt Danish surrender the German 'peaceful occupation' started. As a consequence, Danish society was to go about its business as unaffectedly as possible, and in the view of the German Government, Denmark was still to be seen as a sovereign nation. This was also due to Germany's image of Denmark as an Aryan country, and the country experienced a much more lenient occupation than many other countries, especially those in Eastern Europe.

The DIF, however, did not feel that it could keep up its collaboration in sports and stopped all international sporting events shortly after the German occupation. This move led to great discontent among the new German occupational force. The Danish unwillingness to continue its sports collaboration made the German attempt to establish a peaceful impression of its occupation of Denmark look less credible. Thus, the NSRL, backed by both Hitler and Goebbels' ministry of propaganda, immediately put pressure on the DIF and the Danish Government to return to its normal sporting relations with Germany.[31]

At first, the DIF managed to avoid a quick return to normal relations. This was the result of a meeting on 29 April 1940 between the German plenipotentiary, Cecil von Renthe-Fink, accompanied by the German press attaché, Karl Frielitz, on the one side, and the DIF's president, Holten Castenschiold, together with his powerful vice president, Leo Frederiksen, who was president of the Dansk Boldspil Union (DBU), the large Danish football federation, and the director of the Danish ministry of foreign affairs, Otto Carl Mohr, on the other. The status of Danish sport under these new conditions had for now found its form.[32] *Der Kicker* quoted the Danish newspaper *Politiken* and the sports magazine *Idrætsbladet* the next day for the news about a ban on international sport in Denmark. The *NS-Pressedienst* estimated correctly in these paragraphs that the Danish federations were likely to toe the line prescribed by the DIF.[33]

Head Start in the Press: Hveger and Bukh

The – on the whole effective – ban on international sports did not, however, lead to an absence of Danish sport in the German press. If no actual sport was available, then at least the press could interview leading Danish sports figures with German sympathies. Their good experiences with or sympathy towards Germany was well suited to illustrating the good relations between the two countries.

Already in mid-May, the press of the occupying power visited the world-famous gymnast and educator, Niels Bukh, who since the Nazi takeover in Germany in 1933 had closely associated himself with the Nazi regime and its ideology. His gymnastics had received positive coverage at the Olympic Games in Berlin in 1936, and during the war he remained a prominent personality for the Germans, who listed him as a candidate for the position of youth minister in the case of a Nazi *coup d'état* in Denmark.[34]

The journalist from the *Völkischer Beobachter*, accompanied by a group of German soldiers, were received by Bukh as 'very welcome guests' at his 'world-famous' Danish folk high school for gymnastics in Ollerup on Funen. In general, Bukh happily spoke to the German media. Here it was possible for him to express his support for the German occupation more clearly than in the Danish press, where the risk of condemnation was higher.[35] The main part of the article dealt explicitly with Bukh's sympathies for Nazi Germany and the Nazi sports movement.[36]

Later that summer the *Reichssportblatt* visited the swimmer, Ragnhild Hveger, in her home town of Elsinore together with two German soldiers. Hveger, the journalist remarked, had visited Germany more than 20 times so 'there was no lack of conversational topics, when two handsome German soldiers made her a return visit' from the Germany which Hveger 'loved' and 'had learned to appreciate'. Hveger even went swimming with one of the soldiers.[37]

These two visits paid to famous Danish athletes who had hospitably welcomed the occupation force could give the reader the impression that peaceful relations existed between Germany and Denmark in accordance with the general peaceful occupation policy. Both Hveger and Bukh had previously represented Denmark in connection with their sporting activities. Now they were interviewed as private individuals, which increasingly came to mark Hveger's press coverage in the course of the war. She even wrote a welcome letter to the German soldiers, which was published in the *Kopenhagener Soldatenzeitschrift*, the magazine for German soldiers stationed in Denmark. The paper also reprinted the article from the *Reichssportblatt*.[38]

The Early Occupation: One Among Germany's Friends

During the summer of 1940 the DIF felt increasing pressure to resume international sport from the German authorities, who were believed to have support from a few Danish federations, among them the swimming federation.[39]

From a political perspective, Germany had only strengthened its position in the late summer of 1940, retaining Denmark in a subdued position. On 10 May 1940, Germany had followed up the invasion of Denmark and Norway with an attack on the Netherlands, Belgium, Luxembourg and France even before Norway's surrender on 10 June 1940. Then, on 22 June 1940, France was the last to surrender after the Netherlands and Belgium. Great Britain was the only German opponent left in Europe, and the new Danish foreign minister, Erik Scavenius, declared in his inaugural speech on 8 July 1940: 'as a result of the great German victories that have struck the world with amazement and admiration, a new time has come to Europe which will bring forth political and economic reforms under German leadership'.[40] Scavenius was inaugurated as minister in an all-party government which came to represent active collaboration with the German occupational authorities.[41]

At a committee meeting on 5 August, the DIF decided to revive Danish participation in international sports, just as other parts of society, such as business, took up their connections with Germany again.[42] Shortly afterwards a heading in *Der Kicker* read: 'Denmark makes peace'.[43] The German press praised, through translations of Danish articles, the drive among Danish athletes despite the war, just as was the case with the continued sports collaboration at the outbreak of the war one year earlier.[44]

The fact that a collaboration between the occupied and the occupier continued to take place was exceptional in Europe, but Germany did not want to stress this as it would only bring to light that an actual occupation was taking place contrary to its 'peaceful occupation' policy. In the next period until June 1941, in which coverage of German–Danish sport reached its peak in the German press, a Nordic discourse was now added to its reporting of events such as the athletics meetings and Ragnhild Hveger's tours in Germany.

The Athletics Begins

The sports collaboration was resumed with an athletics meeting in Copenhagen on 22 August 1940 with the participation of German athletes from the *Luftwaffe Sportverein*, Berlin. The Copenhagen Athletics Federation was the initiator behind the meeting. It was headed by Johannes Bojesen Barsøe, who, just like the director of the national athletics federation, Svend Jensen, had Nazi sympathies.[45] With the event on 22 August he flew in the face of the DIF's own plan for the normalization of international sports relations, which had aimed at a soft start with a football match against Sweden.[46]

The meeting attracted little attention in the German press, but a film recording found its way into the newsreels with the help of the German plenipotentiary, Renthe-Fink.[47] He himself was present at the stadium together with the commander-in-chief of the German forces in Denmark, General Lüdke, which further underlines the political importance attached to the event by the Germans. On 4 September already, the clip had made its way through censorship and was released as a part of the *Deutsche Wochenschau*.[48]

The continuation of German–Danish collaborative sport in this way reached a far larger audience than any print media could have provided. The clip showed a sports meeting in which only the pictures of happy German soldiers among the spectators bore witness to the war still in progress. Everything was just as it should be. The pictures of Danish and German athletes in a generous competition sent out, and were a strong signal to the German filmgoer, that a cemented and lasting friendship existed between the two countries. This impression was further supported by the relatively peaceful occupation policy pursued by the German forces in Denmark.

Athletics meetings were often used by the German press in this period as occasions to send signals of friendship, not only between Germany and Denmark but between Germany and other Scandinavian and neutral countries when later Swedish athletes also took part in the meetings. The newspapers often illustrated their articles with portraits of German and Scandinavian athletes posing arm-in-arm and fraternizing, which could be seen as underlining the bonds between Germany and a strong Aryan Scandinavia.

The release of the film in September 1940 showed how much importance the German propaganda apparatus ascribed to the meeting at a time when the sports section of the newsreel was experiencing a dramatic reduction (to almost nothing) compared with pre-war levels. The position of the film at the centre of the newsreel also indicates the relatively high priority given to it by the editor.[49]

On the Danish side, the press hoped that the strong German athletes could put pressure on the Danish participants and open the way for new sporting records. They also expressed an overall happiness about once again welcoming international athletes to Denmark. The Nazi oriented newspaper *Fædrelandet* characterized the event as a 'great success', but also *Idrætsbladet* felt that it had been successful, not least owing to the performance of the German participants.[50]

The meeting was soon followed by other meetings in wrestling and team handball. Here the press coverage was more filling. Especially publications such as *NS-Sport*, *Reichssportblatt* and *Völkischer Beobachter* were marked by the new German–Danish relationship 'welcoming' 'the Danish sportsfriends' 'with the great Scandinavian peoples' cross on the left side of the chest'.[51] Now a 'real friendship was in place'.[52] This was overall much more enthusiastic compared to the occurrences in the conservative *Frankfurter Zeitung*.

Ragnhild Hveger and Germany

Hveger had difficulty agreeing to stay in Denmark when international sports relations were interrupted over the summer of 1940; all the more, then, did she make use of the new opportunities for travelling to Germany, which coincided with the continued collaboration in August 1940.[53]

In the spring of that year the Danish and German swimming federations had already started preparing a German tour for Hveger and the breaststroker, Inge Sørensen, who was a bronze medallist at the Olympic Games in 1936. The German invasion, however, had interrupted the planning temporarily, but the Germans did not fully abandon the idea and repeated their invitation in May 1940, which was declined by the Danish swimming federation.[54]

With the renewed relations, the way was now paved for an acceptance of the offer, and Hveger toured Germany several times in the following years, each time with close coverage in the German (and Danish) press.[55]

In October 1940, when Hveger went on her first German tour during the war, photographs of her arm-in-arm with her German opponents were taken and used by the press to create the impression of good German–Danish relations, as was the case at the athletics meetings. Hveger was portrayed strolling in the city with her German sports friends, who held 'the magnificent Ragnhild very dear',[56] and during a visit to a market garden, where she inspected rubber plants dressed in fur and a bathing cap. Hveger was not only attractive in the swimming baths but also as a private individual, with the bathing cap pointing to her primary occupation.[57] In the same way *Reichssportblatt* also visited Hveger in her hometown Elsinore, not only reporting on swimming but also her dog, and her garden, thus emphasizing a close connection to nature.[58]

The tendency to speak of her as '*our* adorable Ragnhild'[59] not only serves to underline Hveger's star quality in the German press but also the already well-established relations between Germany and Denmark, or Scandinavia. The good relations came to an end, though. The trigger was, of course, a sporting event, more precisely a certain football match on Danish Constitution Day, 4 June 1941.

Intermezzo: Unrest, Summer 1941

The big, and at the same time shocking, sports event for German–Danish sports collaboration took place in Copenhagen that summer with a series of football matches between selected Danish teams and the recognized Austrian teams, Admira and FK Austria, at the end of May and the beginning of June 1941. Admira had a long (and victorious) history in Denmark, and the press welcomed them when the team returned in 1941 after five years of absence.[60]

After the first matches had been played without incident, the match between the Danish team and Admira on Constitution Day (5 June), 1941 ended in tumult, caused partly by Danish anger over losing decisively and partly provoked by the demonstrative Hitler salute from the Austrian players.[61] The Danish historian, Hans Bonde, has aptly baptized the affair 'The revolt in the Park' (Park being the common name for Denmark's national stadium, Idrætsparken).[62] As a consequence, the remaining international matches with Danish participation that summer were cancelled by the German authorities. When, shortly after, Germany invaded the Soviet Union on 22 June the interruption of the German–Danish sports collaboration was prolonged, with the German Government stopping all German participation in international sport until October 1941.

That summer the impression that Germany could win the war was still predominant. This made historian Hans Bonde speculate whether this impression could have been a factor in the Danish tumults in combination with the more general national feeling which influenced Denmark in the same period. (For example, the community singing. Here thousands of people would come together and sing first and foremost patriotic songs.)[63]

Despite, or perhaps because of the extent of the riots, the episode was conspicuously absent in all German media except the Wehrmacht's own magazine in Denmark (*Kopenhagener Soldatenzeitschrift*), which was angered by the Danish spectators' behaviour. The Danish press, on the other hand, was disappointed that the last match against the Austrians was cancelled. It only briefly mentioned the political consequences, i.e. that the Danish minister of justice was forced to resign and the government to give an apology.[64]

Sharpened Rhetoric: Autumn and Winter from 1941 to 1942

The German Government resumed its international sports collaboration in September 1941, and a football match in Dresden on 16 November was a highlight for Danish sport. Even though the programme was similar to that of autumn 1940, the political situation had changed dramatically not least due to Germany's invasion of the Soviet Union.

The tumult on Constitution Day meant that German national teams no longer played in Denmark; therefore, Dresden was chosen as a venue. In Denmark the period was marked by the first occurrences of illegal actions against the German occupation after the internment of Danish communists which followed the invasion of the Soviet Union.

From the German perspective, the expected quick victory over the Soviet Union which did not come to pass meant that the German press started to see entertainment and sport as more important distractions from reports from the front than the presentation of good relations between Germany and Denmark.[65] Thus, stories of victory and continued German strength in sports became increasingly important to disseminate to the German people.

In September 1941, the propaganda ministry in Germany had already made preparations for a steady supply of 'entertainment and relaxation' for the Germans over the winter. The NSRL also had a part to play and was allocated large sums of money for a national 'campaign of events' in the autumn of 1941,[66] which included a football match against Denmark.

A Shaken Germany

The war's increasing demand for more resources made it still harder for Germany to pick strong teams for its matches. Whereas in the autumn of 1940 the *Völkischer Beobachter* focused on the careful Danish preparations prior to the matches,[67] the focus in the autumn of 1941 shifted to the German preparations.

Der Kicker already began to discuss the German line-up at the end of October only a short time after Denmark had beaten Sweden,[68] but months prior to the match against Germany. Sweden had beaten Germany, and *Der Kicker* eagerly discussed the result as the match between Denmark and Germany came closer. The German football federation, however, did not announce the line-up early, as it usually did. Probably the war was making itself felt and made it difficult to present a proper line-up, which was not mentioned in the press, though. The federation just wanted to avoid any gambling against Denmark and that was all, they commented.[69]

In the end, the line-up was presented and the match played. But very disappointingly for the German sports press, the match ended in a draw: 1:1.[70] The *Reichssportblatt* even said, that 'with an opponent like Denmark, the draw looks like a defeat'.[71] Again the question about the team rose, but *Der Kicker* swiftly responded: 'The best sportsmen – the best soldiers'. They would not even, so the magazine said, wish to stay behind (and play).[72]

Generally, all mentions of friendship had now disappeared and the nickname 'northerner' was replaced by the more neutral 'redshirt', with reference to the colour of the Danish players' shirts, in the same way as the Italian players were dubbed the 'Azzuri' because of their azure shirts.[73] This shift of focus away from friendship was due to the lack of German military victories. To replace these, sport had to stand in for German strength (for example, with an increased focus on the *German* preparations for the match). Because of the result, the press could not apply the picture of a strong Germany to the match itself.

Instead they could, as the *Deutsche Wochenschau* did, use the match as entertainment. It was the only sports clip in the newsreel two weeks later in the lighter first part of the show. The clip was introduced with the heading 'Pictures from home'. The focus of the clip was not so much the result of the match but rather entertainment, with pictures of happy spectators at the football match, and only the soldiers in uniform among them reminded the viewers of the war.[74] Pictures of the many soldiers among the civilians were common in newsreel sports clips in order to illustrate a connection between them.[75]

However, it took the press more than a week to discuss the disappointing result of the match. The debate continued as magazines and newspapers tried to make the end result acceptable for the readers.

The *Reichssportblatt* tried to play it down and revive the friendship theme in the coverage: 'They [international matches] are just games! Much more important are the ties of sporting friendships which are made at these matches'.[76]

The *Völkischer Beobachter*, on the other hand, wanted to re-establish the picture of a strong Germany when on 22 November it analyzed a number of European countries and their football capabilities.[77] The article gave the impression of reviewing the season although Germany still had a match scheduled against its close ally, Slovakia, on 7 December.

The article concluded, of course, that Germany was still to be regarded as the leading football nation in Europe. Despite the absurd title of 'unofficial European champions' which Denmark was awarded at the beginning of the article, it went on to say that only Hungary and Switzerland could be numbered among 'the real elite in European football'. That Denmark had played a draw against the German team was pure luck according to the *Völkischer Beobachter*: 'When you look at the full picture, Germany should still be seen as having the leading position, especially since it also has definitely played the most international matches'.[78] After the match the *Völkischer Beobachter* continued to support the discourse of a strong Germany, as was the case before the match, with the focus on the German football federation's preparations. This 'strength' angle was new compared with the earlier coverage of the matches against Denmark in the war.

The last match between Danish and German athletes was the so-called wartime European boxing championship in January 1942. The German press material about the event was a lacklustre affair for Denmark: the Danish participation drowned in German mentions of all the other small countries' participation. But they still provided an attractive number of participants for the *Völkischer Beobachter*: 'The championship 1942 with 11 nations is for all of them a symbol of friendship and readiness together to build a new Europa'.

However, Italy and Germany won most of the titles and publicity. Denmark only received a little attention when a Danish boxer gained a controversial victory over the strong local favourite Rudolf 'Rudi' Pepper in the semi-final of the championship. The surprising German defeat might have been a political decision: a sort of recognition for Denmark's participation.[79]

When the boxing championships ended, so, too, did all high-level sporting events between Danish and German athletes.[80] For the remainder of the war Danish sport in the German press had to do without German opponents.

1942: Alone in the German Press and Newsreels

The sports collaboration came to a complete end in the course of 1942 when German military expansion came to a halt. The invasion of the Soviet Union had stalled, and the battle of Stalingrad would begin in the autumn of the same year. The Wehrmacht's advance in North Africa was also put on the defensive by the British forces at El-Alamein.

Germany's ally, Japan, was being held in check by the USA, which in December 1941 joined the Allies, and over the summer of 1942 managed to get the upper hand in the Pacific after its victory near the Midway Atoll.

The resistance movement in Denmark became increasingly active that year, albeit still on a small scale, and the so-called Telegram Crisis over the summer of 1942 worsened German–Danish relations even further. The crisis was triggered by the Danish king's terse acknowledgement of the personal letter sent by the German *Führer*, Adolf Hitler, congratulating the king on his birthday. A disruption of diplomatic relations between the countries immediately followed, and as a consequence later that autumn the Danish Government was forced to step down. Supported by the German occupation forces, the Danish minister of foreign affairs, Erik Scavenius, became the new prime minister, succeeding Vilhelm Buhl. On the German side the plenipotentiary, Renthe-Fink, was replaced by SS-officer Werner Best. At first, Best and Scavenius would continue the policy of collaboration, which lasted until the outbreak of riots in the summer 1943, compelling the German occupational forces to declare a state of emergency in Denmark. In the following period a government through the heads of departments took power. This put an end to the 'peaceful occupation' and the German wish to keep up appearances in Denmark, although the administrative collaboration continued between the German military administration and the heads of departments.[81]

From 1942 onwards and for the remainder of the war Danish sports only made appearances in the German press when Danish athletes were able to attract attention on their own: this meant first and foremost Danish swimmers and, among them, especially Hveger and the long-distance swimmer, Jenny Kammersgaard. The coverage of Kammersgaard and Hveger was, however, mainly focused on their personal sporting achievements and not their nationality. In August 1942 *Reichssportblatt* visited Denmark reporting from the national swimming championships on 'the Nordic fairies with the red-white Dannebrog [the Danish flag] on their bathing suits'.[82]

Hveger continued in her attempts to set new world records, and even when these failed, the German press still showed interest.[83] In 1943, she also found work in Kiel as a swimming instructor and moved to Germany for the rest of the war.[84] Jenny Kammersgaard, who had been well known before the war for her long-distance swimming in the 1930s, was photographed in 1942 for a picture story about the benefits of winter bathing,[85] as well as for a newsreel.[86] The narrator explained that the 'Danish record swimmer' had come to Germany at the invitation of *Reichssportführer* Tschammer, the NSRL director. Kammersgaard's distance-swimming records prior to the war had attracted much attention in Germany.[87] Among other feats, she swam from Gedser in Denmark to Warnemünde in Germany in 1938. In October 1940, she finished her training as a swimming instructor in Germany.[88] She found work there, too, before returning to Denmark in 1942, where she continued working for the Germans.[89] After the war she was linked with the smuggling of prisoners of war to Sweden, which the Danish Red Cross regarded as a possible escape route for German war criminals. She also continued working with her manager until he was sentenced to five years' imprisonment in 1946 for collaboration with the Germans.[90]

In newsreels the situation was slightly different from that of the print media in the years from 1942 to 1944. In the former, Danish sport was given an entertaining role as amusement for the audience. Sport had almost disappeared from the newsreels during the first war years, but now it experienced a modest comeback in the *Deutsche Wochenschau* despite the general decrease in the amount of sports played in German society. New editions of newsreels also came into being such as *Sport-Sport* in 1943, which covered sport only. Here, Danish athletes appeared twice: at the cycle race, Stjerneløbet ('the Star race' named after its shape) and the Hubertusjagt (the Hubertus hunt) in 1943 and 1944, respectively. Sport had disappeared as a unifying factor for the German people or the representation of a strong Germany, but it now offered variety and a touch of normality instead.

Conclusion: Sport's Many Roles

From the point of view of the German press, Danish–German sports collaboration proved to be a useful political tool. The collaboration was highly adaptive as press material and could be used in a wide range of messages depending on the German Government's sports policy at a given time. The press coverage changed as the German Government adjusted its goals for its international sports policy from entertainment and competition to German–Danish solidarity.

At the beginning of the war until the German occupation of Denmark on 9 April 1940, Danish sport enjoyed a high status in the German press as a consequence of the decision taken by the Danish sports authority, DIF, to continue its sports cooperation with Germany, contrary to the policy of the other neutral Nordic countries, Norway and Sweden.

The coverage in this period gave high priority to a discourse emphasizing the friendship between neutral Denmark and militarily belligerent Germany, which through the sports exchange was portrayed as peaceful and fair, oriented to both the world and its own people. This stage also exemplifies the tendency, that papers like *NS-Sport* and *Völkischer Beobachter* overall had a more enthusiastic coverage compared to the *Frankfurter Zeitung*, for example, which in general also gave sports a lower priority.

Other examples show how Danish press material from this period was used by the German press. It was a two-way exchange and not only from Germany to Denmark as described in *Football with the Foe*. German newspapers translated and printed Danish articles praising the continuation of German sport after the outbreak of the war. The enthusiasm in the Danish press, which is also shown in *Football with the Foe*, is highly reflected by its German counterpart. As the present paper's analysis of the whole war shows, the praise here was strongly dependent on the war situation.

The occupation of Denmark at first led to a (temporary) disruption of the two countries' cooperation in sport. The German press showed its ingenuity as it 'overlooked' the disruption when they interviewed the internationally famous representatives of Danish sports, the swimmer, Ragnhild Hveger, and the educator, Niels Bukh. This made it possible for the German authorities to back its wish for a 'peaceful occupation' of Denmark prior to the official continuation of the sports exchange.

The DIF, encouraged by the German occupation authorities in Denmark and some of the Danish federations, allowed a resumption of the German–Danish sport collaboration on 5 August 1940. The period from August 1940 until June 1941 became the collaboration's most active phase during the war despite the fact that Denmark was no longer neutral and an emphasis on this therefore this could no longer be emphasized in the German press. It was replaced by putting a stronger emphasis on the friendship in the press coverage as a part of the Nazi regime's work on promoting the perception of its occupation of Denmark as a successful 'peaceful occupation'. The fact that the press was able to adapt the sports coverage for a wide range of agendas puts the paper by the German researcher Claudia Kaiser into a larger frame. Her study of the tone used in *Der Kicker* in its coverage of international matches during the war concludes that the nationalistic rhetoric and focus on German strength remained the same throughout the war. This paper shows that this was an exception in the German press.

The emphasis on the Nordic discourse in the collaboration and the good relations with Denmark in the German staging of the collaboration diminished remarkably during the autumn of 1941. The friendship had faded following the football riots at Idrætsparken, the Danish national stadium, on Constitution Day (4 June) 1941, and the new pressure on Germany caused by its invasion of the Soviet Union on 22 June 1941 heightened the need for success stories. German strength and possible success in sport now marked the sporting press in general. Only the unexpected draw in the football match between Denmark and Germany on 16 November 1941 made the *Reichssportblatt* return to a discourse of friendship, perhaps to play down the impression of a weak German performance.

In the last years of the war from 1942 to 1944, Danish sport was reduced to articles about individual athletes. Especially Ragnhild Hveger managed to hold the attention of the press as a result of her numerous world records. Even before the war she had been in high favour with the German press, and during the war, even before she moved to Germany, the German press almost started to think of Hveger as one of their own. This might explain the markedly stable press coverage of Hveger's activities throughout the war in contrast to the fluctuations observed in the case of Danish sport in general.

Notes

1. Hans Bonde, *Football with the Foe: Danish Sport Under the Swastika* (Odense: University Press of Southern Denmark, 2008), 50.
2. The sports collaboration was stopped again shortly afterwards, following the German invasion of Denmark and Norway and only definitively resumed in May 1940. Hans Joachim Teichler, *Internationale Sportpolitik im Dritten Reich* (Schorndorf: Hofmann Verlag, 1991), 271–3.
3. Hans Bonde, *Fodbold med fjenden: Dansk idræt under hagekorset* (Odense: Syddansk Universitetsforlag, 2006), 46; 96; 122.
4. Hans Bonde, *Oprøret i parken: Dansk idræt under hagekorsets tegn* (Odense: Syddansk Universitetsforlag, 2008).
5. Rudolf Stöber, 'Presse Im Nationalsozialismus', in Bernd Heidenreich and Sönke Neitzel (eds), *Medien Im Nationalsozialismus* (München: Fink, 2010), 279.
6. Erika Martens, *Zum Beispiel Das Reich: zur Phänomenologie der Presse im totalitären Regime* (Köln: Verlag Wissenschaft und Politik, 1972), 29; 49.
7. A discussion of the variations in the coverage of the various German sources (newspapers, illustrated sports magazines and newsreels) in Danish internally and between the types is available in Christian Tolstrup Jensen, 'Fodbold Med Vennerne?' (Price thesis, University of Copenhagen, 2014), 94.
8. Norbert Frei and Johannes Schmitz, *Journalismus im Dritten Reich* (München: C.H. Beck, 1989), 35.

9. See ibid., first published in 1989 (latest reprint 1999).

10. Siegfried Weischenberg, *Die Außenseiter der Redaktion: Struktur, Funktion u. Bedingungen d. Sportjournalismus: Theorie u. Analyse im Rahmen e. allg. Konzepts komplexer Kommunikatorforschung* (Bochum: Studienverlag Brockmeyer, 1976).

11. Erik Eggers, '"Deutsch wie der Sport, so auch das Wort!" Zur Scheinblüte der Fußballpublizistik im Dritten Reich', in Markwart Herzog and Andreas Bode (eds), *Fußball zur Zeit des Nationalsozialismus: Alltag, Medien, Künste, Stars* (Stuttgart: Kohlhammer, 2008), 167.

12. The football magazine *Der Kicker* with its huge print run is an exception here.

13. Eggers, 'Deutsch wie der Sport', 167–8.

14. Magazines not consulted: *Deutsche Rugby-Zeitung, Der Bergsteiger* and *Tischtennis*. See Bernett's list of sports magazines (Hajo Bernett, 'Sportpublizistik im totalitären Staat 1933–1945', *Stadion: internationale Zeitschrift für Geschichte des Sports*, no. 11 (1985), 270–1.) Magazines covering disciplines where existing research and other sources have indicated no collaboration were not consulted in the research process. (Report on the Sander period, with its own reports from federations concerning collaboration. Dansk Idræts-Forbunds arkiv, Rigsarkivet [The Danish National Archives], Pakke 196, Copenhagen. Bonde, *Football with the Foe*.).

15. Claudia Kaiser, '"Lustig im Winde flatterten die Hakenkreuzfähnchen …" Die Berichterstattung über die Länderspiele der deutschen Fußballnationalmannschaft am Beispiel "Der Kicker"', in Markwart Herzog and Andreas Bode (eds), *Fußball zur Zeit des Nationalsozialismus: Alltag, Medien, Künste, Stars* (Stuttgart: Kohlhammer, 2008), 183–94.

16. Bonde, *Fodbold med fjenden*, 143.

17. Hans Joachim Teichler and Wolfgang Meyer-Ticheloven, *Filme und Rundfunkreportagen als Dokumente der deutschen Sportgeschichte von 1907–1945: Verzeichnis archivierter Film- und Tondokumente und eine Filmographie des Sports in Deutschland mit Studien zum Verhältnis von Film, Sport und Gesellschaft* (Schorndorf: Hofmann, 1981).

18. Kaiser, 'Lustig im Winde'; Arnd Krüger, 'Germany and Sports in World War II', *Canadian Journal of History of Sport* 24, no. 1 (May 1993), 52–62.

19. Eggers, 'Deutsch wie der Sport', 172.

20. Nils Havemann, *Fußball unterm Hakenkreuz: der DFB zwischen Sport, Politik und Kommerz* (Frankfurt; New York: Campus, 2005); Lorenz Peiffer, *Hakenkreuz und rundes Leder: Fußball im Nationalsozialismus* (Göttingen: Verlag Die Werkstatt, 2008).

21. Bonde, *Football with the Foe*, 244–5.

22. Ibid., 48–9.

23. Teichler, Internationale Sportpolitik im Dritten Reich, 271–3.

24. 'Dänen Über Den Deutschen Sport', *NS-Sport*, 12 November 1939; 'Deutscher Kriegssport Im Urteil Des Auslandes', *NS-Sport*, 24 December 1939.

25. 'Mars Regiert Die Stunden', *NS-Sport*, 8 October 1939.

26. 'Gegen Dänemarks Starkes Angebot', *Völkischer Beobachter*, 3 December 1939.

27. 'Willkommen Dänische Sportkameraden!', *Handball*, 2 October 1939.

28. 'Die Dänen Erobern Leipzig', *Reichssportblatt*, 17 October 1939.

29. One of them was Heilig Vaterland, a song often used by the Hitler-Jugend. Martin Rüther, 'Lieder Zur Überhöhung von Volk Und Vaterland', *Jugend! 1918–1945*, http://www.jugend1918-1945.de/thema.aspx?s=4923 (accessed 18 January 2016).

30. 'Willkommene Gäste', *NS-Sport*, 15 October 1939.

31. Bonde, *Football with the Foe*, 70–1.

32. Ibid., 63–5.

33. 'Kosmopolitana', *Der Kicker*, 30 April 1940.

34. Bonde, *Fodbold med fjenden*, 134.

35. Bonde, *Oprøret i parken*, 65.

36. 'Deutsche Soldaten Besuchen Niels Bukh', *Völkischer Beobachter*, 18 April 1940.

37. 'Den Flotte Ragnhild', *Reichssportblatt*, 23 July 1940.

38. Bonde, *Football with the Foe*, 57.

39. Ibid., 70–1.

40. Quotation in Bonde, *Football with the Foe*, 110. Author's own translation.
41. Aage Trommer, 'Danmark – Historie (1940–45)', Den Store Danske Encyklopædi, http://www.denstoredanske.dk/index.php?sideId=219103.
42. Ibid.
43. 'Hier Spricht Die Reichshauptstadt', *Der Kicker*, 13 August 1940.
44. 'Blick Über Die Grenzen', *NS-Sport*, 20 October 1940; 'Blick Über Die Grenzen', *NS-Sport*, 19 January 1941; 'Gespräch Über Die Dänische Leichtathletik', *Der Leichtathlet*, 30 September 1940.
45. Bonde, *Football with the Foe*, 97, 144.
46. Ibid., 97.
47. Ibid., 99.
48. 'Deutsche Wochenschau', no. 522, 4 September 1940.
49. The share of sports items in the DW increased from 0.2% in 1942 to 4% in 1944, a relatively large increase, but still far from the pre-war levels (19% in 1939). Ulrike Bartels, *Die Wochenschau Im Dritten Reich. Entwicklung Und Funktion Eines Massenmediums Unter Besonderer Berücksichtigung Völkisch-Nationaler Inhalte*, (Peter Lang, 2004), 325; 424–7.
50. Bonde, *Fodbold med fjenden*, 99.
51. 'Es hat (noch einmal) geklappt', *Reichssportblatt,* 19 November 1940; 'Zweimal gegen Dänemark', *Völkischer Beobachter,* 15 November 1940; 'Hier spricht die Reichshauptstadt', *Der Kicker,* 12 November 1940.
52. 'Zwei Länderspiele gegen Dänemark', *NS-Sport,* 24 November 1940.
53. Bonde, *Football with the Foe*, 57.
54. 'Die Dänischen Hallen Geöffnet', *Der Schwimmer*, 22 May 1940.
55. For example, '[Hveger on the frontpage]', *Reichssportblatt*, 25 March 1941; 'Drei Siege Ragnhild', *Frankfurter Zeitung*, 1 October 1940.
56. 'Reizende Ragnhild', *Reichssportblatt*, 8 October 1940.
57. 'Sport Überall', *Reichssportblatt*, 1 October 1940.
58. 'Hier ist Ragnhild Hveger im Haus', *Reichssportblatt,* 3 December 1940.
59. 'Reizende Ragnhild', *Reichssportblatt*, 8 October 1940. Emphasis added.
60. Bonde, *Football with the Foe*, 132.
61. Ibid., 132–5.
62. Bonde, Oprøret i parken.
63. Bonde, *Football with the Foe*, 135.
64. Ibid., 131; Bonde, *Fodbold med fjenden,* 240–1.
65. Bonde, *Football with the Foe*, 151.
66. Teichler, Internationale Sportpolitik im Dritten Reich, 325–7.
67. 'Zweimal gegen Dänemark', *Völkischer Beobachter*, 13 November 1940.
68. 'Was Haben Wir von Der Dänenelf Zu Erwarten?', *Der Kicker*, 28 October 1941; 'Dänen Noch Stärker!', *Der Kicker*, 21 October 1941.
69. 'Wer Spielt Gegen Dänemark?', *Frankfurter Zeitung*, 13 November 1941.
70. 'Nur Ein Unentschieden in Dresden', *Frankfurter Zeitung*, 18 November 1941.
71. 'Am Sieg Vorbei', *Reichssportblatt*, 18 November 1941.
72. 'War die deutsche Elf schlecht aufgestellt?', *Der Kicker,* 18 November 1941.
73. 'Was Haben Wir von Der Dänenelf Zu Erwarten?', *Der Kicker*, 28 October 1941; 'Triumphfahrt Der Azzuri', *Völkischer Beobachter*, 22 May 1939.
74. 'Deutsche Wochenschau', no. 586, 26 November 1914.
75. Bartels, *Die Wochenschau Im Dritten Reich*, 445.
76. 'Wetten, Daß, Wenn', *Reichssportblatt*, 25 November 1941.
77. 'Wer Führt Im Europäischen Fußball', *Völkischer Beobachter*, 22 November 1941.
78. Ibid.
79. Bonde, *Football with the Foe*, 161.
80. A few athletes, in particular cyclists, continued to compete against German opponents, although attracting very little press coverage. Bonde, *Football with the Foe*, 172.
81. Trommer, 'Danmark – Historie (1940–45)'.

82. '800 Einwohner 4500 Zuschauer', *Reichssportblatt,* 11 August 1942.
83. 'Sport-Ostern: Ragnhild Hveger', *Reichssportblatt*, 7 April 1942; 'Ragnhild Hveger vollbrachte', *Völkischer Beobachter*, 5–6 April 1942.
84. Bonde, *Football with the Foe*, 200.
85. 'Jenny – Weit Unter Dem Nullpunkt', *Reichssportblatt*, 24 February, 1942.
86. 'Ausland-Tonwoche', no. 548 (February 1942). The German voice-over in this newsreel seems to indicate, that the edition was distributed in Switzerland or the German controlled General Government in Poland and Ukraine. Both these areas received editions of Ausland-Tonwoche in German. Roel Vande Winkel, 'Nazi Newsreels in Europe, 1939–1945: The Many Faces of Ufa's Foreign Weekly Newsreel (Auslandstonwoche) versus Germany's Weekly Newsreel (Deutsche Wochenschau)', *Historical Journwal of Film, Radio & Television* 24, no. 1 (March 2004), 33.
87. Bonde, *Football with the Foe*, 39–43.
88. Ibid., 117.
89. Ibid., 202.
90. Ibid., 227.

Disclosure statement

No potential conflict of interest was reported by the author.

Between Survival Strategy and Bloody Violence: Boxing in Nazi Concentration and Extermination Camps (1940–1945)

Doriane Gomet

ABSTRACT

Concentration and extermination camps were micro-societies characterized by inequality: the SS reigned supreme over a multitude of prisoners who were either exterminated upon their arrival, or died of hunger and ill-treatment while a few privileged ones enjoyed much more decent living conditions. This disturbing reality is studied here through a singular cultural practice: boxing. The way the SS exploited the talent of prisoners with boxing skills for training purposes and boxing events testifies to their own corporal culture, which was itself a product of the strict order and discipline imposed on German society by the Nazi regime through sport. Concentration camp prisoners' bodies were mere tools that could be put to use for ideological and leisure purposes. Boxing turns out to be a compelling match from which to analyze the social structure of concentration camps: boxing was a leisure activity and a power game to some, a livelihood to others, a torture for the prisoners who were the underdogs, but also a means for a very small minority to escape their plight. It also is an opportunity to bring to light the connections existing between control over and destruction of bodies, between survival and staying power.

Introduction

Concentration camps were one of the most potent tools of repression created by high-ranking Nazi dignitaries during the Third Reich. Although Dachau concentration camp opened as early as March 1933 in the vicinity of Munich, the concentration system was established only gradually as its two main creators, Heinrich Himmler and Reinhardt Heydrich, rose in the *Schutzstaffel*, the Nazi paramilitary organization usually abbreviated as SS. When Himmler appointed Theodor Eicke chief of the Concentration Camps Inspectorate in July 1934 – meaning he actually managed the incipient concentration camp system[1] – the poorly planned camps of the early days of the Nazi regime were replaced by full-fledged institutions all over the national territory: Buchenwald was created in 1937, Flossenbürg in 1938. Camps were a repressive tool wielded by Nazis to outlaw from society all those they saw as an internal threat for the regime: political opponents, social misfits and all those considered deviant because of their crimes, sexual mores, or creed. Under cover of 'rehabilitation', they were ill-treated so as to break their moral and physical resistance. In the system designed by Theodor Eicke SS guards specially trained for that purpose obviously had a key function in the methodical destruction of prisoners, but the role of inmates holding responsibilities within the camps should also be underlined. The latter wielded substantial power over their fellow prisoners, thus taking a significant part in the repression that crushed them down. When the war broke out, this system became more complex. As their population of inmates became more international, a new agenda was set for the camps and extermination measures intensified against Jews. The deportation to concentration camps as non-racial repressive measures was supplemented by deportation to extermination camps as racial persecution.[2] Besides, as the war dragged on along the Eastern front, camp prisoners became a workforce that Nazis could exploit at will in the service of their war machine. The *Rassentheorie*,[3] at the core of the Nazi ideology, was all the more salient: the 'race' and nationality of prisoners – easily identified thanks to a triangle they all wore on their coat – determined to a great extent their chances of survival in the camp.[4] The men and women who were plunged into the camp system were all without exception stripped of their identity and humanity, subjected to systematic violence on a daily basis, and crushed by the unlimited power of their guards who saw them as nothing more than sub-human creatures.[5]

However, in an environment that was as horrendous as it was absurd, cultural practices such as music, cinema or theatre did exist. This is borne out by the fact that no later than 1941 Daniel Curt published an article in the *Theatre Arts* review expounding the multi-faceted goals of theatre in Dachau and Buchenwald.[6] Eugen Kogon, an inmate at Buchenwald, also referred to it in his autobiographical narrative.[7] And while David Rousset described punitive practices that he refers to as 'sports' rather at length,[8] Tadeuz Borowski did mention actual sports activities at Auschwitz, and notably a boxing game in the main camp:

> This afternoon I attended a boxing game in the large *Waschraum* from which the first convoys left for the gas chambers … The boxing ring had been set up in the large waiting room. Vertical lighting, a referee, internationally famous boxers …[9]

How can we make sense of such cultural practices in places given over to the deliberate extermination of human beings? This study proposes to consider the camps as a social framework in their own right and to focus our analysis on boxing. Obviously the general public has now become quite knowledgeable about the subject thanks to several films inspired by the life of champions detained in the camps as well as comic-strip books.[10] However the fact is that beyond the description of the most famous matches, we remain puzzled by two central questions: what purpose did the so-called 'boxing' serve in an environment that allowed extreme discipline and the power of life and death over people to coexist? And what were the motives driving the actions of those individuals living in this environment?

We draw here from Michel Foucault's work, and in particular his concepts of discipline,[11] sovereign power and bio-power,[12] to try and understand the role of sports in camps established by a State that, if we are to believe Foucault:

> … makes the field of the life it manages, protects, guarantees, and cultivates in biological terms absolutely coextensive with the sovereign right to kill anyone, meaning not only other people, but also its own people.[13]

Another fulcrum has been the work of Giorgio Agamben and more particularly his concept of *Homo Sacer*, that is someone who can be killed with complete impunity and thus without the killer being regarded as a murderer.[14]

Several camps have been examined for the present survey: Buchenwald,[15] Neuengamme,[16] Mauthausen,[17] and Auschwitz.[18] It covers the years 1940–1945 and concentrates more particularly upon French prisoners.[19] It makes use of research on the general history of the camp system (Martin Broszat,[20] Olga Wormser-Migot,[21] Falk Pingel,[22] Karin Orth[23]) as well as camp monographies (Wolfgang Benz and Barbara Distel,[24] productions of the Auschwitz Museum, Fabrice Fabréguet).[25] Among other things these works help us understand the organization of camp life, as exemplified by Marc Schemmel's account about Neuengamme.[26]

The data used for this paper were drawn from several archives and research centres, especially the French National Archives, the Contemporary Jewish Documentation Centre, the French Institute of Contemporary History (IHTP), the Bureau of Former Victims of Contemporary Conflicts, the German Federal Archives in Berlin as well as the museums of Mauthausen, Dachau and Buchenwald camps.[27] These archives complement and cross reference each other well, thus allowing a thorough study of the role and use of boxing in the camps. We also used the records of post-war trials such as the *Auschwitz trial* that took place in Frankfort.[28] Beside archives, numerous narratives published up to 10 years after the end of the war have also been drawn upon.[29] We should also mention the testimonies of prisoners gathered after the war came to an end by the *Comité d'histoire de la Seconde Guerre* mondiale (Committee on the History of the Second World War).[30] Our research has also been complemented by three semi-structured interviews with camp survivors. Most accounts used are from French prisoners but other nationalities are also represented, notably Poles.

The aim of this paper is to study boxing as an element of a specific system within which prisoners are only considered as *Homo Sacer*. We will discuss the possibility that boxing in the camps could be linked to the German corporeal culture. This focus will be complemented by two other themes: the actual function of boxing to control prisoners and its role in the Nazi project for a methodical destruction of human beings. Broadly speaking we will look into the multiple types of power-play at work in the camps and the extremely unequal and deadly pyramid-like prison society generated by the camp system.

The Boxer's Body: A Toy Put to the Service of SS Ideological Leisure Activities

Bodies for Entertainment

Young Perez, a French Jew born in Tunisia, and crowned middleweight world champion in 1931, was arrested in June 1943 for not wearing the yellow star.[31] He was imprisoned in Drancy (France) before being sent as a Jew to a concentration camp in October 1943 in convoy No. 60.[32] Upon his arrival, he was sent to Auschwitz III-Monowitz. A few weeks later, the boxer, who had now become No. 157 178,[33] began to take part in matches in a tidy setting. After giving a *demonstration* of shadow boxing, the French champion had to fight against an SS, 'a big middleweight, about 165 lbs and 5.9 ft', in a three-round match referred by a 'stout blond SS'.[34] He was assigned a 'second', Paul Steinberg who eventually survived the Holocaust. Before the match, he was given additional food rations and authorized to train. Although almost unreal, this fight was not an anecdotal report. Tadeusz Pietrzykowski, No. 77 at Auschwitz, would have fought 40 to 60 fights, between 1941 and 1943 at the Auschwitz main camp.[35] This boxer was in particular bantamweight vice-champion of Poland. As he inflicted defeats on German deportees, and more particularly on the *Kapo* Walter Dunning, he rapidly became 'famous',[36] and 'the most renowned champion in the main camp'.[37]

In Mauthausen, Segundo Espallargas, a Spanish republican also called 'Paulino', fought 'organized fights' every Sunday in front of the SS, at the initial request of Franz Ziereis, the SS camp commandant.[38] He had so many victories that he was called 'the valiant, undefeated boxer of Mauthausen'.[39] In Neuengamme, the SS Lütkemeyer ordered Johann Trollmann to fight in the ring.[40] To spot potential fighters, the SS could consult the prisoners' card files or ask the latter to make themselves known. At Drancy, Young Perez mentioned 'boxer' as his profession on his admission file,[41] and he did the same at Auschwitz.[42] Noah Klieger reports that in Auschwitz III, the SS interrogated newcomers as they were put in quarantine to enrol potential boxers.[43] Concerning the practical organization of fights, survivors describe almost similar scenes: rings were set up, fighters had genuine gloves, and even sometimes seconds. Fights generally took place on Sunday, had just a few rounds and were refereed with official rules. A large audience – first and foremost the SS and some privileged inmates – attended them.[44]

The fact that guards resorted to the inmates' physical and boxing skills may seem first and foremost a logical, pragmatic solution for seeking entertainment in a context of geographical isolation. Outside their duty hours the SS were entitled to some leisure time during which they could enjoy various entertaining activities,[45] but concentration camps were built away from urban areas. Auschwitz is a case in point: the camp was set up at the confluence of the rivers Sola and Vistula, which according to Franciszek Piper made its seclusion from 'the rest of the world' easier.[46] As they could not go to shows, the SS used what was on hand for them inside the camp, namely inmates. After the Liberation, SS *Rapportführer* Wilhelm Clausen made no secret of it in his testimony and was reported to have encouraged sports among inmates for entertainment purposes, and to have organized most sports events in the camp.[47] The keen interest of the SS in boxing was obvious: in his testimony, Georges Séguy indicated that boxing fights were 'most appreciated'[48] by the SS in Mauthausen, and Hermann Langbein even uses the term 'favourite sport'.[49] This is hardly surprising since, after the First World War, boxing matches had become highly popular, profitable shows in continental Europe where they got extensive media coverage.[50] When Hitler came to power in Germany, boxing matches became an integral part of the powerful Nazi propaganda machine. They helped establish the theory of racial superiority, and promote sports activities while also offering the masses a state-controlled outlet to let off steam. The victories of Max Schmeling,[51] and of other German boxers like Hervert Runge and Willi Kaiser, at the 1936 Olympics were widely exploited by Nazi propaganda. Accordingly, it is no surprise that the SS were huge fans of boxing matches in the camps, all the more so as cultural entertainment was a real concern for their hierarchy. The *Inspektion der Konzentrationslager* aka ILK (the concentration camps inspectorate) and the *SS-Wirtschafts-Verwaltungshauptamt* aka SS-WVHA (SS economic and administrative department) allocated funds every year, as was the case for instance in 1939, for the SS entertainment within the camps themselves,[52] and Department VI for *Fürsorge, Schulung und Truppenbetreuung* (SS staff welfare and training) went to great lengths to organize all sorts of cultural activities for them.[53] In Auschwitz, Department VI was created at the beginning of 1942, as reported by the *SS-Obersturmführer* Karl Höcker in his Auschwitz trial statement,[54] and supported by Alesander Lasik's findings.[55] That camps had boxing equipment and the SS provided gloves to inmates and attended their fights therefore makes perfect sense: in the particular environment of camps, inmates were only a medium at the service of ideology-filled entertainment and activities rife with ideology which were an integral part of the body culture of the 'master race'.

Bodies as Instruments

The SS also used inmates for their own boxing practice. In his testimony, Moshé Garbarz mentioned an Auschwitz SS who dealt out punches for training purposes.[56] He himself was beaten up by a guard who used techniques typical of boxing.[57] In Neuengamme, the light heavyweight world-champion Johann Trollmann was ordered by *SS Schutzhaftlagerführer* Lütkemeyer to take part in the guards' training every day in the boxing gym.[58] The same goes for Leen Sanders who had to spar with the SS,[59] and Young Perez who, according to Gabriel Burah, would have given 'boxing lessons to some SS'.[60]

The interest the SS showed for their training sessions is directly linked to the importance of boxing in the moral and physical instruction of the perfect Aryan whom they supposedly epitomized. Because it contains in itself essential educational values – in particular the face-to-face encounter with the harshness of life and the necessity of a never-ending fight[61] – boxing was part of a young German's curriculum from a very early age. The book written by Hitler between 1924 and 1925, *Mein Kampf*,[62] emphasized its educational value that was also underlined by Nazi theoreticians like Heinrich Meusel, who dedicated over 20 pages to it in a book recommended by the *Reichssportführer*.[63] Whole books were written about boxing such as Gerhard Voigt's *Der Boxsport im Schulturnen* published in 1934,[64] and Konrad Stein's, *Boxen der Jugend* in 1938.[65] The *Reichsstelle für den Unterrichtsfilm* (the Reich educational film board) even produced *Boxen der Jugend*, a film about boxing training for the young.[66] Logically it was taught at school,[67] and it was a salient feature of *Hitlerjugend's* (Hitler youth) sporting activities, as reported in Kurt Abels' testimony.[68] It obviously played a major part in the elite schools of the Party such as the NPEA (*Nationalpolitische Erziehungsanstalten: the political institutes of education*) and the *Adolf-Hitler-Schulen* (Adolf Hitler schools).[69] The training schools for Nazi leaders such as the *Ordensburgen* were even more demanding. In such schools, sport was considered a national institution, as exemplified in *Vogelsang Ordensburg* where the future Black Order leaders would spend eight hours a week boxing, fencing and parachuting.[70] Boxing was deemed indispensable to inculcate boldness, bravery and a fighting spirit.[71] Once they joined the SS,[72] men carried on training so as to be the worthy representatives of the Nazi sporting ideal.[73] To that end, they were regularly subjected to tests they had to pass successfully.[74] A 1936 document stated for example that the SS belonging to the *SS-Verfügungstruppe* (combat support force) had to spend five hours a week practicing a sport, including one and a half hours of combat-related activities.[75] From 1935 to 1936 onwards, the *Reichsführung* SS (the SS High Command) demanded that all SS soldiers and officers should take the tests of the *SA-Sportabzeichen* (SA sports badge), and also possibly those of the *Reichssportabzeichen* (Reich sports badge). Obtaining these certificates meant that officers could then wear the relevant badges testifying to their sporting skills.[76] SS camp guards, from rank and file to officers alike, were subject to similar requirements as shown in the personal file record of one of the Dachau commandants: Hans Loritz. Among other information his file contains his sports scores when he received the *SA-Sportabzeichen*.[77] It seems that in the camps, the SS made use of the bodies and boxing skills of inmates for their sparring sessions, and thus fulfilled their hierarchy's demands. Two power dynamics clearly meet here: a bio-power willing to give the SS the highest possible body strength and an absolute power through which the right to kill is granted to guarantee the well-being of the superior race.

Broken Bodies

If making use of inmates seemed apparently inconsistent with the German *Rassentheorie* and the organized mass murder of prisoners, it actually revealed the 'banality of evil'[78] prevailing in the camps and the potency of the racist prejudice that shaped the Nazi mindset . Boxing bouts entertained the guards but significantly decreased the inmates' life force energy – something about which a Nazi sports audience could not care less. Inmates were only *Homo Sacer* in the sense given by Giorgio Agamben: someone who could be killed with the killer's complete impunity, someone who had to fight according to sports regulations at the risk of their own life. Also their sparring sessions with and multiple victories over former boxing world champions reinforced the SS guards' feeling of racial superiority and their self-belief in the Aryan sports supremacy: the weakness of Jews was exposed for all to see as in the boxing ring at least they could no longer hide behind a corrupt system they had helped to establish before the war. In any event, once one of their 'toys'[79] was broken, the Nazis would look for another inmate to replace the former. If no inmate fitted the part, they would choose one at random without a second thought for the outcome. An example is a totally unbalanced confrontation organized by the SS in December 1943 at the Loibl-Pass North *Kommando,* pitting a member of the kitchen *Kommando* against a very weak Pole. The latter reportedly lost his life.[80]

Those fights had multiple but rather paradoxical consequences for former boxing stars. The SS, who wished to add spice to boxing events and make a pretence of equal opportunities, granted privileges to the boxers as long as they ensured a good show. They were given extra rations of food and assigned to less demanding work *Kommandos*. It is necessary to bear in mind that virtually all prisoners were subject to slave labour in quarries, armaments plants, forest clearance or earthmoving activities in the vicinity of the camps. Their daily calorie intake was inadequate,[81] with for instance a maximum of 1700 calories at Auschwitz.[82] However a small minority remained within the camp where they were employed in administrative and economic tasks – workshops, warehouses, kitchens, parcel sorting offices, secretarial offices and medical units.[83] All such assignments offered advantages, especially because prisoners were not exposed to the elements and had easier access to food, medicines and clothes.[84] In return for his fights, Young Perez was appointed to the kitchen *Kommando* where he received extra rations through the autumn of 1943.[85] As for Tadeusz Pietrzykowski, he was assigned to the cowshed *Kommando*, one reputedly offering better food. Tadeusz Borowski underlines in his account the privileges granted to boxers at Auschwitz I: 'Auschwitz and boxing. The champions train in facilities located in the camp itself. They are fed accordingly, and well taken care of'.[86]

Some of them like Tadeusz Pietrzykowski, Salamo Arouch or Jacques Razon survived the camps. It seems therefore that boxing skills could be considered an asset, in the meaning given to the word by Wolfgang Sofsky, that offered sportsmen a greater chance of survival in the camps.[87]

However, such protection did not come easy. Having a referee, rounds, and judges to decide on the winner, allegedly gave boxing matches the status of regular fights, but the fact remains that those fights were totally unbalanced because of their frequency, the non-respect of weight divisions, and more particularly the living conditions of inmate boxers. Together with ill-treatment, lack of food, poor living conditions and the inescapable atmosphere of death and violence, the fights drained their forces despite the significant advantages they derived from them. For Serge Smulevic, boxing had no little bearing on the former champion's gradual decline[88] and his death during the 'Death Marches.'[89] Prisoners at Neuengamme remember that Johann Trollmann's fights were always most unequal. Although he was weak and injured, his opponents would always be healthy SS so his strength soon faded away.[90] His state of health led the camp resistance to pretend he was dead and then manage to send him to a *Kommando* where he was to die eventually.

In short the boxing matches organized in the camps were the tangible expression of the discipline that weighed upon the SS. Their appetite for boxing was but the result of a process of indoctrination that started when they were quite young, a process that advocated a combative mindset and refused any form of weakness. Still, the fights as well as the training sessions reveal another characteristic of the ideology that pervaded their education: first the fact that human beings belonged to various categories organized in a hierarchy, and second a total lack of compassion for those that were considered sub-humans. Camp prisoners were mere *Homo Sacer*, and according to the Nazi ideology, their bodies could be used freely as an instrument by the master race for their leisure activities.

Between Unconscious Imitation and Resistance: Boxing, an Activity for Inmates Within the 'Grey Area'[91]

Boxing, a Leisure for the Camps' 'Happy Few'

Beside the fights organized by the SS, other boxing events were also staged in camps by prisoners themselves with the agreement of their guards. At Loibl-Pass South, a *Kommando* depending on Mauthausen, '… Boxing fights or football matches were sometimes organized on a Sunday afternoon'.[92] These sports events supposedly started during the summer of 1943 and only involved those inmates who wished to participate. In this specific case, there was no obligation imposed by the SS and champions were not compelled to go into the ring. The same could be observed in most concentration camps. At Buchenwald boxing expanded rapidly from 1943 onwards. According to Otto Halle, fights were organized in the camp's cinema or in the woods outside the camp.[93]

It seems quite unbelievable that boxing fights could be organized when you think of the prisoners' living conditions and the fact they worked from sunrise to sunset.[94] However certain prisoners enjoyed much better living conditions, thus enabling them to box and even organize boxing events. To understand how this was possible requires going back to the very origin of concentration camps. The so-called 'self-administration' established in 1933 by Theodor Eicke in Dachau was then generalized to all camps. It was based on the assignment of certain duties to prisoners so the camps could operate. The latter were duly selected by the SS according to their 'race', their skills or the reason why they were in the camps. Those prisoners enjoyed much better living conditions than others, at least in the short term, in return for their involvement.[95] Among the positions of responsibility were those linked to the administration and economic organization of camps mentioned above, but also maintaining order jobs. The *Lagerältester* is the Elder of all inmates of a camp. Under him are *Kapos* whose job it is to keep under close watch their fellow inmates during working hours and *Blockältester* who were overseers in charge of order and discipline in the bunkhouses. It resulted in a deeply unequal camp society embracing starving, beaten up prisoners and privileged inmates called '*Prominente*',[96] who enjoyed particular living conditions: 'moderately hard work, as well as better food, clothes and sleeping equipment'.[97] Boxing was one of their huge privileges. At Auschwitz III-Monowitz *Lagerältester* P. Kosmara was well known for his interest in the organization of fights.[98] When he was asked about this *Lagerältester's* interests and incentives, Serge Smulevic answered: 'Kosmara liked sports, all of them, but boxing was his favourite. He was crazy about it and boxing events in the camp were a thrill to him'.[99]

At Loibl-Pass South, just like in Auschwitz, the inmate holding the highest position in the camp hierarchy, Fridolin Bipp, prompted most boxing matches and was assisted by a few other inmates also holding senior positions.[100]

Still the reason why boxing events mainly developed from 1942 to 1943 remains to be determined. Answers have to do both with economic and military realities. Although the aim set out when they were originally created was to break prisoners so as to 're-educate' them, camps eventually became a key element in the war production, and especially from 1942. Prisoners were then available for manufacturing plants in which working hours matched more or less those of regular German factories. Sunday was normally a day-off when some inmates were allowed to participate in recreational activities:[101] 'Sunday was a day off for most *Kommandos* … The orchestra would sometimes give a concert … A few boxing events were even organized'.[102]

Also, while prisoners' lives were hitherto wasted against a background of general indifference, the SS High Command decided that the mortality rate should decrease so as to make the most of larger and more productive manpower, and SS camps commanders received orders to that effect: larger food rations, easier access to the inmates' hospital, the possibility for some inmates to receive Red Cross packages,[103] go to brothels[104] or see films.[105] Such measures give us an inkling of the sheer complexities of the camp system. Although they were borrowed from social organizations founded on bio-power, they were applied to individuals refused any right to live by Nazis, and while they can be credited with a decrease in the death rate at Mauthausen,[106] they actually mostly benefited the prisoners with responsibilities. The latter improved their daily life stealing from prisoners' parcels,[107] and also enjoyed a wider variety of leisure activities.

Privileged Prisoners with Mixed, Complex Motivations

As for the motives of those privileged prisoners, they were far from identical: they actually varied significantly according to their status in the camp. The prisoners in supervisory positions were chosen above all else for their violent behaviour and slavish obedience. Most prisoners in this category were German common law criminals who had been detained from the very creation of camps and bore a green triangle.[108] Although they had the power of life and death over their fellow inmates, theirs was a very precarious situation as the SS and other higher ranking prisoners could dismiss them as quickly as they had been appointed.[109] To keep their privileged positions, they would stick at nothing and developed a strategy of 'mimetic servility' in all aspects of camp life including boxing.[110] This is hardly surprising since, even before they were arrested, that sport was part of their cultural world, a world they actually shared with the SS.

Just like the SS who compelled former prize fighters to partake in the big boxing events, the privileged inmates recruited prisoners to participate in less important boxing bouts in exchange for a few benefits in kind. After participating in a boxing exhibition against a *Kapo* who asked him to, Gabriel Burah got 'a double ration of soup and triple ration of bread'.[111] The *Kapos* could also ask inmates to fight each other, often to the death. Georges Dudal remembered a Polish prisoner who organized fights in *Block* 8A. When entertainment was not the order of the day, prisoners' bodies could also be used by *Prominente* for sparring purposes, as the SS did. Serge Miller remembers a *Blockältester* who had been a boxer in his youth and enjoyed using prisoners as a punching bag when he trained.[112] At Loibl-Pass Karawanken, the *Blockältester*, whose nickname was 'The Tattooed Man', often liked to hone his skills by hitting prisoners compelled to stay put.[113] Sometimes, boxing was nothing short of a pretext for killing. Also in Auschwitz Raymond Montégut reports the evening 'dances of death' during which *Blockältester* would beat up Jewish prisoners - at times to death.[114] By imitating their superiors, organizing or participating in activities highly valued by the latter, showing their total adherence to the Nazi ideology, the *Prominente* endeavoured to keep their privileges. We can see this logic at work in whatever task they were asked to perform: killing, torturing, organizing or participating in boxing bouts or music shows.[115]

However, the *Prominente* progressively came to include inmates who strove to resist the Nazi rational effort for their extermination. Initially, the prisoners in supervisory positions were systematically chosen among German common law prisoners. However this policy was to change as the war wore on and recruitment became more diversified, eventually including prisoners not so likely to comply as submissively with the Nazis' every wish. Two main explanations can be put forward. First, the very dynamics at work within the prisoner society: the massive inflow of political prisoners from 1942 to 1943 and the creation of resistance groups brought about a redistribution of power within the camps.[116] Second, the motivations of the SS since the 'all-out' war context urged them to diversify their recruitment strategy to foster inmate productivity. The fierce struggle between 'red' and 'green' prisoners exemplifies this struggle,[117] and so does the lot of the Spaniards in Mauthausen.[118] When better living conditions befell them, these newly privileged prisoners gained considerable power. They used that power not to ill-treat their fellow-countrymen but quite on the contrary to protect them from the worst acts of violence and keep them alive until the camps were liberated. To achieve that goal, they controlled the food rationing, made it possible for the weakest among them to be admitted to the prisoner hospital, and limited the use of physical violence. To keep up the prisoners' morale, they used notably cultural and corporal activities as a protection against degradation. This was the case of the Spanish survivors at Mauthausen, who organized musical events and engaged in sports activities.[119] From 1944, when the French inmates finally organized themselves in the camps, what little cultural entertainment they could initiate was aimed at boosting the survivors' morale.[120] Here, the testimony refers to the 'Committee for French Interests' created in June 1944 at Buchenwald. According to Frédéric-Henri Manhès, its main leader, the Committee aimed at 'enabling the largest number of his fellow citizens to go back to France in the best physical condition possible, and ruining the German war production'.[121] Boxing matches were sometimes scheduled. At Loibl-Pass South, after some hesitations, the clandestine resistance committee decided to promote boxing events with French fighters so as to 'give inmates the opportunity to break with the dullness of daily routine'.[122] In such instances, boxing appears to be a cultural landmark that gave men faced with a dehumanizing process the strength to reconstruct an identity and to feel they did belong to a group. In the main camp at Mauthausen, Michel de Bouard noted: 'In the summer of 1944, the victories of such and such Frenchman helped … boost our national prestige within the strange, closed world of the K.L.M'.[123]

These various facts highlight the utmost complexity of camp life and the various forms of power at work there. Because of the very system of camp management, the SS had the opportunity to transform some privileged inmates into devoted accomplices capable of horrific violence against their fellow prisoners. Concerning this point, Olga Wormser-Migot says: 'the unreality of this hellish experience, although so painfully felt by the inmates, had annihilated the SS' and inmates' awareness that killing one or several individuals was actually a murder'.[124] Additionally, the world of concentration camps induced the privileged inmates to reproduce the entertainment patterns and customs of their masters, whenever the latter gave them the opportunity to do so, and consequently to use sports as an expression of their authority. But sport was also one of the means used by other *Prominente* for resisting the degradation they were submitted to. Finally, sport was an opportunity for a few underprivileged prisoners to scrounge for some means of subsistence.

Conclusion

Boxing was overwhelmingly acclaimed by the Nazi regime and proved especially popular with SS guards and officers in the camps. The latter eagerly used prisoners to set up pugilistic spectacles, which they considered nothing less than a pleasurable pastime. Through unconscious imitation, privileged camp inmates also organized boxing matches, a fact undeniably showing that cultural activities are a marker of concentration camp hierarchy. We can even assert that the incentives to participate in those matches differed according to the inmates' status in the camp system: for those belonging to *Kapocracy*,[125] the aim was to please their superior obediently while also consolidating their supremacy. Others strove to regain an identity that was denied in every possible way – personal, social, cultural and national. As for the most underprivileged in the camp hierarchy, they considered it a means of subsistence as they could trade off whatever boxing skills they possessed.

When the camps were liberated, learning of such practices was disturbing. How could anyone conceive of such unnatural association without playing down Nazi crimes? How could champions become popular icons again after taking part in such a travesty of sport? While the cruelty of the fights is pointed out in all accounts and camp narratives, the champions' willingness to resist is also widely emphasized: Young Perez for instance was presented as a brave, altruistic person who did not hesitate to take advantage of his position to steal food and thus help save lives.[126] Still there remains the fact that their boxing skills allowed certain prisoners to survive[127] in an environment where they were from the start destined to die, and this appalling fact remains disturbing to this very day.

Disclosing the existence of boxing activities in concentration camps leads us to examine another aspect that cannot be avoided: what is the real meaning of sports in relation to supremacy, power, discipline and violence. In summary, this study shows how complex it is to understand sports practices in concentration camps because of the porous boundaries between two antagonistic forms of power established by Foucault: sovereign power and bio-power. Within the specific reality of concentration camps, the Nazis severed the organic link that existed between regulated sports events and the limits imposed on physical violence. In the camps, rules only existed so the fights would become part of the Nazi culture of sports and the Nazi personnel could more easily control the emotions the fights stirred up, regardless of the consequences on the bodies of prisoners.

Notes

1. Martin Broszat, 'Nationalsozialistische Konzentrationslager 1933–1945', in Hans Buchheim, Martin Broszat, Hans-Adolf Jacobsen and Krausnick Helmut (eds), *Anatomie des SS-Staates* [Anatomy of the SS State] (München: Deutscher Taschenbuch Verlag, 2005), 362; Joseph Billig, *L'hitlérisme et le système concentrationnaire* [Hitlerism and the Camp System] (Paris: PUF, 1967), 210–11.

2. The word 'inmate' refers to individuals who have been held in a Nazi concentration camp (Annette Wieviorka, *Déportation et génocide. Entre la mémoire et l'oubli* [Deportation and Genocide. Between Memory an Oblivion] (Paris: Hachette, 2003), 27–9; Laurent Joly, Annette Wieviorka, and Tal Bruttmann, *Qu'est-ce qu'un déporté? Histoire et mémoires des déportations de la Seconde Guerre mondiale* [What is a Concentration Camp Prisoner deportation] (Paris: CNRS, 2009). To grasp fully the concentration camp system, it is essential to acknowledge the difference between 'racial deportation as persecution measures' and 'non-racial deportation as repressive measures'. Fondation pour la Mémoire de la Déportation, *Livre-Mémorial des déportés de France arrêtés par mesure de répression et dans certains cas par mesure de persécution 1940-1945, IV vol.* [Memorial Book of French people deported as repressive measures and sometimes as persecution measures, 1940–1945] (Paris: Editions Tirésias, 2004), 15–6.

3. Nazi racism fed on the works dealing with the existence of human races. Those works were quite abundant in the late nineteenth century with writers such as A. Gobineau, Vacher de Lapouge and H.S. Chamberlain among others. Nazi racism also drew on the *völkisch* movement. The race theory was founded on the belief that races were not equal and perpetually struggling with each other. In this context, Aryans were at the top of the hierarchy but were endangered by the Jews, a race that was considered at once inferior, parasitic and evil-minded (George. L. Mosse, *Les racines intellectuelles du Troisième Reich. La crise de l'idéologie allemande* [The Crisis of the German Ideologie] (Paris: Calmann-Levy; Mémorial de la Shoah, 2006); Ian Kershaw, *Qu'est-ce que le nazisme? Problèmes et perspectives d'interprétation* [The Nazi Dictatorship. Problems and Perspectvies of Interpretation] (Paris: Seuil, 1997)).

4. See how Michel De Bouard describes the various groups of prisoners: Michel De Bouard, 'Mauthausen', *Revue d'histoire de la Deuxième Guerre mondiale,* nos. 15–16 (1954), 57–8.

5. Wolfgang Sofsky, *L'organisation de la terreur* [The Order of terror. The Concentration Camp] (Paris: Calmann-Lévy, 1995), 147–81.

6. Daniel Curt, 'Theatre in the German Concentration Camps', *Theatre Arts* (1941), 801–7.

7. Eugen Kogon, *L'Etat SS. Le système des camps de concentration* [The SS State] (Paris: Editions de la Jeune Parque, 1947), 145–52.

8. David Rousset, *L'univers concentrationnaire* [The Universe of the Concentration Camp (Paris: Hachette, 2005), 54.

9. Tadeusz Borowski, *Le monde de pierre* [The World of Stone] (Paris: Christian Bourgeois Editeur, 2002), 181.

10. Several movies relate the fate of the famous boxers in the camps. *The Boxer and Death* is a Slovak film directed by Peter Solan, released in 1963 under the original title *Boxer A Smrt. Triumph of the Spirit* is an American film directed by Robert M. Young released in 1989. *Victor Young Perez* is a film by Jacques Ouaniche released in November 2013 after being shown at the Colmar film festival '7 jours pour le 7ème art'. There are also numerous comic strip books: Reinhard Kleist, *Le boxeur* [The Boxer] (Paris: Casterman, 2013); Eddy Vaccaro and Aurélien Ducoudray, *Young: Tunis 1911- Auschwitz 1945* (Paris: Futuropolis, 2013).

11. Michel Foucault, *Surveiller et punir* [Discipline and Punish: The Birth of the Prison] (Paris: Gallimard, 1975), 161.

12. Michel Foucault, *Il faut défendre la société* [Society Must Be Defended] (Paris: Gallimard/Seuil, 1997), 216.

13. Ibid., 232.

14. Giorgio Agamben, *Homo Sacer, Tome 1. Le pouvoir souverain et la vie nue* [Homo Sacer: Sovereign Power and Bare Life] (Paris: Seuil, 1998); Giogio Agamben, *Ce qui reste d'Auschwitz. Homo Sacer III* [Remnants of Auschwitz. The Witness and the Archive] (Paris: Editions Payot et Rivage, 2003).

15. The creation of Buchenwald had been decided by the end of 1936. It was established near Weimar in central Germany. The first group of prisoners arrived on 16 July 1937. As in the case of Dachau, the majority of prisoners were Germans at first but became more diversified in the course of the war. The prisoner count at the end of 1943 was 34,643, whether they were in the main camp or in one of its satellites. In March 1945 the figure had risen to 84,651. It is estimated that a total of 250,000 people were detained in Buchenwald, 56,000 of whom died. The camp was liberated on 11 April 1945.

16. Neuengamme was located in northern Germany, more precisely to the south-east of Hamburg. Initially a satellite of Sachsenhausen from which prisoners were sent as from December 1938, Neuengamme became a camp in its own right in June 1940. The prisoners were at first Germans and Austrians but many more nationalities were represented later when the Second World War started. The number of satellite camps also increased: In August 1943 the main camp population was 5500 while another 4000 were held in satellites. All in all 106,000 inmates were detained in Neuengamme and 55,000 of them died. The camp was liberated on 5 May 1945.

17. When Austria was annexed by the German Reich in March 1938, the Nazis decided on the creation of a camp 25 km from Linz. The first inmates, mostly Austrian common law detainees and social misfits, arrived in Mauthausen in August 1938. The camp population totalled approximately 200,000 between 1938 and 1945, with a death count estimated to be between 95,000 and 118,000. Mauthausen was liberated in early May 1945.

18. Auschwitz I (the main camp) was opened on May 1940 and was intended for men exclusively. It was initially established as a traditional concentration camp, but the implementation of the Final Solution scheme deeply altered its objectives and turned it into both a concentration and extermination camp. In autumn 1941 the ever-increasing number of deportees sent to Auschwitz resulted in the construction of a second camp, Auschwitz II, 3 km away from the main camp. The first deported prisoners arrived there in spring 1942. Finally, the Buna Monowitz *Kommando*, located 7 km from the main camp, became a self-governing camp as from November 1943 and was renamed Auschwitz III – Monowitz. The number of prisoners recorded between 1940 and 1945 in the Auschwitz camps reached 400,355, all nationalities included. All the prisoners held in Auschwitz camps were evacuated by the SS in mid-January 1945 and transferred to other camps.

19. Although the occupation of France began in June 1940, mass deportation to Nazi camps did not start until March 1942. Before that date, only two groups of prisoners were sent to the camps: Spanish Republicans in July 1940, and miners from northern France in July 1941.

20. Martin Broszat, 'Nationalsozialistische Konzentrationslager 1933–1945', in Hans Buchheim, Martin Broszat, Hans-Adolf Jacobsen and Krausnick Helmut (eds), *Anatomie des SS-Staates* [Anatomy of the SS State] (München: Deutscher Taschenbuch Verlag, 2005), 423–45.

21. Olga Wormser-Migot, *Le système concentrationnaire nazi* [The Nazi Camp System] (Paris: PUF, 1967).

22. Falk Pingel, *Häfltlinge unter SS-Herrschaft. Widerstand, Selbstbehauptung und Vernichtung im Konzentrationslager* [Prisoners under Nazi Rule: Resistance, self-assertion and extermination in the Concentration Camps] (Hamburg: Hoffmann und Campe Verlag, 1978).

23. Karin Orth, *Das System der nationalsozialistischen Konzentrationslager: Eine politische Organisationsgeschichte* [The Nazi Concentration Camp System: History of a political organization] (Hamburg: Hamburger Edition, 1999).

24. Wolfgang Benz and Barbara Distel, *Der Ort des Terrors. Geschichte der nationalsozialistischen Konzentrationslager* [Place of Terror. History of the Nazi Concentration Camp]. *Band 4 : Flossenbürg, Mauthausen, Ravensbrück* (München: C.H. Beck, 2006).

25. Michel Fabréguet, *Mauthausen. Camp de concentration national-socialiste en Autriche rattachée (1938–1945)* [Mauthausen. A National Socialist Camp in Annexed Austria (1938–1945)] (Paris: Honoré Champion Editeur, 1999).

26. Marc Schemmel, *Funktionshäftlinge im KZ Neuengamme. Zwischen Kooperation und Widerstand* [Prisoners and Positions of Power in the Neuengamme Camp. Between Cooperation and Resistance] (Saarbrücken: AkademikerVerlag, 2012).

27. The archives used are from the French National Archives in Paris (AN, 736MI; AN, F/9/); the Contemporary Jewish Documentation Centre (CDJC) in Paris; the Bureau of Former Victims of Contemporary Conflicts (AC, deportation records); the German Federal Archives in Berlin (BAB); the museums of Mauthausen (GMa), Dachau (GDa) and Buchenwald (GBu) camps.

28. The Auschwitz trial is published in its entirety in a DVD: *Der Auschwitz-Prozess* (Berlin: Digitale Bibliothek, 2005).

29. The testimonies we studied are as follows: 23 from former Auschwitz inmates; 20 from Mauthausen; 25 from Buchenwald; 23 from Dachau and 14 from Neuengamme.

30. All these testimonies can be found at the French National Archives in Paris in document AN, 72aj.

31. AN, F/9/5622. Jewish individual file of Paris Prefecture. Victor Young Perez' card: 'Drancy 18-6-43. Not wearing his yellow star'.

32. Serge Klarsfeld, *Le mémorial de la déportation des Juifs de France* [The Memorial of the Deportation of French Jews] (Paris: Paris: B et S Klarsfeld, 1978).

33. A.C. Young Perez personal file.

34. Paul Steinberg, *Chronique d'ailleurs* [Chronicles from Elsewhere] (Paris: Editions Ramsay, 2000), 40–1.

35. Johanna Ciesla and Antoni Molenda, *Tadeusz Pietrzykowski 'Teddy': 1917–1991* (Oswiecim: Oddz/ Wojewodzki, 1995).

36. Wieslaw Kielar, *Anus Mundi, Cinq ans à Auschwitz* [Anus Mundi: Five Years in Auschwitz] (Paris: Robert Laffont, 1980), 128.

37. Hermann Langbein, *Hommes et femmes à Auschwitz* [People in Auschwitz] (Paris: Fayard, 1975), 129.

38. Luis-Garcia Manzano, *La Rondalla de Mauthausen* [A Spanish Rondalla at Mauthausen] (Paris: Privat, 2013), 78.

39. *Mauthausen. Bulletin de l'Amicale de Mauthausen-Déportés, Familles et amis* 330 (2012), 15.

40. Roger Repplinger, *Leg dich, Zigeuner. Die Geschichte von Johann Trollmann und Tull Harder* [Lie down, Zigeuner. The History of Johann Trollmann and Tull Harder] (Berlin: Piper Ebooks, 2012), 277.

41. AN, F/9/5622. Jewish individual file of the Paris Prefecture, Victor Young Perez personal record.

42. Steinberg, *Chronique d'ailleurs*, 33.

43. Noah Klieger, *La boxe ou la vie. Récit d'un rescapé d'Auschwitz* [Boxing for your life. The Story of a Survivor from Auschwitz] (Paris: Editions Elkana, 2008), 44.

44. Steinberg, *Chronique d'ailleurs*, 38.

45. Fabrice D'Almeida, *Ressources inhumaines* [Inhuman resources] (Paris: Fayard, 2011).

46. Franciszek Piper, 'La genèse du camp', in Aleksander Lasik, Franciszek Piper, Piotr Setkiewicz and Irena Strzelecka (eds), *Auschwitz, 1940–1945 (vol. 1)* (Oswiecim: Musée d'Etat d'Auschwitz-Birkenau, 2011), 71.

47. Langbein, *Hommes et femmes à Auschwitz*, 130.

48. Georges Seguy, *Résister: de Mauthausen à mai 68* [Resisting: From Mauthausen to May 68] (Paris: L'Archipel, 2008).

49. Langbein, *Hommes et femmes à Auschwitz*, 129.

50. André Rauch, *Boxe, violence du XXᵉ siècle* [Boxing, a 20th Century Violence] (Paris: Auber, 1992).

51. Roger, I. Abrams, *Playing Tough: The World of Sports and Politics* (New England: Northeastern University Press, 2013), 73–100.

52. BAB, NS 3/479. Haushaltsvoranschlag der Konzentrationslager für das Haushaltsjahr 1939.

53. D'Almeida, *Ressources inhumaines*, 125.

54. *Der 1. Frankfurter Auschwitz-Prozeß*, Das Verfahren: Vernehmungsprotokolle der Angeklagten', 3788 (vgl. Blatt 7737).

55. Aleksander Lasik, 'La structure organisationnelle du camp d'Auschwitz', in Aleksander Lasik, Franciszek Piper, Piotr Setkiewicz and Irena Strzelecka (eds), *Auschwitz. vol 1.* (Oswiecim: Musée d'Etat d'Auschwitz-Birkenau, 2011), 319–22.

56. Moshé Garbarz and Elie Garbarz, *Un survivant* [A Survivor] (Paris: Editions Ramsay, 2006), 69.

57. Ibid., 89.

58. Repplinger, *Leg dich, Zigeuner*, 276–8.

59. Braber, *This Cannot Happen Here*, 152.

60. Gabriel Burah, *Bibi* (Paris: Fayard, 1970), 264.

61. Gustav Schäfer, 'Der Boxsport und seine erzieherischen Werte', in Mildner Friedrich (ed.), *Olympia 1936 und die Leibesübungen im Nationalsozialistischen Staat* [1936 Olympics and Physical Exercices in Nazi Germany] (Berlin: Buchvertrieb Olympiade 1936), 313–19.

62. 'There is no sport that, like this, promotes the spirit of aggression in the same measure, demands determination quick as lightning, educates the body for steel-like versatility … Thus the meaning of sports is not only to make the individual strong, versatile and bold, but it has also to harden him and to teach him how to bear inclemencies'. Adolf Hitler, *Mein Kampf*. Translation by J. Gaudefroy-Demombynes and A. Calmettes (Paris: Nouvelles Editions Latines, 1934), 70–1.

63. Heinrich Meusel, *Körperliche Grundausbildung* [Basic Physical Training] (Berlin: Weismannsche Verlagsbuchhandlung, 1940), 172–92.

64. Gerhard Voigt, *Der Boxsport im Schulturnen: Ein Methodischer Aufbau der Boxübungen für den Massenunterricht* [Boxing in School: A Methodological Approach to Boxing Exercises for the Masses] (Leipzig: Quelle and Meyer, 1934).

65. Konrad Stein, *Boxen der Jugend. Grundschule des Faustkampfes in der Leibeserziehung in Jungenschulen* [Boxing for the Young: Boxing in Boy's Schools Physical Education] (Berlin: Weidmannsche Verlagsbuchhandlung, 1938).

66. Archives from United States Holocaust Memorial Museum (USHMM): German Education film: *Instructional Film on Boxing Techniques*, Story RG-60.3654, film ID: 2596.

67. Roland Naul, 'History of Sport and Physical Education in Germany', in Roland Naul and Ken Hardman (eds), *Sport and Physical Education in Germany* (London and New York: Routlege, 2002), 25.

68. Jean-Denis Lepage, *La Hitler Jugend* [Hitler Youth] (Paris: Jacques Grancher, 2004), 89: 'Boxing was a particularly stimulating sport for aggression, it developed addiction to violence and resistance to fear and punches'. See also Arndt Krüger, 'Die Rolle des Sports bei den Kriegsvorbereitungen des nationalsozialistischen Deutschlands', in Sven Güldenpfennig and Horst Meyer (eds), *Sportler für den Frieden : Argumente und Dokumente für eine sportpolitische Bewusstseinsbildung* [Athletes for Peace: Arguments and Documents for Consciousness Raising in Sports Policy] (Köln: Pahl-Rugenstein, 1983), 137–51, and Kurt Abels, *Ein Held war ich nicht* [I Was No Hero] (Köln: Böhlau, 1998), 13.

69. For the NPEA, see Herma Bouvier and Claude Geraud. *Napola. Les écoles d'élites du troisième Reich* [NPEA and the Nazi Elite Educational Institutions] (Paris: L'Harmattan, 2009), 140. For the Adolf-Hitler-Schule, see Wolf-Dieter Mattausch, Wolf-Dieter, 'Sport', in Wolfgang Benz, Hermann Graml and Hermann Weiss (eds), *Enzyklopädie des Nationalsozialismus* [Encyclopedia of Nazism] (München: Deutscher Taschenbuch Verlag, 2007), 282.

70. Jean Neff, *Le National-socialisme et l'éducation sportive. Thèse de 3ème cycle* [National Socialism and Physical Training. PhD Dissertation] (Paris: Université de Paris VII, 1974), 195.

71. Franz-Albert Heinen, *Ordensburg Vogelsang. Die Geschichte der NS-Kaderschmiede in der Eifel* [Vogelsang Castle. The History of Nazi Elite in Eifel] (Berlin: Ch Links Verlag, 2014), 65.

72. With regard to sport and physical education in Nazi garrisons, see Berno Bahro, *Der SS-Sport: Organisation, Funktion, Bedeutung* [Sport in the SS: Organization, Function, Meaning] (Paderborn: Schöningh Ferdinand Gmbh, 2013).

73. Franz Pisecky, 'Leibesübungen in der SS', in Friedrich Mildner (ed.), *Olympia 1936 und die Leibesübungen im Nationalsozialistischen Staat in 1936* [Olympics and Physical Exercices in Nazi Germany] (Berlin: Buchvertrieb Olympiade 1936), 513.

74. Berno Bahro, 'Der Sport und seine Rolle in der nationalsozialistischen Elitetruppe SS', *Historical Social Research,* no. 32 (2007), 78–91.

75. BAB, NS 31/348. Sonderanweisung für die Sportreferenten und -warte im Sommerausbildungsabschnitt 1936, 17.4.1936. Ebenso die Richtlinien für die Ausbildung der SS-Verfügungstruppe in Leibesübungen für die Zeit vom 1.5.-31.10.1935, Chef des SS-Hauptamtes, 6.5.1935. Quoted by Bahro, 'Der Sport und seine Rolle in der nationalsozialistischen Elitetruppe SS', 80.

76. Meusel, *Körperliche Grundausbildung*, 224–43.

77. BAB. NS DA 40. Loritz' Personal Papers.

78. Annah Arendt, *Eichmann in Jerusalem: A Report on the Banality of Evil* (New York: Viking Press, 1963).

79. Greg Lamazères, *Dernier round à Neuengamme* [Final round at Neuengamme] (Toulouse: Privat, 2009), 191.

80. Christian Tessier and Janko Tisler, *De Mauthausen au Ljubelj (Loibl-Pass)* [From Mauthausen to Ljubelj (Loibl-Pass)] (Paris: l'Harmattan, 2005), 166.

81. De Bouard, 'Mauthausen', 61.

82. Iwasko, 'Le logement, les vêtements et l'alimentation des détenus', 65.

83. As from 1942, a decision was made that a maximum of 10% of prisoners should work within the camp (Reimund Schnabel, *Le dossier des SS. Les pièces du dossier* [The SS File. The Case Documents] (Paris: Perrin, 1967), 115).

84. Franciszek Piper, 'L'exploitation du travail des détenus', in Tadeusz Iwasko, Kubica Helena, Francizek Piper, Irena Strzelecka and Andrzej Strzelecki (eds), *Auschwitz 1940–1945 (vol. 2)* (Oswiecim: Musée d'Etat d'Auschwitz-Birkenau, 2011), 110.

85. Testimonies agree on this point, even though it is impossible to know how long he worked in the kitchen *Kommando*. See: Steinberg, *Chroniques d'ailleurs*, 68; Burah, *Bibi*, 264; A.C. Young Perez' political prisoner file: Letter of Doctor Elmedik dated 3 December 1945.

86. AN, 72aj/318. An account in French of a book written in Polish: 6643 Janusz Nel Siedlecki, 75817Krystyn Olszewski and 119198 Tadeusz Borowski, *Byliśmy w Oświęcimiu* (Oficyna Warszawska na obczyznie, 1946).

87. Sofsky, *L'organisation de la terreur*, 157–59.

88. Serge Smulevic's testimony taken at his home at Onglet on 25 May 2006.

89. A.C. Young Perez' political prisoner file.

90. Lamazères, *Dernier round à Neuengamme*, 193–4.

91. The concept of 'grey area' was created by Primo Levi, a survivor from Auschwitz III It refers to those inmates who, for various reasons, escaped the most horrific living conditions by holding various positions inside the camps See Primo Levi, Les naufragés et les rescapés Quarante ans après Auschwitz [The Drowned and the Saved] (Paris: Gallimard, 1989), 36–68 Olivier Lalieu then used it in his works on Buchenwald: Lalieu, La zone grise? Many researchers are currently working on the history of concentration camp society, such as Philippe Mesnard and Yannis Thanassekos, La zone grise: Entre accomodement et collaboration [The Grey Area, between Acceptance and Collaboration] (Paris: Editions Kimé, 2010)

92. Tessier and Tisler, *De Mauthausen au Ljubelj (Loibl-Pass),* 165.

93. GBu. Gruppe 31. Bericht. N° 31/142: Otto Halle, *Sport im Buchenwald*: 'The fights took place in the woods but also in the cinema hall, and they instantly became very popular in the camp until they were forbidden'.

94. Primo Levi, *Si c'est un homme* [If This is a Man] (Paris: Julliard, 1987), 49.

95. Sofsky, *L'organisation de la terreur*, 182–91. About Buchenwald: Kogon, *L'Etat SS*, 62–9; about Mauthausen: Fabréguet, *Mauthausen*, 517–26.

96. Levi, *Si c'est un homme*, 139.

97. Robert Waitz, 'Auschwitz III-Monowitz', in *De l'Université aux camps de concentration, témoignages strasbourgeois* (Strasbourg: Presses universitaires de Strasbourg, 1996), 479.

98. Ibid., 480.

99. Serge Smulevic's testimony taken at his home at Onglet on 25 May 2006.

100. Tessier and Tisler, *De Mauthausen au Ljubelj,* 165.

101. Strzelecka, 'La journée de travail des détenus', 77. Irena Strzelecka, 'La journée de travail des détenus', in Tadeusz Iwasko, Kubica Helena, Francizek Piper, Irena Strzelecka and Andrzej Strzelecki (eds), *Auschwitz 1940, 1945 (vol. 2)* (Oswiecim: Musée d'Etat d'Auschwitz-Birkenau, 2011), 71–8; Marsalek, *Mauthausen,* 52; Fabréguet, *Mauthausen,* 276.

102. De Bouard, 'Mauthausen', 60.

103. BAB. NS 4 NA 3 DI/Az.: 14d 4/ot. /U. Packetsendungen an Häftlinge, 29.10.1942, Himmler.

104. BAB. NS 3/426. Dienstvorschrift für die Gewährung von Vergünstigungen an Häftlinge, 15.5.1943, Himmler.

105. BAB. NS 3/426. Nachtrag zur Dienstvorschrift für die Gewährung von Vergünstigungen an Häftlinge, 14.2. 1944, Pohl.

106. Fabréguet, *Mauthausen,* 177.

107. Charles Sandron, 'A l'usine de Dora', in *De l'Université aux camps de concentration. Témoignages strasbourgeois* [From University to Concentration Camps. Testimonies from Strasbourg citizens] (Strasbourg: Presse Universitaire de Strasbourg, 1996), 17.

108. The reality is more complicated. Some privileged inmates bore also a rot or a black triangle. They were German but also Polish, Hungarian or a lot of other nationalities. See Jean Laffitte, *Ceux qui vivent* [Those Alive] (Paris: Editions hier et Aujourd'hui, 1947), 264.

109. On this matter, Hermann Langbein quotes Himmler's words in a speech to Wehrmacht Generals, dated 21 June 1944: 'Those German political prisoners and second offenders, some 40,000 … are my "non-commissioned officers" for the camp society. We have appointed what we call *Kapos* … The minute they do not meet our expectations, they go back to the bunkhouse with their men. From that very moment, those former *Kapos* know the other prisoners will kill them the very next night'. Langbein, *La résistance dans les camps,* 38. The author refers to the following archives: MA 315 bl. 3949 f. (Institute of Contemporary History, Munich).

110. Sofsky, *L'organisation de la terreur,* 172.

111. Burah, *Bibi,* 284.

112. Serge Miller, *Le laminoir* [The Steamroller] (Paris: Flammarion, 1947), 284.

113. Gaston-G. Charlet, *Karawanken, le bagne dans la neige* [Karawanken, A Forced Labour Camp in the Snow] (Limoges: Impr. Rougerie, 1955), 28.

114. Raymond Montégut, *Arbeit macht frei* [The Work Makes Free] (Ury: Ed du Paroi, 1973), 116.

115. François Wetterwald, *Les morts inutiles. Un chirurgien français en camp nazi* [The Pointless Dead. A French Surgeon in Nazi Camps] (Paris: L'Harmattan, 1999), 53.

116. Krysztof Dunin-Wasowicz,. *Resistance in the Nazi Concentration Camps 1933–1945* (Warszawa: Polish scientific publishers, 1982); Langbein, *La résistance dans les camps,* 67–71; Henrik Swiebocki, 'Les caractéristiques principales de la résistance dans le camp', in Henrik Swiebocki (ed.), *Auschwitz 1940–1945 (vol. 4)* (Oswiecim: Musée d'Etat d'Auschwitz-Birkenau, 2011), 13–27; Kogon, *L'Etat SS,* 341–66; Fabréguet, *Mauthausen,* 562–87.

117. Hermann Langbein, *La résistance dans les camps de concentration nationaux-socialistes (1938–1945)* [Resistance in the Nazi Concentration Camps, 1938–1945] (Paris: Fayard, 1981), 52–66; Olivier Lalieu, *La zone grise? La Résistance française à Buchenwald* [The Grey area? French Resistance in Buchenwald] (Paris: Tallandier, 2005) 87–94.

118. The first Spanish republicans arrived at Mauthausen on 6 August 1940, after fighting with the French army and being imprisoned in a normal *Stalag.* Other Spaniards coming from France soon rejoined them. During the second half of 1940, some 2239 individuals were sent to Mauthausen. In 1941, 4681 Spanish newcomers were recorded there. After a period of systematic extermination, survivors enjoyed a significant improvement of their lot. While some of them organized active units for mutual protection, others were promoted to important positions in the camp. Fabréguet, *Mauthausen,* 118 and 564; Michel Fabréguet, "Les "Espagnols rouges" à Mauthausen (1940–1945)", *Guerres mondiales et conflits contemporains,* n° 162, (1991), 77–98.

119. Manzano, *Rondalla de Mauthausen*; Paul Tillard, *Mauthausen* (Paris: Editions Sociales, 1945), 54.
120. AN, 72aj/323. Testimony of M. Delattre, communicated to the WWII history committee, no date, 5.
121. Frédéric-Henry Manhès, *Buchenwald. L'organisation et l'action clandestines des déportés français 1944–1945* [Buchenwald. Organization and Underground Action of the French Prisoners, 1944–1945] (Paris: FNDIRP, 1947), 19.
122. Tessier and Tisler, *De Mauthausen au Ljubelj,* 166.
123. De Bouard, 'Mauthausen', 60. K.L.M stands for *Konzentrationslager* Mauthausen.
124. Olga Wormser-Migot, *Le système concentrationnaire nazi* [The Nazi Camp System] (Paris: PUF, 1967), 479.
125. Pierre De Froment, *Un volontaire de la nuit dans l'enfer des camps nazis* [A Night Volunteer in the Hell of Nazi Camps] (Paris: Lavauzelle Graphic, 2005), 68.
126. A.C. Young Perez personal file.
127. Segundo Espallargas, Tadeusz Pietrzykowski, Leen Sanders, Salamo Arouch and Jacques Razon were among those who survived the camps.

Disclosure statement

No potential conflict of interest was reported by the author.

Reshaping Spanish Football Identity in the 1940s: From Fury to Tactics

Carlos García-Martí [ID]

ABSTRACT

National playing styles are part of national identities. During the 1940s, a series of defeats questioned the virtue of the Spanish playing style, known as the *Spanish Fury*, characterized by improvisation, genius, courage and enthusiasm. Isolated from international football trends, Spain has despised the use of man-marking and tactical discipline. Analysis of both official documents and the Spanish press would show that Francoism was sympathetic to the *fury's* discourse, being close to the regime's narrative itself, but needed victories to gain internal support and international recognition in a critical moment of diplomatic pressure and isolation. Therefore, the dictatorship forced the football authorities to undergo a modernization process, which involved abandoning the traditional discourse of the *fury*, at least momentarily.

Introduction

Throughout the evolution of football, the nations where football became a mass phenomenon created a particular tradition and a particular way of understanding the game. This gave birth to a series of national playing styles that were also expressions of the national identity. These identities were constructed mainly through contact with and opposition to the others, especially through international games. Disappointing performances created identity crises used by different interest groups to alter or challenge the previous consensus.

In Spain, one of these periods was the 1940s, when after the civil war the construction of a national style narrative coherent with the dictatorship values in the first years of the 1940s confronted the need for a tactical upgrading after a series of defeats experienced by the Spanish national side in the years 1946 and 1947, forcing the incorporation of the British WM tactic by the end of the decade, in time to qualify for the 1950 World Cup. The Spanish playing style, far from the current *tiki-taka*, was then known as the *Spanish fury*, and became harshly questioned. It was an especially interesting moment because this crisis took place in a critical political moment for the Spanish dictatorship, diplomatically isolated, that found in sports one of the few ways of acquiring international recognition.

After winning the Spanish Civil War (1936–1939), general Franco had to secure his fragile leadership, a task he successfully undertook by splitting the power between the different factions of the regime – the Catholics, the monarchists, the traditionalists known as Carlistas,[1] the army and the fascist-inspired movement Falange – and by acting as the referee between them in their constant battle for hegemony.[2] Firstly, these different political sensitivities were all forced to merge during the civil war under only one political party, named Falange Tradicionalista y de las JONS (FET-JONS). FET-JONS was in fact the formal result of the unification of the original Italian fascist like Falange, founded by José Antonio Primo de Rivera, and the Carlista Comunión Tradicionalista, the two political organizations backing the coup.[3] During the years of the civil war, when the reliance on and the alliance with the Axis powers were at its heights, and especially with the Mussolini regime, the original Falange members came to dominate the new-born party under Franco's brother-in-law's leadership, the prominent figure of Ramón Serrano Suñer, nominated chief of the FET-JONS and Foreign Office minister.[4]

The original Falange was a relatively small party with limited influence in Spanish politics before the war, but in the first years after the war its members came to dominate Spanish politics under Serrano Suñer's leadership and the alliance with the Axe powers, initializing the transformation of Spain into a fascist regime, in the so-called 'blue period'. This prominent position started to decline in 1941, when the dictator designated a new FET-JONS leader, José Luis Arrese, appointed to definitely submit the party to his personal authority, and definitely in 1942 after a falangista terrorist attack over a carlista demonstration which ended with Serrano Suñer dismissed from all his positions. These series of political crisis caused by the tensions between the different political sensibilities allowed Franco to definitely secure his personal leadership.[5]

Although the falangistas became subjected to Franco's personal authority, the regime did not give up the fascist discourse right away, and the Spanish foreign policy remained one of open germanophilia, despite official neutrality. However, the following Allied progress in the Second World War forced a turn into a more neutral position. Once the war concluded with the Allies' victory, Franco started seeking the support or at least the tolerance of the winners by a more clear defascistization process. To do so, he appointed the ultra-catholic Alberto Martín Artajo as Foreign Affairs Minister in 1945, and reinforced the Catholic and anticommunist profile of the regime, trying to seduce both the Vatican and the U.S.A.,[6] by recycling the fascist ideology into was what latter known as nationalcatholicism.[7] The regime also developed a legal and institutional infrastructure to build a traditionalist legitimacy.[8] While Franco avoided economic sanctions or any military intervention, Spain suffered a rigid diplomatic isolation from the very end of the Second World War throughout the end of the decade, including the exclusion from the UN in December 1946 and the withdrawal of all ambassadors immediately after.[9] In that sense, sport constituted from the very first moment an exception to this isolation. In fact, Franco's side achieved first FIFA's recognition and then the IOC's recognition during the war, despite the fact that the republican side represented the legitimate government.[10]

As for the institutional organization of sports, they came under the Spanish single-party FET-JONS's control, dominated by the falangistas. The falangista ideology praised the exceptional nature of the Spanish race – from a cultural, not a genetic point of view – as the result of its exceptional history, and its role as guardian of Catholicism and spiritual values facing the ruling modernity and rationalism, and therefore being openly anti-liberal.[11] Sport had therefore the mission of giving birth to a physically and spiritually healthy new Spanish generation, ready to sacrifice for the motherland. Consequently, Falange's initial idea of sport was strongly related to mass participation and the amateur ideal, and therefore was suspicious of professionalism. An article published in the DND bulletin titled 'Falange and Sport' clearly stated it:

> We cherished sport as much as it serves to strengthen the spirit and creates great men to render service to Spain. By itself, considered only in the individual aspect of the champion or privileged minorities, it is of no interest.[12]

However, there were never the economic resources or the political will for such an ambitious programme, and it remained simply part of the regime's propagandistic agenda. Quite on the contrary, sport remained underdeveloped and sporting practice very limited all along Franco's reign and professional football became one of the few entertaining options for a suffering population in what was later known as the culture of evasion.[13] Therefore, there was always a 'contradiction between the transcendental project and the sport inner dynamic, fuelling competitivity and show business'.[14]

The institutional structure developed was characterized by the Estate take over of sport. Under the control of the party, the Delegación Nacional de Deportes (DND), in charge of the traditional, club and federation-based sport, was created, but also the party's organization of sporting activities,[15] including military sport. As for traditional, competitive sport, a completely hierarchical structure emerged, where the DND had the authority to appoint directly the federation's presidents, and the DND president was also the president of the Spanish Olympic Committee (SOC). The DND also sought to take control over professional clubs by appointing their presidents through the football federation up to 1948, when limited elections were instated.[16] There was, consequently, no formal autonomy whatsoever in sport.[17]

Again, as every other institution, sports suffered an ideological purge that included professional football.[18] The Spanish press suffered also its own purge, including a sporting one, and was firmly controlled by censorship, as Viuda-Serrano's research has proved, refuting the established opinion of a greater freedom in the field.[19] Also, Falange created a media company, known as *Prensa del Movimiento*, publishing several newspapers, including the official journal of the regime, *Arriba*, and the bestseller and most important sporting newspaper at the time, *Marca*.

Reconstructing the Spanish National Side After the War: The Blue Side, 1941–1942

The first years after the war under Falange's hegemony are known as the blue period, the colour of their uniforms. The alliance with the Axis powers was so obvious, that the Nazi salute was adopted for the international matches, and the customary red shirt was substituted by a blue one.[20] A war hero was appointed as DND president, general Moscardó, who remained in office until his death in 1955.[21]

If the DND ever had the intention to favour amateurism over professionalism, they were quickly aware of the social and economic importance of professional football, as was later to be acknowledged by the first football federation president, colonel Troncoso (1939–1940):

> Once in the Federation, professionalism itself, with its quick development, sweep us along and we could do nothing but submit to its demands with the hope of normal channeling.[22]

At the same time, it is also clear that the dictatorship was quickly aware of football's importance, and its links to the inner and outer public image, as of its propagandistic potential. Days after a defeat against Italy in 1942, an order came from the censorship to the press not to mention the national side whatsoever, being 'all dead individually and collectively'.[23] This all meant that although the falangistas would have been more comfortable celebrating the exploits of amateur Spanish athletes in the Olympics, they accepted the money-driven, uncontainable football as the best way to promote their nationalistic credo, at least in the international confrontations, where professional footballers could be treated as amateurs defending national pride.

The football community helped this trend by hanging on to a discourse about the Spanish style appropriate for the political atmosphere of those blue years. It established, in the first term, the existence of a peculiar Spanish style, a component of the broader Latin style. It was characterized by its enthusiasm, will and the creative and improvizing qualities of the Latin genius; the *Spanish Fury*. The name was coined by a foreign journalist in the Amberes 1920 Olympics and was later popularized by the Spanish journalist Alberto Martín Fernández, known as Juan Deportista, in his 1922 book, *The Spanish Fury*.[24] It was supposed to summon up the spirit of the Spanish side who reached the silver medal in those Olympics. Besides, it was considered that before the war Spain was a football power, as proved by its performance in the 1934 World Cup, the unbeaten record home until 1936, and the victory over England in 1929.[25]

This *fury* theme was therefore created decades before the civil war, but there is no systematic historical work about its role in the Spanish playing style during the twenties and thirties. What is clear is that it was highly coherent with the Falange's ideology, since the Spanish race superiority was also established in its courage, genius and sacrificial will, and therefore it was the privileged approach in those first years after the war. The regime's critique of republican football was based on the over-development of professionalism and the regional rivalries, but it never questioned the talent of the past 'aces' or the performance of the national side.[26] On the contrary, the most ideologically committed and best connected commentators considered the 1930s as a golden age, and understood that Spanish football, after being destroyed by the war as the rest of the country was, had the sacred mission of reaching up to the privileged position held before the conflict.[27]

However, in this blue period the chances for re-emergence were quite few, due to the international conflict. There were only international matches against the Axis powers and neutral countries: two matches against Portugal and one against Switzerland in 1941, and matches against occupied France, Germany and Italy in 1942. The Spanish national side manager, Eduardo Teus, knew clearly the path to victory:

> I count nothing on the national side team play. Moreover, it has never existed. Spanish football has always shined because of its individual values … that brilliant improvisation spirit and individualism typical of our race.[28]

The 2–2 draw against Portugal was saluted as a corroboration of 'the gay re-emergence and … [return] to its summit' of Spanish football. Journalists, however, were alert about possible deviations.[29] One year later, despite beating Switzerland 3–2, Spain had apparently failed to show enough determination and had adopted a defensive play against which Juan Deportista admonished:

> Spanish superiority prevailed through the old and fruitful paths of resolution and enthusiasm … [Let] no one forget it, although, fortunately, the manager has been the first to take good notice of it.[30]

Opposing him, the senior sporting newspaper *El Mundo Deportivo* editor, José Carlos Lasplazas:

> There was a glorious time in which every Spanish victory was credited to its famous 'fury', and therefore it was denied any technical virtue, which never deranged the majority, but only a minority … However, our utter satisfaction will come the day we'll see the national team winning out of pure technique, without having to bring into play the mad enthusiasm and the exuberant speed which inflame the masses, but are not admired as the chess-like English or South American football.[31]

Unfolded in front of us are the two central trends in the Spanish football debate throughout the 1940s. On the one side, the champions of the *Spanish Fury* understood it as a racial feature binding the traditional patriotism and the fascist will of triumph; on the other side, the advocates of the technical and tactical instruction, who were keen to plan and rationalize the game.

Both attitudes are supported by individuals clearly and deeply adhered to the regime, so there are no political differences between them. Neither did they represent distinctive professional collectives, such as managers or journalists. In fact, the football community was somehow limited in numbers in those years, most of the people combining position both in the press, the federation and the clubs, or jumping from one sector to the other. For example, Juan Deportista was a reporter for the ABC journal and also the public relation manager at the DND; Eduardo Teus was also a journalist before being appointed national manager, and resumed journalism after that; editor Lasplazas would also be national manager in the years to come. It was then a matter of an internal struggle between those prioritizing the individualistic and spontaneous playing style linked to the Spanish nationalism and the Falange racial discourse, and those, also conservatives, but aware of the urge for a pragmatic stance on the game and the substitution of the nostalgic nationalism by a tactical revolution.

Back to Internationals: From Imagined Hegemony to Undeniable Crisis, 1945–47

After this first series of competitions, war prevented any further tests until 1945. In those years, optimism about the Spanish re-emergence was widely spread among the football community. In 1943, Basque federation president and pundit José María Mateos openly played with the idea in the DND bulletin. Given the necessary halt in the countries involved in the conflict, and the sustained progress in the peaceful Spain, it was not foolish to think about an international hegemony:

> And therefore, since there is a basis, we expect that, when the moment arrives for international competitions, back to business as usual, we would have a national team able to give lessons … to those who gave them to us previously.[32]

However, by 1945 the international context had changed dramatically in two ways. The Allies' victory had meant the regime's diplomatic isolation and an international boycott. While Spain was a FIFA member, only Portugal's allied dictatorship and Catholic Ireland were willing to play against the national side. Although the falangistas had lost their prominent position on behalf of the army and the Catholic Church and the regimen was experiencing a defascistization process, an evolution made explicit in football by the abolition of the fascist salute and the reinstatement of the traditional red shirt in 1945,[33] these cosmetic changes did not prevent foreign nations identifying Spain as a Nazi Germany ally.

On the other side, the great majority of European nations had adopted a revolutionary tactic, the WM, in the previous years. Despised by the isolated Spaniards, who considered the WM to be 'absolutely inefficient against the Spanish aggressive and sharp speed',[34] it was in fact a Copernican change in the way the defence was understood.

Up until that moment, all over the world teams played in what was known as the Pyramid System, what nowadays would be classified as a 1–2–3–5. The two backs would balance being outnumbered by using the offside rule, which established that the attackers should be behind at least three defenders. The one back system meant that one of the two defenders would seat deep, while the other would go up front to challenge the ball, almost to the half line, pushing the attackers back. Its perfection meant the rise of goalless draws until the International Board was forced to change the offside rule and limited to two the number of necessary defenders between the attackers and the goal-line in 1925.

This in turn generated a tactical evolution perfected by Herbert Chapman's Arsenal in the 1930s, the aforementioned WM or 1–3–2–2–3. Centre-half would seat deep between the two backs, becoming a centre back, the wing halves would centre their positions, and the two inside forwards would retreat to midfield to help the midfielders. Besides the retreating of the centre half, the great novelty in the WM was that, by deploying the same number of defenders and attackers in the same positions, it naturally led to the assignment of one attacker for each defender, responsible for following him all over the pitch. Thus man-marking was born, and along with it, the end of a certain degree of liberty for both defenders and attackers, especially for the centre half, up to that moment the charismatic leader of the team, contributing both to the defence and the offence, and now reduced to following the opposite centre forward. This tactical change generated polemics all around the world throughout the 1930s and 1940s, especially in those countries where the national playing style was called into question, such as in Italy or Argentina. There were even attempts by some Nazi sporting officials to abandon the WM because of its 'democratic', 'pacifist' or 'English' character. However, the WM tactic had been widely adopted throughout the world by 1945 when Spain resumed internationals.[35]

When the new series of internationals came, WM was known in Spain, but it was understood that both the centre half and the improvization room for defenders and attackers were part of the Spanish identity; the *fury*. When the newly appointed national manager, Jacinto Quincoces, used the WM in a draw against Portugal in 1945, he was severely warned by the press.

> This is Spain and nothing else. It has its unique genius and figure. Pretending to have any other physiognomy seems to go against our personality. It would have sufficed our genius to win. Football is attacking and playing; it cannot be a premeditated geometry in the chalkboard or keeping bounded to a theorem resolved theoretically.[36]

It is clear in this excerpt that the WM was associated with decadent values, such as rationalization and planning, ways of limiting the Spanish genius for improvization. In this sense, it expresses the profound antiracionalist mistrust shown by fascism.

It is the beginning of a public debate, in which terms and extension were controlled by censorship, but is not until 1946 that the football crisis took the centre of the stage. First, Spain would lose against Ireland, 0–1, in Madrid; soon after, the Argentinean side of San Lorenzo de Almagro would beat two training national sides during a tour; finally, in March 1947, Spain will lose for the first time against Portugal, 4–1, in Lisbon.

The first defeat, against Ireland, was absolutely unexpected, since it was considered a minor opponent. Some journalists tried to blame it on the 'physical energy' and 'courage' of the Irish,[37] but the use of the WM technique was considered the key to their success.

There was no doubt about it among those supporting the immediate adoption of the WM. This group was composed of journalists and professionals, and among them at least three key figures: the aforementioned José Luis Lasplazas; the former national manager, Eduardo Teus, who had completely changed his mind; and the FIFA referee, chairman of the referees and the most popular figure in Spanish football, Pedro Escartín. They were no mavericks; in fact they were well connected among sporting powers. Moreover, Escartín published his critical articles in *El Alcázar*, the property of DND president, general Moscardó. In these articles, Escartín – besides presenting himself as an anglophile, which would had been impossible a few years earlier – stated that against the Irish tactical planning, Spaniards 'came out to play gaily and without thinking'.[38] His colleague M. Monasterio added that players and coaches must reckon that the player 'is simply a pawn or a piece in the gears that make the machine work'.[39] As for the enemies of the necessary modernization, Escartín pointed out to the managers, who considered the WM inferior to the *Spanish Fury* and rejected tactics as a whole, as confirmed by Paco Bru, the former manager in the glorious 1920 silver medal:

> Our unique style, made out of fury and combativeness, has no equal. It may be defeated when things don't come our way, but it is unbeatable when they do.[40]

Along with the managers, a great number of journalists and pundits showed disbelief, as did the international referee Ramón Melcón and the journalist Gilera:

> The goal of these inventors will be attained: all the eleven men will be perfectly shadowed in the pitch; none will be able to move without the shadow of an opponent following and obstructing him. But to do so the opposite team will have rendered itself useless … The spectators, filled up with technique, but eager for real football, will have to abandon the stadiums.[41]

> Nevertheless, it is very difficult for us to adapt, not to this, but to any other discipline, because of our temper and because we have played so well for so many years, without any need for an alphabet.[42]

That is to say that tactics, whatever they may be, were always defensive, denied improvisation and genius and turned players into automatons and football into a boring technical exercise. Moreover, tactics were considered against the Spanish temper, against their most intimate self.

The public debate continued, without reaching any consensus. Movement among the football federation also started. One month after the defeat, the newly appointed president, Agustín Rivero Meneses, came out with a plan for improving Spanish football, and in the case of elite football, referred to a will to improve the fitness of representatives and the instruction of managers.[43] However, the most significant measure was to request permission from the DND to hire foreign players and managers specifically to 'assimilate new playing styles and to help the technical advance of our players'.[44] DND, who had banned foreign participation in the Spanish sport on patriotic grounds, were to open the borders in December not to improve Spanish sport, but to 'adjust our laws to those in force in each particular international federation', in a clear concealment of reality.[45] Here is another sign of the downplaying of the falangista amateur ideal under the pressure of football popularity and propagandistic needs.

As it was mentioned earlier, it is worth noting that the football crisis was taking place among an increasing international isolation. In July 1947, Spanish sports attained a diplomatic victory when the plea for its exclusion from FIFA on political grounds, made by Yugoslavia, was rejected thanks to the support of president Jules Rimet, the same man responsible for recognition during the war.[46] It is another proof of diplomatic pressure on Spain, which attained its peak in December 1946, when the UN asked for the withdrawal of all ambassadors. With the departure of the English ambassador, only the ones from Ireland, Portugal, Switzerland and the Vatican remained in place. These were the very same countries, with an exception made of the Holy See, who were willing to play against Spain. International pressure, guerrilla actions and economic crisis gave the regime its worst year, with internal movements for a monarchic restoration.[47]

Spain's only diplomatic victory in December 1946 was the Argentinean support, made clear with the appointment that same month of a new ambassador.[48] His arrival hit the front pages and coincided with the San Lorenzo de Almagro tour. In fact, his first public event was to assist, along with Franco, the second of the friendly matches opposing San Lorenzo to a training Spanish side, not the official one, in preparation for the coming internationals. The Spanish side was demolished 1–6, just like the first side, who had lost 5–7 days before, exacerbating the crisis and the debate, with some specific features: their passing game and their technical mastery. In fact, Argentineans dazzled Spaniards with their mastery with the ball, to the point that one of the Spanish players, Bravo, said:

> You see, you consider yourself the top of your profession after all these years running the ball, just to find out now that you know almost nothing.[49]

Nevertheless, it was all just about the WM. While some looked at their technical skills, the modernizers preferred to focus on their shadowing and slipping skills, their use of the WM – a notion that would be highly contested in Argentina:

> We have no system, we don't know how to mark nor to slip, and we don't have the Amberes enthusiasm anymore. There are no excuses, since all the footballers had played against the Argentineans one moment or the other during their tour. If they knew how they played and couldn't stop them, is it because they are unable to follow a tactic and grasp it?[50]

On the other side, there were those who considered that, confronted by their 'ultra scientific' game, only the *Spanish Fury* could have been victorious:

> The Spanish side could only have secured a minimum victory or a draw drawing upon the authentic Spanish fury. However, this fury has almost completely disappeared, substituted by the so called tactics ...[51]

Both happened to agree on the absence of enthusiasm, that is to say, of players mastering the *fury*, but what for Monasterio was part of a natural decline, for Subirán it was clearly the result of the imposition of tactics.

The real problem, though, is that the debate was drifting to a questioning not just of the *fury's* usefulness, but of its very own essence: '... the so called fury – let's acknowledge it sincerely – it's nothing but rough game, more or less treacherous ...'[52]

This last remark coincided with those made by the Argentinean players, who publicly declared that Spanish forwards could not excel because they must be cautious of the Spanish defenders' rough game. Such a criticism could have been offensive to the Spanish national pride, but it was repeatedly published and backed by journals and pundits. In fact, the DND had tried for years, under its amateur ideal mandate, to refrain violence in the professional game, especially indiscipline among players and fans, unsuccessfully.

Moreover, it was not just that the Argentineans' opinion strengthened the DND policy, or the due respect to the masters of the ball, but mainly the politically strategic character of the visit that explained the reactions. As a sign of it, the DND dedicated almost a complete issue of their official magazine, *Antorcha*, to praise the San Lorenzo tour, including a revealing editorial note:

> Whatever the outcome of the matches, what we – the DND and the Spaniards – actually will remember it is the deep, wide, intimate meaning of a visit that have left an unforgettable mark in the Spanish soul, offering an sporting excuse to joyfully show the love between Spain and the Argentinean nation. The football trip, so judiciously organized by the Spanish Football Federation, has offered some tangible outcomes, which are not to be discussed or judged by us.[53]

Although the DND seemed to neglect the national side performance and favored the political interpretation, the Federation took matter into its own hands, knowing that another defeat in March 1947 against Portugal, who had never defeated Spain, would be untenable. For the first time, the Spanish championship was called off so the players could train together for two weeks before the match.[54]

Spanish manager Hernández Coronado, an eccentric and popular character, had tried to play down the crisis but recognized the superiority of the WM. He had to choose between sticking with the Pyramid System or trying a WM, still unfamiliar to the players. He finally improvised a WM and suffered an overwhelming defeat, 4–1, raising alarm bells. Portugal cast doubt on the Iberian hegemony, the only one remaining for an isolated and depressed country. Criticisms were aimed more than ever at the Spanish idiosyncrasy, seen no longer as a guarantee of genius, but of failure:

> We are Spaniards … and we like improvising. We give too much credit to our temperamental character –which is an evident trait, but not decisive in any human activity – and we completely dismiss those technical developments coming from outside our country. In doing so, our football has become totally obsolete.[55]

That is to say, genius and enthusiasm could not stand in for the lack of planning and instruction. Escartín went even further, titling his editorial opinion piece 'Our Football is Collectively Sick and Must be Saved'.[56] Surprisingly, the term 'sick' had evident political connotations at the time, since it was a notion used to describe the Republican regime, while Francoism was in a moral regeneration crusade. Yet, Escartín had an impeccable track record, being responsible for the purge among the referees after the war and, as it has already been said, published his piece in a journal of the DND president, in a country with a preventive censorship system in place. These criticisms can only be understood as officially permitted.

We can then assume that reformists were, at that point, leading or at least guiding the federation and the DND. The shared diagnosis in the reformist side was clear: Spanish managers were not only completely outdated, but so were their tactics. As a consequence, players were being trained in the same way as 15 years before, while football had evolved and Spain had been left behind to the point of losing against Portugal. Public intervention was mandatory to put Spanish football back on track.

Although the need for an evolution was evident, conservative forces were always willing to reclaim the traditional discourse. The seemingly honourable defeat 3–2 to Ireland in Dublin two months later allowed them to vindicate themselves and reject any foreign influence:

Pessimist augurs judged our football in a declining line, close to its collapse ... It has even been made the case for the foreign scion in our teams, and there were managers beyond the Pyrenees ready to provide new lifeblood to our classic fury. ... We are where we stood, and the aged virtues of this Spanish race, which will never get rid of the heart in its efforts, are an integral part of this success.[57]

In fact, decisions probably had already been taken. If the humiliation against San Lorenzo had not generated any official reaction, the defeat against Portugal proved to be very different. Actions had to be undertaken, and only a month later, the DND accepted Rivero Meneses' resignation and appointed a new president, Armando Muñoz Calero, with no experience whatsoever in sports. He, in turn, appointed a new manager, the former international goalkeeper Guillermo Eizaguirre. A volunteer and war hero, he also lacked any prior experience as a manager.[58]

The Path to Modernization, 1947–1949

Results were no longer secondary to the friendship among nations. Defeats had become a problem of domestic policy and of the regime's public image. Winning was now mandatory and the DND explicitly acknowledged the turn with an unprecedented gesture: in the very same meeting when Calero was appointed, the DND released a memo which urged sporting officials to take any necessary measure to 'improve the standards in those sport[s] who may need it'. Officially, it is a generic admonition, but it is not difficult to imagine their actual recipients in a country where only football got public interest. Moreover, it should be noted that the memo also asked for the internationals to be accepted 'after seriously considering and with all guarantees'.[59]

Again, the very same day the memo was published in the press, Calero granted an interview to Marca to set the official stance in the new era. The new president had the mandate to improve the national side's performance, key to the public image inside and outside the country, by modernizing Spanish football. However, even though racial, patriotic discourse was no longer at its heights, it could not be completely abandoned, since it was an integral part of the official ideology. Therefore, Calero had to keep the balance when diagnosing the ills of Spanish football:

> Essentially, since the game has derived in a team effort in which individual strokes of genius are frustrated, an harmonic team effort has not yet been successfully implemented. Something is missing, something that would be unwise for me to judge, but must be related to the training routines, or to the moral fibre of the players, or to other factors that need to be identified.[60]

As for the tricky issue of foreigners, those are necessary, but only to incorporate 'all those lessons appropriate to our unique idiosyncrasy'.[61]

In the long run, it was not even a question about tactics, but about priorities. Calero had the political mandate to impose the pre-eminence of the national side over the professional clubs. Although their presidents were appointed by the federation, they had profited from the aforementioned DND disdain to work with relative autonomy in everyday operations. Calero's appointment was the sign of the shift in political priorities. In July, the Federation came out with a plan for the national team including the right for the national manager to call in the international players at any given moment, and the direct medical control of the player by the federation. Eizaguirre could even prevent a player taking part in a particular game if he considered there was a risk for the footballer's health. Finally, the federation scheduled four week-long stages during the 1947/48 season in order for the national side to train, rearranging the championship calendar.[62]

It is clearly a centralization movement for a professional sport that was officially under public control but actually had a wide degree of autonomy. For example, days after the defeat against Portugal, Hernández Coronado had set up a meeting with all professional managers to unify tactical criteria, that is to say to make them all play the WM, according to the press.[63] The day after the meeting, the press published that the manager 'exchanged views with the managers', but unfortunately 'no summary of the meeting could be obtained' or, in other words, the managers had rejected the plan.[64] This anecdote confronts us with the limits of the Francoist authoritative power facing professional football aforementioned by Troncoso: managers resisted the pressure since they could not risk a defeat in the home championship due to the priorities of the national side. In fact, unified tactical criteria had to be abandoned, and the task postponed to the work of the coming Escuela Nacional de Entrenadores and the informal pressures coming from the press and officials. This also matches the testimony collected by Shaw of a continuous confrontation between the clubs and the federation all along the dictatorship, always subdued but always in place.[65]

Calero's modernizing plan included setting up a bigger number and more prestigious internationals, linking diplomatic and sporting goals. After failing to set in place an international match against England, the Federation announced negotiations with the federations of Switzerland, Holland, Sweden, Belgium and Ireland.[66] However, in 1948 they would only manage to appoint games against the usual nations: victories against Portugal, 2–0, and Ireland, 2–1, in Spain, and a 3–3 draw against Switzerland in Zurich. Just before the game against Portugal, Calero set up the new official position:

> I do believe that the 'fury' must be of great service to the tactics. We come out [to] the pitch with a preconceived idea; yet we do not believe that Spanish football can be … brilliant without the enthusiasm, without the determination so typical of our race …[67]

That is to say that although *fury* was not cast into oblivion, it was now auxiliary to tactics. This in turn implied the rule of reason over faith, reversing the order established by the Spanish Catholic Church and the fascist Falange. In order to assume this ideological transfiguration it was necessary to turn to the totalitarian side of the dogma. The individual genius, pride of the Spanish race, must be sacrificed and disciplined for the sake of the common good and the nation, the ultimate aspiration of the new order.

> Our football, established under old and glorious individualistic grounds, has always achieved its greatest victories relying on the personal inspiration of our best players. Spain, as in any other field, had to be known as a country of individual singularities. Yet war, among all its evils, has brought some benefits: today we the Spanish people make up a great team, and our success and our setbacks depend only on our collective soul.[68]

Although the performances were far from convincing, the chosen path had been selected by the public authorities, and therefore was completely out of reach of any criticism. It was only possible to subtlety remind people of the official origins of the change:

> … the new systems that have been imposed and that, whether we like it or not, must be accepted and practiced if we want our football to shine again as in the old days against the foreign nations …[69]

The successes of 1948 constituted a turning point in the Spanish sports diplomatic strategy. First, Spain had the opportunity to participate in the London Olympic Games – the early recognition of the new regime by the IOC being already mentioned – in what constituted a great opportunity to show some normality.[70] At the same time, after the diplomatic pressure climax, the opposition weakness and the new Cold War scenario were changing the western strategy towards Franco: in February, France reopened the border,[71] and almost immediately Rimet started talks for an international match between the two countries.[72]

Moreover, in January 1949, Spain definitively got to set in the Copa Latina project, a tournament facing the league champions of France, Italy, Portugal and Spain. The Copa Latina final agreement in May stated that it would be held each year by one of the countries, starting with Spain in 1949, which meant another diplomatic success.[73] Also, internationals were confirmed against Belgium, Italy and France, as well as the customary Portugal and Ireland, for the coming year.

Public opinion was not enthusiastic after two consecutive draws against Belgium (1–1) and Portugal (1–1), yet the biggest setback was a crushing defeat against Italy in Madrid (1–3) in March 1949. This could be a question mark against the official plan, but it could not be the case in a firmly controlled dictatorship. The players may be harshly criticized, but the plan could only be supported. The only questioning allowed was over the opportunity for international games. Maybe they could have been abandoned until victory could have been guaranteed. This was the point of view expressed by Marca's editorial staff, always worth remembering it was the most important sporting newspaper and property of the only legal party. For Marca, football's increasing social significance demanded its protection from negative outcomes:

> The game is now so Spanish that has become a national concern. It may be said, as an hyperbole, that is now an essential good. And this in turn calls for social and political responsibilities. The hope of the people cannot be disappointed. Let's play home until we can guarantee a victory.[74]

The calls for isolation were disregarded, both for sporting and diplomatic reasons. The only change was to call Benito Díaz as coach, being considered the greatest WM advocate and expert after spending the civil war playing and managing in France.[75]

The change was a clear success, shown in two stunning performances in June 1949, and the first two victories abroad after the war ended all criticism: first against Ireland (1–4) and weeks later against France (1–5). Reformists could now call the polemic over:

> Today, as I understand it, an hiatus has been closed and a new time for our international football has begun. The era of doubts and tactical polemics lies behind us.[76]

And so they believed the conservatives, who somehow embarrassed, even dared to praise the team's intelligence:

> The explanation [for the victories] lies in the coach thaumaturgy powers and his efforts, being able in only fifteen days to transform those heavy players into men [superior] … to their enemies in strength, speed and command. And, why not, in intelligence.[77]

The coach Benito Díaz's central role was clear to everyone. The racial discourse, however, could not be abandoned right away, so Arriba said that he had proven that the modern tactics 'are not at odds with our traditional enthusiasm and nerve'[78] and three days later that:

> [Benito Díaz] represents the Spanish managers who, clearing their minds of alien doctrines and criteria, come from the shadows of confusion to the light of what is adequate among Spanish race players.[79]

Although these kind of contradictory statements were still in place, something had changed without a doubt. The clearest evidence was the role of hero played by Díaz, who was carried out shoulder-high by his players in Paris.[80] Also, the statements from the players undoubtedly showed the change from an improvised racial football to the meticulous planning and tactical discipline of modern football, as evident by this comment by goalkeeper Eizaguirre:

> A few of our players had orders to, in certain given moments, look at him in the bench. Also, he ordered me to pass the ball always to a close teammate in every goal kick, since he believes we should always start our plays from behind. However, if we had a clear advantage in the score, I was supposed to kick the ball as far away as possible on the sideline. I remember that in Colombes [France's national side stadium at the time] having a 3–0 lead, I mistakenly pass the ball to a close teammate and Benito right away made me a sign of disapproval. It goes without saying that I rectified in the next action, kicking the ball far away.[81]

The game against France was, also, a huge diplomatic success heavily stressed by the press. As it was the case for the London Olympics, from the foreign policy view the strategic goal was just to be there, and to give proof of the return to normality. Everyone was aware that the game being played was already a success. Arriba declared on the front page:

> Sporting literature has raised it incense and has not refrained in its politeness and its honorable mentions to Spain. We appreciate this friendly attitude from our French colleagues. We return them, and we are happy to go beyond the limited field of football. And we hope so.[82]

Arriba completed this opinion piece with an article on the Spanish football fans travelling to Paris, who strengthened the success and the back-to-normality attitude:

> Football has made [it] possible for the Spanish national hymn to be played in front of 60,000 people so strongly that [it] would have upset Vichinsky's eardrums [a former soviet diplomat]. And thanks to football, samples of what is known abroad as the 'Spanish issue' have appeared in the boulevards of Paris. After so much fuss, the world didn't know what to expect anymore. If, instead of Spaniards, African Bushmen or two-headed humans had appeared, it would have been no surprise to them.[83]

In terms of football, players were now persuaded of the need for discipline and tactical orders from managers. The managers were, therefore, the last remaining source of resistance. In order to submit them to the new dogma, the Escuela Nacional de Entrenadores was finally put in place in the summer of 1949, with José Carlos Lasplazas as chairman and the mandate to issue the new mandatory manager licence to practice. All first and second division managers were forced to be involved with the first summer course, which had the teaching of the WM as its main goal.[84] The Escuela Nacional de Entrenadores also created the first official guide to coaching in 1950, edited by the federation, with the tactics chapter written by Benito Díaz, who also became a member of the staff.[85]

A year later, after qualifying for the 1950 World Cup in Brazil, Spain overcame England with a goal by Spanish centre forward Telmo Zarra to finish fourth, the best outcome in a World Cup until the victory in 2010. After years trying to win the favour of the FA, Muñoz Calero became nationally famous for declaring 'we have beaten the perfidious Albion', which was a completely politically inappropriate statement.[86] The official propaganda could then reinstate the more politically adequate *fury* theme, making this victory the epitome of the *fury's* success for the remaining decades of dictatorship.[87] In fact, this performance was the outcome of a deep and intricate modernization process, a process of rationalization and planning not just unconnected, but in open contradiction, to the *Spanish Fury*.

Conclusion

Somehow, the football debate described in this paper is similar to others taking place around the world. The opposition between individual creativity and team discipline has always been central in the football debate, and was fundamental in the birth of football national identities such as the Argentinean or the Brazilian.

In the Spanish case, this debate was shaped by its political context, as was the case in Nazi Germany.[88] Francoism quickly acknowledged the political possibilities of professional football, which had become a mass phenomenon without any public intervention. Yet, football underwent a deep crisis, and the solution needed a compromise between the ideological grounds of the regime and the modern tactical needs of the game. Just as the dictatorship abandoned its fascist traits when the international context demanded it, it also transformed its sporting discourse to achieve triumphs associated with football propaganda.

Notes

1. Carlistas were a traditionalist political faction who reclaimed the establishment of a separate line of the Bourbon dynasty, but above all defended a reactionary and anti-liberal ideology.
2. Paul Preston, *Franco: Caudillo de España* (Barcelona: Grijalbo, 1995).
3. Javier Tusell, 'La evolución política de la zona sublevada', in Santos Juliá (ed.), *República y guerra en España, 1931–1939* (Madrid: Espasa, 2006).
4. Juan María Thomàs, 'La Falange. De la revolución al acomodamiento', in Ángel Viñas (ed.), *En el combate por la historia. La república, la guerra civil y el franquismo* (Barcelona: Pasado y Presente 2012).
5. Preston, *Franco*.
6. Stanley G. Payne, *El franquismo: 1939–1950. La dura posguerra* (Madrid: Alianza, 2005).
7. Hilari Raguer Suñer, 'El nacionalcatolicismo', in Ángel Viñas (ed.), *En el combate por la historia. La república, la guerra civil y el franquismo* (Barcelona: Pasado y Presente 2012), 547–64.
8. Glicerio Sánchez Recio, 'La construcción del Nuevo Estado: una dictadura contra viento y marea', in Ángel Viñas (ed.), *En el combate por la historia. La república, la guerra civil y el franquismo* (Barcelona: Pasado y Presente 2012), 517–30.
9. Juan Carlos Pereira Castañares, 'De "Centinela de Occidente" a la conspiración masónica-comunista. La política exterior del franquismo', in Ángel Viñas (ed.), *En el combate por la historia. La república, la guerra civil y el franquismo* (Barcelona: Pasado y Presente 2012), 659–78.
10. Julián García Candau, *El deporte en la guerra civil* (Pozuelo de Alarcón, Madrid: Espasa Calpe, 2007).
11. Stanley G. Payne, *Franco y José Antonio: El extraño caso del fascismo español: Historia de la Falange y del Movimiento Nacional (1923–1977)*, translated by Joaquín Adsuar Ortega (Barcelona: Planeta, 1997).
12. José María Gutiérrez del Castillo, 'La Falange y el Deporte', *Boletín oficial de la Delegación Nacional de Deportes de F.E.T. y de las J.O.N.S.* 11 (1944), 3.
13. Raymond Carr, *Spain: Dictatorship to Democracy* (London: HarperCollins Academic, 1991).
14. Carles Santacana i Torres, 'Espejo de un régimen. Transformación de las estructuras deportivas y su uso político y propagandístico, 1939–1961', in Xavier Pujadas i Martí (ed.), *Atletas y ciudadanos: Historia social del deporte en España (1870–2010)* (Madrid: Alianza Editorial, 2011), 214.
15. FET-JONS developed a specific sporting and leisure organization, Frente de Juventudes, as a tool for the youth political indoctrination, inspired fundamentally by the German Hitler Jugend and by the Italian Opera Nazionale Balilla, with the monopoly of Under 18 sport. The German influence is emphasized by Juan Carlos Manrique Arribas in 'Actividad Física y juventud en el franquismo', *Revista Internacional de Medicina y Ciencias de la Actividad*

Física y el Deporte 14, no. 55 (2014): 427–49, and José Ignacio Cruz Orozco, 'Falange, Frente de Juventudes y el nuevo orden europeo. Discrepancias y coincidencias en la política de juventud durante el primer franquismo', *Revista de Educación* 357 (2012), 515–35, while the Italian one is critical for José A. Cañabate in 'La pugna entre la Iglesia Católica y el Frente de Juventudes en el ámbito educativo. Referencias internacionales, antecedentes y trayectoria general durante el primer franquismo', *Historia de la Educación* 22–23 (2003–2004), 105–21.

16. Carlos Fernández Santander, *El fútbol durante la Guerra Civil y el franquismo* (Madrid: San Martín, 1990).

17. Teresa González Aja, 'La política deportiva en España durante la República y el franquismo', in Teresa González Aja (ed.), *Sport y autoritarismos: La utilización del deporte por el comunismo y el fascismo* (Madrid: Alianza Editorial, 2002).

18. Julián García Candau, *El deporte en la guerra civil* (Pozuelo de Alarcón, Madrid: Espasa Calpe, 2007).

19. Alejandro de la Viuda Serrano, 'Deporte, censura y represión bajo el franquismo', in Xavier Pujadas i Martí (ed.), *Atletas y ciudadanos: Historia social del deporte en España (1870–2010)* (Madrid: Alianza Editorial, 2011), 273–321. Viuda-Serrano proves after studying the censorship archives that there were censorship and political orders in the Spanish sporting press, contrary to a general sense of freedom reflected in former literature, especially in Duncan Shaw's *Fútbol y Franquismo* (Madrid: Alianza Editorial, 1987).

20. Duncan Shaw, *Fútbol y franquismo* (Madrid: Alianza Editorial, 1987); Santander, *El fútbol durante la Guerra Civil y el franquismo*; Teresa González Aja, 'La política deportiva en España durante la República y el franquismo', in Teresa González Aja (ed.), *Sport y autoritarismos: La utilización del deporte por el comunismo y el fascismo* (Madrid: Alianza Editorial, 2002), 169–202; and Santacana i Torres, 'Espejo de un régimen' in Pujadas i Martí *Atletas y ciudadanos* 205–32.

21. Jordi Rodríguez Virgili, 'La cooperativa del diario "El alcázar" (1945–1948)', *Historia y Comunicación Social* 5 (2000), 171–87. General Moscardó had endured a military siege during the Civil War on the Alcazar fortification in Toledo which became a mythical tale for the winning side. In recognition of their sacrifice, survivors and Moscardó himself received permission to edit a newspaper, called *El Alcazar*.

22. Félix Martialay, *Las grandes mentiras del fútbol español* (Madrid: Fuerza Nueva, 1997), 243.

23. Viuda Serrano, 'Deporte, censura y represión bajo el franquismo', in Xavier Pujadas i Martí (ed.), *Atletas y ciudadanos: Historia social del deporte en España (1870–2010)* (Madrid: Alianza Editorial, 2011), 273–321.

24. Juan Deportista, *La furia española* (Madrid: Renacimiento, 1940).

25. Pedro Escartín Morán, *Técnica y estrategia en el fútbol de hoy y un manual de entrenamiento para la juventud* (Madrid: Pueyo, 1947).

26. González Aja, 'La política deportiva en España durante la República y el franquismo', 169–202.

27. Fielpeña, *Los 60 partidos de la selección española de fútbol (1920–1941): Síntesis histórica de los equipos adversarios, olimpiadas de Amberes, París, Ámsterdam y Berlín, copa del mundo de Uruguay, Italia y Francia* (Valladolid: Maxtor, 2005).

28. Fielpeña, *Los 60 partidos de la selección española*, 7–9.

29. Carlos Cardo, 'Los equipos de España y Portugal empataron a dos tantos en Lisboa', *Mundo Deportivo*, 19 January 1941.

30. Juan Deportista, 'Fútbol', *ABC*, 31 December 1941.

31. José Luis Lasplazas, 'Por 3 a 2 España triunfó en su encuentro con Suiza, *Mundo Deportivo*, 30 December 1941.

32. José María Mateos, 'Panorama de nuestro fútbol', *Boletín oficial de la Delegación Nacional de Deportes de F.E.T. y de las J.O.N.S.* 3 (1943), 17.

33. González Aja, 'La política deportiva en España durante la República y el franquismo', 169–202.

34. Juan Deportista, 'La selección española venció a la francesa por cuatro tantos a cero', *ABC*, 17 March 1942.

35. The invention of the WM and the consequences for football can be seen in authors like Tony Say, 'Herbert Chapman: Football Revolutionary?', *Sports Historian* 16 no. 5 (1996),

81–98; Pablo Hernandez Coronado, *Las cosas del fútbol* (Madrid: Plenitud, 1955); Dante Panzeri, *Fútbol: Dinámica de lo impensado* (Madrid: Capitán Swing, 2011); Alejandro Scopelli, *Hola, míster: El fútbol por dentro* (Barcelona: Juventud, 1962); Jonathan Wilson, *Inverting the Pyramid: The History of Football Tactics* (London: Orion, 2009); M. Herzog, 'German Blitzkrieg Football Against the English "Wall Tactic": The Football System Dispute in the German Empire 1939–1941', *The International Journal of the History of Sport* 31, no. 12 (2014), 1489–508.

36. Hefeces, 'Portugal y España empataron a uno en un partido que debimos ganar', *Marca*, 12 March 1945.

37. Juan Deportista, 'La selección de Irlanda venció a la española en el estadio metropolitano por un gol a cero', *ABC*, 25 June 1946.

38. Pedro Escartín, 'El Generalísimo presenció el encuentro internacional España-Irlanda y fue aclamado por la multitud', *El Alcázar*, 26 June 1946.

39. M. Monasterio, 'Con las tácticas hemos topado …', *El Alcázar*, 25 June 1946.

40. Mencheta, 'El secretario técnico del Español cree que ni los entrenadores ni los jugadores extranjeros pueden enseñarnos nada', *Marca*, 3 August 1946.

41. Ramón Melcón, 'Menos tácticas defensivas y más ataque', *Marca*, 12 July 1946.

42. Gilera, 'Consecuencias del España-Irlanda', *Marca*, 25 June 1946.

43. 'Acuerdos del Comité Directivo de la Federación Española', *Boletín oficial de la Delegación Nacional de Deportes de F.E.T. y de las J.O.N.S.* 40 (1946), 11–8.

44. Ibid.

45. 'Acuerdos de la Delegación Nacional de Deportes y de sus organismos integrantes', *Boletín oficial de la Delegación Nacional de Deportes de F.E.T. y de las J.O.N.S.* 45 (1947), 3–5.

46. 'Acuerdos del Comité Directivo de la Federación Española', *Boletín oficial de la Delegación Nacional de Deportes de F.E.T. y de las J.O.N.S.* 40 (1946), 11–8.

47. Payne, *El franquismo*.

48. Preston, *Franco* 710.

49. Carlos Cardo, 'El San Lorenzo de Almagro bordó ayer una lección de gran fútbol en Las Corts', *Mundo Deportivo*, 2 January 1947.

50. M. Monasterio, '6–1 vencieron los argentinos al combinado español', *El Alcázar*, 17 January 1947.

51. Subirán, 'En Barcelona el San Lorenzo de Almagro venció a un combinado español por 7–5', *Marca*, 2 January 1947.

52. Carlos Cardo, 'El San Lorenzo de Almagro bordó ayer una lección de gran fútbol en Las Corts', *Mundo Deportivo*, 2 January 1947.

53. 'Argentina y España', *Antorcha* 9 (1947), 7.

54. 'Acuerdos del Comité Directivo de la Federación Española', *Boletín oficial de la Delegación Nacional de Deportes de F.E.T. y de las J.O.N.S.* 47 (1947), 7–10.

55. Carlos Cardo, '¿Sabremos aprovechar La lección de Lisboa', *Mundo Deportivo*, 29 January 1947.

56. Pedro Escartín, 'Nuestro fútbol se haya colectivamente enfermo y hay que salvarlo', *El Alcázar*, 29 January 1947.

57. 'Estamos donde estábamos y conservamos nuestras virtudes deportivas y las características de raza', *Marca*, 3 March 1947.

58. 'Acuerdos de la Delegación Nacional de Deportes y de sus organismos integrantes', *Boletín oficial de la Delegación Nacional de Deportes de F.E.T. y de las J.O.N.S.* 50 (1947), 3–7.

59. Ibid.

60. Cronos, 'Aspiro a que los jugadores adquieran la necesaria autodeterminación', *Marca*, 8 May 1947.

61. Ibid.

62. 'Acuerdos del Comité Directivo de la Federación Española', *Boletín oficial de la Delegación Nacional de Deportes de F.E.T. y de las J.O.N.S.* 52 (1947), 9–14.

63. 'Los entrenadores de Primera División, invitados a una reunión en Madrid', *Arriba*, 2 February 1947.

64. 'Después del partido de Dublín, la Federación Española se preocupará intensamente de mejorar nuestro fútbol', *Arriba*, 5 February 1947.

65. Shaw, *Fútbol y franquismo*.

66. 'Acuerdos del Comité Directivo de la Federación Española', *Boletín oficial de la Delegación Nacional de Deportes de F.E.T. y de las J.O.N.S.* 52 (1947), 9–14.

67. 'Muñoz Calero piensa que la "furia" debe ser gran servidora de la táctica', *Arriba*, 21 March 1948.

68. 'Se habla de Guillermo Eizaguirre' *Arriba*, 21 March 1947.

69. Ramón Melcón, 'España venció a Irlanda por la mínima diferencia', *Marca*, 31 May 1948.

70. Alejandro Viuda-Serrano, 'A Diplomatic Mission: Spain and the 1948 London Olympics', *The International Journal of the History of Sport* 27 no. 6 (2010), 1080–103.

71. Payne, *El franquismo*.

72. 'Acuerdos del Comité Directivo de la Federación Española', *Boletín oficial de la Delegación Nacional de Deportes de F.E.T. y de las J.O.N.S.* 59 (1948), 18–9.

73. 'Acuerdos del Comité Directivo de la Federación Española', *Boletín oficial de la Delegación Nacional de Deportes de F.E.T. y de las J.O.N.S.* 70 (1949), 18–20.

74. 'Otro mal paso', *Marca*, 28 March 1949.

75. Scopelli, *Hola, míster*.

76. José Luis Lasplazas, 'España bate a Irlanda por 4 a 1', *Mundo Deportiv*, 13 June 1949.

77. Juan Deportista, 'Balance y comentario final al partido Francia-España, en Colombes', *ABC*, 22 June 1949.

78. 'Benito Díaz', *Arriba*, 14 June 1949.

79. Alcaraz, 'Tendremos preparadores y tendremos profesores', *Arriba*, 17 June 1949.

80. Ramón Melcón, '¡Goleada en Colombes!', *Marca*, 20 June 1949.

81. Cronos, 'Ignacio Eizaguirre quedó maravillado del trabajador del entrenador de la Real', *Marca*, 1 July 1949.

82. 'España-Francia', *Arriba*, 19 June 1949.

83. Antonio Valencia, 'Españoles en París', *Arriba*, 19 June 1949.

84. Scopelli, *Hola, míster*.

85. Benito Díaz, *Manual del preparador* (Madrid: Real Federación Española de Fútbol, 1950).

86. Julián García Candau, *El fútbol, sin ley* (Madrid: Penthatlon, 1980).

87. Liz Crolley and David Hand, *Football and European Identity: Historical Narratives Through the Press* (London: Routledge, 2006), 96–115.

88. Herzog, 'German Blitzkrieg Football Against the English "Wall Tactic"'.

Disclosure statement

No potential conflict of interest was reported by the author.

ORCiD

Carlos García-Martí ⓘ http://orcid.org/0000-0001-9075-6941

How the Touring Club de France Influenced the Development of Winter Tourism

Pierre-Olaf Schut

ABSTRACT

The link between sport and tourism is closely related in outdoor sports and it is worth considering the development of these physical activities in conjunction with the tourist infrastructures that facilitate access to the activity areas. The purpose of this paper is to reveal the major role played by the Touring Club de France (TCF) in the launching of winter sports in France through its promotion of tourist infrastructures and support of the related activities. The TCF played an innovating and most efficient part through its action on three essential aspects: equipping sites for tourists; developing the manufacture of winter sports equipment; and promoting winter sports, thus bringing new life to mountain resorts. In taking into account the crucial role of the TCF in this study, the main sources used are related to the club itself: its archives and the monthly review from 1908 to 1914. On a larger scale, an explanation on how the TCF acted as a lever to generate dynamics beneficial to local development of the mountain areas will also be provided.

The history of skiing in France presents useful perspectives for analysis as the activity is central to many interests that have all contributed to its fast expansion. Skiing is a sports activity,[1] and it plays a full part in the history of alpine societies, for example, the French Alpine Club (Club Alpin Français, CAF).[2] But the history of skiing is not restricted to this society only and should be more widely understood, in particular concerning its development through the army,[3] its role in creating national identities[4] (notably through prominent figures),[5] and also its encounter with the Olympic Games of 1924.[6] Therefore its growth combined the efforts of several institutions.

In addition to the action of these contributors, the infrastructures should also be considered in order to understand all the factors at stake. Obviously, skiing is an outdoor sport that requires seasonal migrations to the mountains. This entails having access to a means of transport and to accommodation at the relevant location. At the beginning of the twentieth century, the demand for sport infrastructures was still limited to competitions. Therefore, the expansion of skiing is closely related to the growth of mountain tourism, especially in winter. This notion has been developed by experts in economic history, for example, Larique,[7] and Bouneau,[8] as well as by geographers such as Debarbieux.[9] Simultaneously, the impact of skiing on local development gave rise to regional interpretations of the phenomenon, whether on the scale of a massif,[10] or of a resort.[11] Thus, skiing has become a physical activity widely taken into account by experts in tourism.[12]

This short historiography shows both the importance of the subject and the abundance of literature on it. However, research on the history of the TCF has revealed two levels of interest that justify the present contribution to the history of how skiing first developed before the outbreak of the First World War. The first one concerns the position of the TCF. As the vocation of this society was to work for tourism development, it acts as an interface between sports people and the local, public, and private contributors in order to support projects. Thus, through its role as an instigator, coordinator or even catalyst of local dynamics, the TCF shows how relationships were established between different people and institutions concerned by the expansion of winter sports.

The second point of interest is related to a weakness in the historiography that frequently mentions the TCF, though often underestimates its importance. The TCF is generally represented as a secondary player as its investments in winter sports came later and therefore appears less important. As a matter of fact, the analysis presented here shows that most of the people concerned by the expansion of skiing were helped by the TCF. In other words, the TCF played a crucial part, not only through its direct action, but also through its indirect involvement as an activator and supporter of initiatives.

The purpose of this research is to highlight the role of the TCF as a lever in the tourist development of winter sports. This was apparent in many ways, as much in the development of presentations, practices, and techniques as in supporting the equipping of mountain areas. For this, the TCF used various complementary means: donations in kind or funding; communication; and lobbying with institutional bodies. This apparently protean involvement actually proved to be extremely efficient as it brought about numerous achievements.

The investments of the TCF in winter sports started in 1908. At that time, skiing was already the focus of many projects. However, the steps taken by the TCF brought about a definite innovative touch. This study follows in the tracks of an earlier research carried out by Drouet,[13] and analyzes it further. Indeed the TCF was a participant in social innovation when it introduced skiing to a new public, tourists, and mountain inhabitants with its twofold view, namely: leisure and utility. The communication programme implemented by the TCF and their direct and indirect contributions to technical innovation through the development of winter sports equipment are especially noteworthy.

To carry out this research, this historical study is limited to the period between 1908 and 1914 and relies for the main part on TCF archives and monthly reviews. As the propagandist language used in the reviews is obviously biased and potentially misleading, meeting reports are more important to this study as they present a more objective view on the actions carried out by the club. In addition, other publications such as the *TCF Directories* will also be quoted as they contain information on hotels and tourist services in French towns and villages.

To make this presentation clearer, the results of the present research are divided into three sections, although the phenomena expounded are connected. First, communication campaigns carried out by the TCF to convince its members of the importance of winter tourism and how it tried to spread the idea of the practical advantage of skiing among the alpine population will be dealt with. Then, the substantial actions of the TCF benefitting winter sports will be presented, with the development of mountain areas being the crux of the matter. Finally and probably the most important, in order to measure their impact, an explanation will be included about the accomplishments of the TCF with public and private stakeholders.

Turning Winter Sports into a Tourist Activity

When skiing first started, it was soon taken over by the army and the CAF.[14] Henri Duhamel, considered as one of the pioneers in this activity, carried out his first experiments during 1878. As an active member of the CAF, he spread the word among the 7,000 mountain enthusiasts of the club to encourage the expansion of the sport. At the same time, the French army appropriated the activity to solve strategic issues and became very much involved in training its soldiers in ski techniques. Despite these bursts of enthusiasm, the impact of skiing on civilian society on the whole remained quite limited. According to soldiers in the Dauphiné area:

> Skiing has been very slowly spreading among the population of Briançon despite the example given by soldiers who have been skiing all over the area since 1900. On 1st January 1906, there were only four or five civilian skiers within a radius of 30 kilometres around Briançon.[15]

The work of the TCF was quite innovative compared to the projects led by the army or the CAF. Indeed, as it was focused on tourism, the TCF broached the development of winter sports from a different angle: it became a pretext for spreading winter tourism in the mountains. From then on, skiing did not only concern the 7,000 mountaineers of the CAF, but the 137,000 members of the TCF.[16] The TCF strategy was even more ambitious as it intended to rely on the local population to ensure the development of the tourism opportunity. Learning and teaching others how to ski was to be a way of breaking the winter torpor affecting the mountain areas. Thus, the programme of the winter tourism committee also aimed at getting the local population to become ski instructors. It planned to support the creation and development of ski schools; pay in kind and in cash schoolteachers, guides, and ski enthusiasts to get them to teach skiing for free to the populations of the villages and hamlets of our mountain areas.[17] Hence, besides the tourists, the population of the mountain areas was also involved in the larger scheme of the TCF in a practical perspective.

A New Plan for the Mountains in Winter

At the beginning of the 1900s, skiing and winter sports were relatively unknown by the public. Consequently, the first step taken by the TCF was to communicate. In such a mission, the TCF excelled.[18] For example, it increased information in favour of winter sports in the columns of its magazine. Every winter, one or several articles attracted attention to winter tourism, broaching the subject from several angles: directly, by praising the value of the activity,[19] or, more ingeniously, by recommending regions where skiing could be practised, underlining the accessibility of these sites.[20] The strength of the TCF was the vast audience of its members, but this was greatly affected by the participation of its members and delegates,[21] who made up an active network all over the country, relaying the TCF messages through publications in newspapers in particular.[22] During the period under study, about 20 articles were published in a number of papers ranging from local newspapers to the most important national dailies: *la Dépêche de Toulouse, La République du Var, l'Echo de Paris, Le Gaulois,*

La Vie à la *campagne, Gil Blas, L'Intransigeant, Excelsior, L'Illustration, L'Auto, Le Figaro,* and *Le Monde*. In addition, the TCF met up with people through its participation in many places where winter sports equipment was displayed.[23] It also sponsored the international exhibition of winter sports industries organized in Luchon at the beginning of 1910.[24] This way, the TCF promoted winter sports and tried to convince not only tourists but also the whole population of their advantages.

This approach was very specific to the TCF: it addressed a vaster public because skiing was not presented as a sports activity only reserved for well-trained experts. All the club members could be interested. In addition, its recruitment policy was much more democratic than that of the French alpine club. Although the leaders of the TCF came from the affluent classes, its membership included 30% of 'middle class employees and self-employed people',[25] yet there were still almost no factory workers or farmers.

The TCF target was wider. The connoisseurs of life in the mountains knew that activity slowed down during the winter, whereas the development of tourism demanded that a certain number of services were maintained all year round. This is why the TCF wanted to develop skiing among the mountain populations, and thus include public services like post-offices and schools. Here, the approach was different: skis were presented as a means of transport. Just like cycling, skiing offered practical mobility for mountain residents:

> The inhabitants of the mountains follow the example given by the army and public services; skis, this wonderful invention that offers 'freedom from the snow', are spreading fast all over the mountains will be for the mountain populations what the bicycle was for those in the valleys.[26]

Only a minute part of this population subscribed to the TCF, so communicating through its review was not sufficient. This is why the TCF also engaged in more direct actions as will be shown in the second and third parts of this study.

Nevertheless, the effort made by the TCF to spread information was enough to reach the heads of the public services. Indeed, after defending the use of skiing to maintain services during the winter, in particular postal delivery, the report of congressman Dalimier made it possible to obtain a credit of 12,000 francs to compensate the 400 postmen for using skis for their job.[27] The use of skiing as a way of getting around was also appropriate for tourists who were eager to discover the beauties of snow-covered mountain landscapes.

The TCF literally accompanied tourists and encouraged them to practice winter sports and ensured they enjoyed their first experience. Guidebooks were published which familiarized city-dwellers with the mountains in winter. For example, in 1908, an article was published to teach people how to dress for winter sports.[28] Sometime later, the TCF participated in the distribution of a technical manual, *Le Ski*, a translation of the book entitled *Der Skilauf* by Hoeck and Richardson.[29] Then, the TCF brought out a guidebook grouping together practical and tourist information necessary for the practice of winter sports.[30]

This way, the TCF got involved in supporting winter sports and, consequently, the development of winter tourism. By promoting a view of skiing as being both, practical and recreational and hence addressing a wider population of mountain dwellers as well as tourists, the TCF aimed at a vast public. Its means of communication enabled it to rapidly contact keen tourists and soon words were followed by actions.

A Flagship Action: The 'Great Winter Sports Weeks'

The concept of 'Great Winter Sports Weeks' was thought up in 1908 and designed to send pioneers to the mountains in winter so they could test practically what had been publicized.[31] If we compare this to the international competitions organized by the CAF during the same season, we can better understand the specific TCF plan of action and reveal its deeper intention. The CAF set up international competitions which closely resembled sports events for professional athletes, whereas the TCF aimed, on the one hand, at convincing the tourists who participated in the games of the attraction of winter sports and, on the other, at showing mountain inhabitants the economic advantages of winter tourism, thus persuading them to develop attractive offers to compete with Switzerland.[32] Indeed, Switzerland already had tourist infrastructures and was considered an often-cited role model.

Originally, the sites chosen for the Great Winter Sports Weeks reveal the TCF determination to cover all French massifs (the Alps in 1909, the Vosges in 1910, and the Pyrenees in 1911 and in 1912), and the Weeks were planned in the Massif Central. Due to bad weather conditions, the event in the Auvergne was cancelled at the last minute,[33] and postponed to the following year – except that the same scenario reoccurred and the Great Winter Sports Week never took place in that massif.[34] It can also be noted that no such event was organized in the Jura, but this does not mean the TCF was not interested in that region which, like the others, benefitted from subsidies and donations. The temporary nature of these Great Weeks is also very important in understanding the intention of the TCF: whereas the CAF sports competitions were meant to take place regularly, these Great Weeks were unique events. While the villages where competitions were held were already well equipped in terms of infrastructures, the TCF set up its events in places with great potential and relied on the lever effect of the event to develop them further. Actually, the projects planned for the selected sites had a more or less long-term effect and depended on a series of situations that would or would not motivate further activity in the area. For example, the Great Winter Sports Week in the Pyrenees in 1911 led to the present-day site of Font-Romeu and two years later, the opening of the Grand Hotel marked the actual launching of tourist activity in that region. It should be noted however that this opening occurred within the strategy developed by the Railway and Mountain Hotel Company and two years after the launching of the electric railway from Cerdagne to Perpignan.[35] Thus, the role played by the TCF was quite often more that of a catalyst than of a contracting authority in mountain tourism.

The mobility of the TCF caravan presented several advantages. First, the 300 tourists taking part in these events were keen to discover the mountains in winter. Thus, mobility was essential in the discovery of new landscapes.[36] Moreover, the TCF was determined to mobilize all the mountain populations to develop many and varied practice sites. This is why it was important to spread its range of action to all the massifs: on the one hand, visiting places already taken over by winter sports to support them in their investment policies, and on the other, discovering sites with a high geographical potential to launch their tourism development.

This is why the venues for Winter Sports Weeks were not planned to be reused. The TCF members acted as pioneers and put little known places on the map. For example, they used sleighs to reach passes not usually open in winter:

> The highlight of the trip will be the unique itinerary from Murat to Salers through the Eylacet and the Peyrol passes. For the first time, this amazing route, one of the most beautiful in France, will be cleared and after going up the sides of the curious volcanic rocky peaks of Murat, our sleighs will venture into this region so strange and so little visited – steppe in the summer and snow desert in the winter – which, through Dienne and La Vigerie, ends up right in the heart of the Cantal massif … This crossing, analogous to our lovely outing to the passes of Peyresourde and Aspin last year, will be a real tour de force worthy of our Association.[37]

But these explorations were not so much the outcome of a physical feat (tourists were more travellers than sports people) than the fruit of the TCF's efforts to mobilize, equip, and develop. Indeed, its caravan was essentially made up of Parisian tourists, often joined by the local elite.

The participation of the TCF in winter sports is not like that of a sports organization. Tourists were taken by sleigh from one site to the next. Most of the time, their sports activity was mainly done by proxy: they watched skiers from the local ski clubs and only occasionally took part on the side-lines, as a recreational activity. Thus, skiing was clearly only optional as these travellers were basically interested in taking leisure trips in beautiful mountain landscapes – a photography competition was organized – and ski events with the possibility of being introduced to winter sports was an additional motivation.[38] This is the genuine 'culture tourism' depicted by Hoibian.[39] From the beginning, the president of the TCF very clearly answered the concern of sports stakeholders regarding the important investments by this powerful tourist Association:

> Winter sports, through the events organized, the attraction and impact of the competitions, are greatly helping the tourism movement. For this, they deserve our full attention and we shall generously offer it to them. However for us they are a means, not an end. We shall certainly give assistance and support to this very precious ally in spreading and expanding ideas. But let's not forget that we were founded to promote tourism, not sport. So sports societies should know that while they are under the patronage of the Touring club, we do not intend to intervene in sports issues, not even managing anything related to sport.[40]

After this declaration, the specific nature of the TCF mission was clear and its action became collaborative. The committee for mountain tourism, which organized the TCF actions, was invested by core members of the CAF board, notably Schrader and Helbronner. Thus, on several occasions, the TCF participated in projects undertaken by the CAF, in particular supporting them financially. For example, they granted a 500 francs subsidy for the organization of its international competition in 1912,[41] and allocated, respectively, 7,000 francs to help with the building of the chalet hotel in the Chavière Pass, and 1,000 francs for the refuge near the Glandon Pass.[42] Both projects were undertaken by local branches of the CAF.

The Great Winter Sports Weeks were the consequence of the TCF endeavour to promote winter tourism. They offered an opportunity to really show how attractive the mountains could be in winter, in particular because of winter sports. Campaigning played an important part in the TCF action, but the members of the committee for mountain tourism took even further steps: they engaged in logistic, financial, and political support to bring to fruition the development of a network of practice sites in every French massif.

Efforts of the TCF in Favour of Developing Tourism in Mountain Areas

Very soon, the TCF became involved in projects coming under the scope of public works by placing signposts on roads, financing cycle tracks and rowboat hatches on dams.[43] The financial resources of the TCF increased as public interest grew,[44] which enabled it to multiply its realizations and become involved in more ambitious projects. This intervention was made possible or facilitated through a close collaboration with the services of the ministry of public works and especially engineers from the highways department, some of whom were members of the club. Finally, the strength of the TCF was closely related to its capacity to mobilize local, public, and private participants who in turn influenced the phenomenon it had initiated. There again the way the TCF operated seems highly efficient.

Actions Oriented Towards Practice Sites

The necessary prerequisite to winter sports is snow. At the beginning of the twentieth century, the growth of the activity firstly relied on existing structures and in particular on mountain towns and villages. There the highest inhabited dwellings were vacant in the winter or lacked the necessary services to receive tourists. Similarly, only a few accommodations existed on the northern slopes of the steepest mountains where the best snow coverage could be found. As a consequence, skiing first took place in the medium-high mountain ranges,[45] around villages where snowfalls could vary from one year to the next, as demonstrated by the lack of snow in January 1912 and 1913 in Puy-de-Dôme, which forced the TCF to cancel its Great Winter Sports Weeks. Thus, it soon became necessary to get not only regular weather reports – a procedure which became quite common during the nineteenth century – but also reports on snow depth in order to inform tourists of the possibility of doing winter sports in the various mountain villages.[46] At first, the TCF planned to rely on its network of delegates to inform its members of snowfalls in the mountain areas and even in the valleys close to large city centres so that they would know of the possibilities for skiing.[47] In reality, it looks as if this service did not operate satisfactorily because the information published in the club monthly review about snow coverage in ski resorts was relatively scarce.[48]

Nevertheless, the TCF equipped some mountain villages with weather stations,[49] and created the necessary conditions for precise, regular, and especially generalized reports on snowfalls in the mountains.[50] Thus, temperatures and snow depths were communicated to the TCF which then relayed the information. The new National Office for Tourism, created in 1910,[51] also ensured this communication service through daily newspapers.[52] And so, the TCF implemented an operational weather forecast service, which was useful for tourists wanting to go skiing in the different French massifs. This service was all the more crucial as most practice sites were located at heights where snowfalls were not certain, even though some benefitted from a connection between the host village and a zone of altitude offering relatively reliable practice conditions, like Aix-les-Bains/Le Revard where the spa resort was connected to the higher domain by a rack train, or Bagnères/Luchon in the Pyrenees.

However, the sites having significant infrastructure were rare. Practically speaking, skiing and tobogganing in their tourist forms required relatively simple facilities. Usually, a large snow field surrounded by gentle slopes was enough to arouse the initial pleasure of winter sports. The TCF participated in making these domains accessible by helping create access roads as for Luchon.[53] Yet, the idea of opening routes soon became a necessity and the TCF was asked to carry out the project.[54] First, it worked at marking out ski runs,[55] and equipping various places in the Chartreuse and Luchon,[56] but then it met the demands of the local players and also financed the realization of ski runs as in the Fraize district (in the Vosges massif).[57] However, these contributions to regional sports facilities were few and represented only a modest part of the resources that the TCF invested in favour of winter tourism.

The most significant part of the funds allocated to works was directed towards the building of refuges. Indeed, these played the most important role in the spreading of winter sports as they facilitated the organization of routes to the heights, ensuring shelter to tourists in case of bad weather, or even accommodation for longer stays. It should also be remembered that the committee for winter tourism founded in 1908 changed names in May 1909. It became the committee for tourism and widened its objectives to include the development of mountain tourism in all seasons as refuges also played an important role for summer holiday-makers.[58] Just before the Great War, TCF investments amounted to 84,000 francs,[59] which made it possible to have nine refuges built: two in the Alps, three in the Vosges, three in the Pyrenees, and one in the Massif Central. Thus, all massifs could benefit from infrastructure facilitating winter sports.

Even though there was a genuine will to fit out all the French territory, there was still a certain inequality in provision between the massifs. In actual fact, investments were strongly influenced by the momentum of the Great Winter Sports Weeks. These events greatly mobilized the human and financial resources of the TCF and, to ensure their success, the TCF leaders directed investments towards the massif where the event was to be held.[60] For example, the Jura, where no event was programmed, was the only massif that did not benefit from the creation of a refuge. On the other hand, coinciding with the Great Winter Sports Week in the Pyrenees, six weather stations were established there at the beginning of the winter of 1910–1911.

In this way, the TCF showed how it intended to play a dynamic role in the development of winter tourism. It offered better accommodation conditions to its members, the followers of winter tourism. It brought a dynamic to the regions through building infrastructure and, through its caravan, showed that these areas were of interest to tourists. Thus, it positioned itself in a favourable light towards the local populations to whom it offered a potential for economic growth and towards the local public authorities which were likely to be influenced by the efforts made by this Parisian association. Generally, the club delegates living in the mountain areas reinforced the activity of the club by representing its arguments in the locality.

The Development of Services

The implication of the TCF in favour of mountain tourism and particularly of winter tourism was not limited to granting subsidies related to the Great Winter Sports Weeks. It was also involved in spreading practical information to tourists so as to facilitate the organization of their stays.

The TCF was also concerned with the conditions in which tourists would be received. Practically speaking, mountain hotels were clearly subject to the seasons and many of them were closed in the winter. This choice – which may be logical considering the rather small number of winter tourists – also contributed to a meagre quantity of hotel establishments. Indeed, as fiscal laws imposed pre-set taxes independently of the length of the working period, these weighed more heavily on hotels which generated their revenue during one season only.

Moreover, a necessary condition for a hotel to be open in winter was the existence of a heating system, which was quite rare before the First World War. From the very beginning of its involvement in winter tourism, the TCF was convinced of the importance of having central heating installed in the hotels which were likely to receive tourists during the cold season. Hence, spreading information about the hotels which could welcome winter sports lovers was essential. As a matter of fact, the TCF was very active in giving tourist information on accommodation facilities as it published a list of all hotels in a yearly *General Directory*.[61] Because of the TCF investment in winter tourism, accommodation descriptions also mentioned the presence of central heating systems.[62] This information was also relayed in the columns of its monthly review. It is thus possible to see how a map of winter tourism sites slowly developed.

The TCF invested not only funds, but also a lot of support in the development of winter sports. It spread tourist information by forwarding it to its members who were likely to organize stays in the mountains and participate in winter sports. It was also directly involved in developing some practice sites, taking responsibility for building several refuges, and giving subsidies to create more. In this way, every French mountain area benefitted from the support of the TCF. Some local stakeholders, public or private, also joined forces with it to broaden the scope of this action in favour of the development of winter sports.

Generating a Dynamic in the Regions

In addition to the direct impact of the actions taken on by the TCF, there was an indirect effect that was even more extensive in terms of quantity, but also in the long term. Indeed, the aim of the TCF leaders was to generate a dynamic in the regions, creating initiatives that could then be taken over and carried on by the local people, thus acting as a lever. The Great Winter Sports Weeks perfectly illustrate this approach as the event was meant to convince and also initiate changes. With this type of events, they could transform an area and reveal to its inhabitants the tourist potential it held – something the locals could then develop by themselves. When this target was achieved, the TCF often received a lot of credit. This positive outcome was based on a system that combined good communications, support, and good public relations with local authorities. The TCF enjoyed a reputation of integrity and was even seen as an authority in the development of tourism. It knew how to motivate people and how to create the essential commercial initiatives for the development of a region.

Lobby Network

The TCF was founded and directed by people from the affluent classes. All the board members had a large social network in Paris, which enabled the club to get the patronage of several successive French Presidents and have one or two ministers regularly present at the annual general meeting, in particular the minister of public works. These Parisian networks had local branches in the provinces thanks to the TCF 'delegates'. This special status was granted to those who played the role of local intermediaries for the club activities.[63] Generally coming from the same social background as the leaders, the delegates enlarged the TCF network. They benefitted from sufficient resources to exchange favours with the local representatives and especially the civil services. As an example, the club delegate F. Brousse,

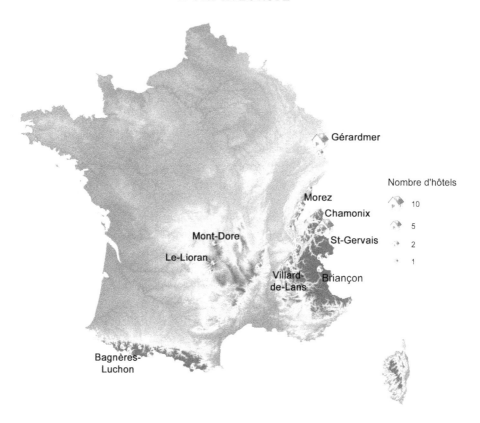

Figure 1. Map of heated hotels open during the winter of 1913–1914.
Source: Revue mensuelle du TCF (November 1913), (December 1913), (January 1914).

who was also and above all deputy of the Eastern Pyrenees, facilitated the organization of the Great Winter Sports Week in the Pyrenees.

The TCF was in contact with the ministry of war because, for strategic reasons, soldiers had been trained in skiing for a long time. The TCF wanted the ministry to increase its efforts to train ski instructors in all the massifs, thus contributing more effectively to its effort to spread skiing as an activity. Indeed, after returning to civilian life,[64] former soldiers represented a large reservoir of ski instructors essential to the teaching of skiing and, consequently, to its development. Local authorities were also contacted as skiing required access to places that were normally covered with snow. This meant that roads had to be cleared, which entailed human and financial resources. For example, on the occasion of the 1910 Great Winter Sports Week, the local authorities spent 8,850 francs to this end.[65] This type of action was often repeated, especially by private companies which faced the same problem, for example, from railway companies.[66]

Mobilizing Tourism Stakeholders

The organization of the Great Winter Sports Weeks relied on railway transport and the managing companies were already implicated in tourist development.[67] The TCF chartered special trains from Paris just to take its own caravan to its destination. The trains were scheduled to make a few stops to enable provincials to hop on. Even though the majority of tourists were probably from Paris, it is not really possible to know the precise composition of the group. For the first Great Winter Sports Week in Chamonix, the snow had to be cleared from the last section of the railway, especially for the caravan. In fact, this railroad was normally used only in the summer. The success of the event led the PLM railway company to put on a special express train leaving Paris at 8.45pm and arriving in Chamonix at 11.00am the following day. The PLM also developed a connection between the Tines station and the Planet Hotel via Argentières that was in service all winter until 30 April.[68] The company thus invested in winter tourism and put emphasis on winter sports in order to promote Chamonix and other places in Dauphiné and Savoie as winter destinations during the cold season.[69]

However, receiving tourists in Chamonix would not have been possible without the cooperation of hoteliers. Even though Chamonix was one of the first tourist towns in the south-east of France,[70] and consequently well equipped with hotels, most of them closed during the winter months. With its caravan, the TCF tried to convince hoteliers that those who stayed open in winter could count on a substantial number of clients to ensure their prosperity. But the issue was quite complex and fairly risky. At the beginning of the twentieth century, receiving well-off tourists in the mountains in winter meant purchasing modern central heating equipment. So the TCF was actually asking hoteliers to invest a lot of money to install central heating and to stay open in winter. It was a hazardous bet considering the French tendency to resist tourist investments compared to their Swiss neighbours.[71] Still, a number of establishments took up the challenge. Two in Gerardmer in the Vosges had central heating put in ready for the TCF Great Winter Sports Week.[72] Their rivals followed and so before the Great War, Gerardmer had four heated hotels open in winter. In Chamonix, seven hotels were equipped in the same way,[73] but only two of them were listed as such in the 1912 hotel directory.

Before the war, the first resorts for winter tourism were recorded this way (see Figure 1). The TCF contributed to this movement later taken up by local entrepreneurs – hoteliers, in this case – who knew that they would get a return on investment.

Now along with hotels, ancillary services were required for the tourists. The TCF soon realized that keeping hotels open was not enough. What was actually needed was a large 'winter awakening'.[74] Snow reduced mobility and the cold slowed down activities, so the mountain regions hibernated in winter. But for the TCF, skiing was the opportunity for mountain-dwellers to remain mobile, thus making it possible to maintain a number of services. This is why the TCF was quick to give out skis, not to tourists but to the local population and all of the public services.

Development of the French Manufacturing of Winter Sports Equipment

During the very first months of its existence, the members of the winter tourism committee reflected on the equipment needed for winter sports activities. It should be noted that, at that time, there was no industrial production of quality skis in France that could compare with those from Norway or Switzerland. So the TCF had to buy from its neighbours,[75] which went against the project of its leaders to enhance the national heritage. In addition, the cost of this imported equipment was quite high,[76] and this economic issue could put a serious brake on the ambition of spreading the idea of skiing for all. For this reason, on the occasion of the first Great Winter Sports Week, the TCF organized a ski-making

Figure 2. Shapes (templates) given out by the TCF
Source: Revue mensuelle du TCF (November 1909), 486.

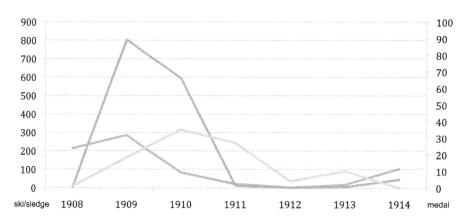

Figure 3. Distribution of material by the TCF
Source: Revue mensuelle du TCF, mountain tourism committee meetings, 1908–1914.

competition. This was meant to stimulate French manufacturing and firms that had the know-how in woodworking present their models. The stakes were quite high as there was not only a prize to win but also a lot of publicity through the advertising associated with the event and the opportunity of a large number of orders. In fact, the TCF promised to buy the equipment that it gave out from the most outstanding manufacturers in the competition.

The requirements were simple: the challenge launched by the TCF consisted in producing high-performance skis comparable to the Norwegian ones, but at a lower cost. The winner of the first competition in 1909 was no other than Abel Rossignol, the founder of the company which is still one of the world leaders on the market today. The TCF was to buy several hundreds of skis from them in the following years. The Coninck Company located in Maison-Laffites also won a prize and became fully involved in ski manufacturing, with significant sales to the TCF and its members as the company regularly published a full-page advertisement in the TCF review. The same idea – a competition to stimulate industrial innovation in France – was adopted at the following Great Winter Sports Weeks with new challenges: making skis for children or ski sticks.[77] Thus, the TCF was a catalyst for innovation, targeting the needs of skiers so as to direct the efforts of industry, which responded positively to these challenges.

The TCF action in this field took many forms. As a major stakeholder in this process, the club not only stimulated industrial manufacturing, but also supported small family businesses. In fact, the ski-making competition was divided into three categories: firms, families, and schools. With the same goal of developing skiing and making it accessible to as many people as possible, small-scale family production offered extra support in the realization of this project. Indeed, the lower income populations could not necessarily afford skis even if they were made in France and thus a little cheaper than imported skis. However, they could get the wood needed for making them at a very low cost. Thus, the aim of the TCF was to encourage people to increase the production of cheaper ski equipment. Soon, the winter tourism committee got directly involved in this process. It started recommending 'shapes', that is to say templates to help to make skis (see Figure 2) and also published a handbook. This way, the TCF took on a major role in ski-making by offering models and advice to all.

Like skis, these templates were given to everyone: inhabitants, public services, and any other applicant. Progressively, more templates were given out than skis (see Figure 3). For the TCF project, the impact of this distribution was potentially more efficient since a single template could generate the production of many pairs of skis. The TCF received a lot of encouraging accounts confirming this.[78]

Thus, the TCF members were innovators and A.G. Staath, secretary of the mountain tourism committee, wrote a ski-making handbook. Several manufacturing drawings were also published in the review, with the same intention to give free templates and enable local populations to make their own equipment at a low cost. This was also the case for the folding sledge developed by L. Auscher, vice-president of the mountain tourism committee, and, more importantly, for the sleigh that was to allow easy mobility throughout the winter in the highest snow-covered areas. Sleighs were crucial to the success of the Great Winter Sports Weeks because they enabled the TCF to reach places that had been neglected because of their difficult access. At the beginning of the twentieth century there were not many sleighs in the French mountains. In fact, there were none at all in the Pyrenees, which forced the TCF to boost their fabrication for the Great Winter Sports Week organized in that massif in 1911. Eventually, the manufacturing of dozens of sleighs made it possible to get over the Casteillou, Peyresourde, and Aspin passes situated above 1,500 metres – a rare thing in winter in those days – and to highlight the beauty of some practice areas that had so far been neglected.

Boosting Local Associations

Tourist Offices (TO) took part in this dynamic. They followed the TCF guidelines and projects. In fact, from the 1900s, the club largely supported the development of Tourist

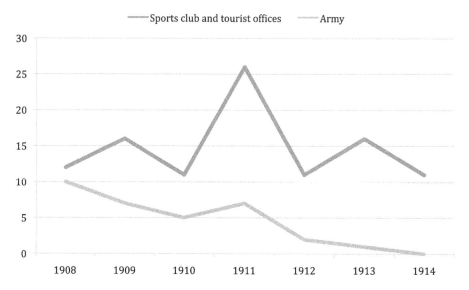

Figure 4. Distribution of the beneficiaries of TCF funding (*Y* axis, number of structures)
Source: Subsidies voted by the mountain tourism committee, *Revue mensuelle du TCF* (1908–1914).

Offices through campaigns leading to their creation and direct incentives from its delegates to organize their own actions.[79]

By taking part in TCF enterprises, some offices tried to highlight the potential of their region for winter sports. For example, the Vivarais TO organized a competition and emphasized that their mountains offered long-lasting snow coverage suitable for skiing.[80] Elsewhere, TO initiatives first aimed at boosting the area by creating events as in the Briançon region, Samoëns,[81] and La Bastide. Thus, the number of local competitions increased and the TCF was part of their success; it granted subsidies and offered many medals and other prizes to the winners (see Figure 3).

TO were not the only organizers of activities. Military ski schools and sports societies also took part in the development of winter sports. Many regiments received equipment and subsidies from the TCF for their role as ski instructors.[82] Others received help to set up ski making workshops.[83] Many other regiments were assisted without explicit mention of the nature of the TCF contribution.[84]

Progressively, through this emulation, the number of civilian clubs organizing skiing activities increased and they gradually replaced the army in projects with the TCF (see Figure 4). They contributed to the implementation of a growing number of local competitions parallel to the international events organized by the CAF. The army, sports societies, and the CAF benefitted from material and financial help of the TCF (approximately 480 francs each) to enable them to function and develop their actions.

Conclusion

At the end of this study, it clearly appears that the TCF did its very best to play a dynamic role in the development of skiing in France. In the short span of time under study, it is obvious that its actions in favour of tourists as well as the mountain populations were ambitious. Clearly, the way skiing was portrayed by the TCF created a more meaningful conception of the activity. Club members discovered the pleasures of snow and winter sports while the local population who benefited from the TCF actions discovered a means of transport adapted to snow-covered areas. Even though the objective was qualitatively clear, it is difficult to quantify the effects of these actions. The subsidies mentioned in the sources make it possible to count the beneficiaries of TCF aid: almost a hundred associations/ sport and tourist societies, about 20 army regiments, 10 tourist offices, a few districts, and a hundred individuals. These organizations and people were mainly located in mountain areas and the nearby towns. Several thousand people benefited from the TCF actions either directly or indirectly. Almost one thousand tourists, mainly from Paris, who participated in any of the Great Winter Sports Weeks, can be added to these numbers.

The TCF actions were also practical: the club gave financial and material resources to local players to enable them to develop winter sports. An assessment of the TCF actions between 1908 and 1914 indicates that 15,600 francs was given as subsidies and prizes and 20,000 francs was dedicated to distributing equipment.[85] Skis, sledges, manufacturing materials, and other equipment were just handed out by the hundreds to a large public. This contribution led the TCF onto the road of technological innovation. In fact, the creation of winter sports equipment benefitted from the TCF projects and the incentive given by its ski-making competitions. In addition, it is important to acknowledge the indirect impact of the TCF actions in order to fully understand its role in the development of winter sports.

The TCF intervened at every level. First, it is impossible to ignore its response to the initiatives of the army, the French alpine club, and other budding ski clubs. Indeed, even if the TCF was not a pioneer in the actual launching of skiing, all these groups benefitted from its support when they developed its actions. More importantly, the TCF played a role in making skiing accessible. This was visible in the way it made skiing equipment available. It focused on having the equipment made and instead of just giving away skis, the TCF gave people the means to make dozens of them. It therefore acted as a lever in the development of the activity.

And last but not least, the TCF – especially through its Great Winter Sports Weeks – contributed to the construction of the first winter sports resorts by encouraging local private participants as well as public bodies and transport companies to make accommodation available to tourists who had recently become interested in this type of holiday. Many initiatives were developed during the period studied and others, postponed because of the war, were realized after the Armistice.

Despite a late implication in the expansion of skiing and an action that may seem fragmented, the TCF encouraged practical and technical innovations that gave it a leading part in the development of winter sports. The hosting of the first winter Olympiad in Chamonix and the leadership of the French industry in winter sports equipment benefitted from this legacy.

Notes

1. Sébastien Stumpp, 'Alsatian Ski Clubs Between 1896 and 1914: An Exploratory Evaluation of the Role of Employees in the German "Sportization" of Skiing', *The International Journal of the History of Sport* 27, no. 4 (2010), 658–74.

2. Olivier Hoibian, *Les alpinistes en France 1870–1950: Une histoire culturelle* (Paris: L'Harmattan, 2000); Dominique Lejeune, *Les alpinistes en France* à la *fin du XIXᵉ et au début du XXᵉ siècle* (Paris: Editions du CTHS, 1988).

3. Rudolf Müllner, 'The Importance of Skiing in Austria', *The International Journal of the History of Sport* 30, no. 6 (2013), 659–73; Yann Drouet and Antoine Luciani, 'A l'origine du ski français, le discours commun de l'Armée et du Club alpin français (1902–1907)', *Revue STAPS* 71 (2006), 71–84; Pierre Arnaud and Thierry Terret, 'Le ski, Roi des sports d'hiver', in Thierry Terret (ed.), *Histoire des sports* (Paris: L'Harmattan, 1996), 159–202; and J.B. Allen, *Le ski en France. 1840–1940* (Saint-Cyr-sur-Loire: Editions Alan Sutton, 2003).

4. Borut Batagelj, 'Slovenian Skiing Identity: Historical Path and Reflection', *The International Journal of the History of Sport* 30, no. 6 (2013), 647–58; Matti Goksøyr, 'Taking Ski Tracks to the North. The Invention and Reinvention of Norwegian Polar Skiing: Sportisation, Manliness and National Identities', *The International Journal of the History of Sport* 30, no. 6 (2013), 563–79.

5. Müllner, 'The Importance of Skiing'; Richard Holt, 'An Englishman in the Alps: Arnold Lunn, Amateurism and the Invention of Alpine Ski Racing', *The International Journal of the History of Sport* 9, no. 3 (1992), 421–32.

6. Pierre Arnaud and Thierry Terret, *Le Rêve blanc. Olympisme et sport d'hiver en France* (Bordeaux: Presses Universitaires de Bordeaux, 1993); E. Monnin, *Un siècle d'Olympisme. De Chamonix à Salt Lake City* (Méolans-Revel: Editions Déslris, 2001); and R. Mugnier, 'Les sports d'hiver à travers les Jeux olympiques de Chamonix Mont-Blanc en 1924', in Thierry Terret (ed.), *Jeux et sports dans l'histoire*, vol. 2 (Paris: Editions du CTHS, 1992), 311–20.

7. Bertrand Larique, 'L'Economie du tourisme en France des années 1890 à la veille de la Seconde Guerre mondiale: Organisation et développement d'un secteur socio-économique' (PhD diss., Université Bordeaux III, 2006).

8. Christophe Bouneau, 'Chemins de fer et développement régional en France de 1852 à 1937: la contribution de la compagnie du Midi', *Histoire, économie et société* 1 (1990), 95–112.

9. Bernard Debarbieux, *Chamonix-Mont Blanc: 1860–2000* (Servoz: Edimontagne, 2001).

10. Yves Morales, *Une histoire culturelle des sports d'hiver. Le Jura français des origines aux années 1930* (Paris: L'Harmattan, 2007); R. Merle, *Histoire du ski dans le briançonnais* (Paris: Ophrys, 2002); M. Achard, *Histoire du ski et des sports d'hiver dans le Massif du Pilat. Loire-Forez de 1892 à nos jours* (Saint-Etienne: Vanity publishing, 1989); and J.-P. Lombard, *L'histoire du ski dans les Alpes-Maritimes de 1909 à 1939* (Nice: Gilletta, 1993).

11. R. Balseinte, 'Megève ou la transformation d'une agglomération montagnarde par les sports d'hiver', *Alpine Geography Review* 47, no. 2 (1959), 131–224; and Françoise Cribier, 'De Venosc aux Deux-Alpes: une station à double saison', *Revue de Géographie Alpine* 49, no. 2 (1961), 293–318.

12. Marc Boyer, 'Comment étudier le tourisme?', *Ethnologie française* 32, no. 3 (2002), 393–404.

13. Yann Drouet, 'Le ski aux frontières: les conditions de possibilité de l'implantation du ski en France (1872–1913)' (PhD diss., Université Paris XI Orsay, 2004).

14. Drouet and Luciani, 'A l'origine du ski français'.

15. Capitaine Dauphin, 'Le ski dans le briançonnais', *0TCF* (December 1910), 543.

16. Numbers in 1913.

17. Winter tourism committee, sitting of 11 February 1908, *Revue mensuelle du TCF* (March 1908), 101.

18. Catherine Bertho-Lavenir, *La roue et le stylo Comment nous sommes devenus touristes* (Paris: Editions Odile Jacob, 1999).

19. E. Meynot ('En Norvège! Tourisme et ski', *Revue mensuelle du TCF* (October 1909), 454–6) spoke about tourist practices in Norway, in particular to underline the fact that activities did not stop during the winter season; they simply relied on other means of transport: skis or sleighs – the former being also a healthy amusement.

20. For example, an article by C. Soullier ('Grande semaine d'Hiver des Pyrénées', *Revue mensuelle du TCF* (December 1910), 536–7), President of the Tourist Office of Eastern Pyrenees, about the Cerdagne area, a short time before the organization of the Great Winter Week of the

Pyrenees or M. Viollette ('Les Alpes en Hiver', *Revue mensuelle du TCF* (October 1908), 460–5) relating his winter wanderings in the mountain to testify to the accessibility of these places in that season.

21. Larique, *L'Economie du tourisme*.
22. The press review realized by the TCF quoted articles published in *L'Auto, Le Figaro, Le Gaulois, Gil Blas, l'Echo de Paris, la Dépêche de Toulouse, L'Intransigeant, Excelsior, La République du Var, L'Illustration, Le Monde, La Vie* à la *campagne*. Some of these texts were written by delegate members of the TCF.
23. Eleventh international exhibition of automobiles, cycles, and sports in November 1908 (*Revue mensuelle du TCF* (November 1908), 506); Eastern France International exhibition in Nancy in June 1909 (*Revue mensuelle du TCF* (May 1909), 205).
24. *Revue mensuelle du TCF* (December 1909), 540.
25. Larique, *L'Economie du tourisme*, 62.
26. *Revue mensuelle du TCF* (December 1912), 532.
27. *Revue mensuelle du TCF* (April 1912), 177.
28. E. Giraud, 'Du matériel du skieur', *Revue mensuelle du TCF* (December 1908), 555–8.
29. Winter tourism committee, sitting of 8 December 1908, *Revue mensuelle du TCF* (January 1909), 10.
30. Winter tourism committee, sitting of 19 October 1909, *Revue mensuelle du TCF* (November 1909), 487.
31. Winter tourism committee, sitting of 9 May 1908, *Revue mensuelle du TCF* (June 1908), 250.
32. Paul Bernard, *Rush to the Alps: The Evolution of Vacationing in Switzerland* (New York: Columbia University Press, 1978); Susan Barton, *Healthy Living in the Alps: The Origins of Winter Tourism in Switzerland, 1860–1914* (Manchester: Manchester University Press, 2008).
33. Winter tourism committee, sitting of 7 December 1911 and 6 January 1912, *Revue mensuelle du TCF* (January 1912), 54–5.
34. 'Great Winter Week in Auvergne', *Revue mensuelle du TCF* (February 1913), 55.
35. Frédéric Bartczak and Johann Rage, 'L'invention d'une destination touristique: l'exemple de Font-Romeu entre 1903 et 1928', *Revue Espace* 189 (2002), 42–8.
36. Pierre-Olaf Schut and Eric Levet-Labry, 'Le Touring Club de France et la conception d'itinéraires: l'exemple de la Grande Route des Alpes', in Laurent Bourdeau, Pascale Marcotte and Mohamed Habib Saidi (eds), *Actes du colloque Routes touristiques et itinéraires culturels, entre mémoire et développement,* vol. 2 (Québec: Presses de l'Université Laval, 2012), 287–303.
37. Léon Auscher, 'La Grande Semaine d'Auvergne', *Revue mensuelle du TCF* (November 1911), 488.
38. Photography contest of the Great Winter Week in the Pyrénées, *Revue mensuelle du TCF* (May 1911), 199.
39. Hoibian, *Les alpinistes en France*.
40. Abel Ballif, 'Sports d'hiver', *Revue mensuelle du TCF* (March 1909), 100.
41. Winter Tourism Committee, sitting of 12 February 1912, *Revue mensuelle du TCF* (March 1912), 107.
42. Winter Tourism Committee, sitting of 21 February 1913, *Revue mensuelle du TCF* (March 1913), 106.
43. Eric Levet-Labry, 'Aménager les rivières et réduire les risques pour développer le tourisme nautique en France (1904–1924)', *Vertigo* 10 (December 2011), doi:10.4000/vertigo.11396.
44. In 1913, TCF receipts amounted to 1.4 million francs, more than half coming from membership fees (*Revue mensuelle du TCF* (November 1913), 490).
45. Later these pioneer villages in the medium-high mountain would be called 'first generation' winter sport resorts (Jean-Pierre Augustin, *Géographie du sport. Spatialités contemporaines et mondialisation* (Paris: Armand Colin, 2007)).
46. Fabien Locher, *Le savant et la tempête. Étudier l'atmosphère et prévoir le temps au XIXe siècle* (Rennes: Presses Universitaires de Rennes, 2008).
47. *Revue mensuelle du TCF* (December 1909), 540.

48. Only a few correspondents regularly sent in information on the snow conditions, i.e. the Vivarais Tourist Office *(Revue mensuelle du TCF* (March 1913), 111).

49. In 1910, the TCF reported on the operational state of the following weather stations: Saint-Pierre-de-Chartreuse, Chamonix, Thônes, Xonrupt (Gérardmer), Ballon d'Alsace, Sainte-Eulalie, Saint-Agrève, Le Rudlin, Campan, Cauterets, Luchon, Samoëns, Col de Voza, Montlouis, Luz-Saint-Sauveur, Gavarnie, Payolle, Arreau, Eaux-Bonnes, Eaux-Chaudes, le Canigou, and le Mont-Dore (*Revue mensuelle du TCF* (December 1910), 538).

50. An announcement stated that the TCF could give information on the temperatures and snow levels of 22 resorts spread over the various French massifs – Anonymous, 'TCF weather stations', *Revue mensuelle du TCF* (December 1910), 538.

51. Bertrand Larique, 'Les débuts et déboires de l'organisation officielle du tourisme en France: l'expérience malheureuse de l'office national du tourisme (1910–1935)', *Entreprises et Histoire* 47 (2007), 73–92.

52. *Revue mensuelle du TCF* (January 1912), 26–7.

53. *Revue mensuelle du TCF* (October 1910), 457.

54. Mountain Tourism Committee, sitting of 4 October 1910, *Revue mensuelle du TCF* (November 1910), 486.

55. Mountain Tourism Committee, sitting of 19 October 1909, *Revue mensuelle du TCF* (November 1909), 486.

56. Mountain Tourism Committee, sitting of 4 October 1910, *Revue mensuelle du TCF* (November 1910), 486 and Mountain Tourism Committee, sitting of 20 October 1911, *Revue mensuelle du TCF* (November 1911), 491.

57. The TCF Board of directors voted a subsidy of 200 francs for the walking committee in the Fraize Canton (Vosges) meant to restore and mark out the paths of the region and the ski runs. Board of directors 23 December 1912, *Revue mensuelle du TCF* (January 1913), 39.

58. The visits to the Wallon refuge in the Pyrenees from 12 January 1912 to 23 April 1913 were described as follows: 84 caravans, that is 185 tourists. Winter 1912: 10; Summer 1913: 158, Winter 1913: 17. *Revue mensuelle du TCF* (October 1913), 465.

59. Mountain Tourism Committee 1908–1923, National Archives, 20000028/51.

60. Indeed, the Baerenkopf and Rheinkopf refuges were opened in the Vosges in 1910 and also the Wallon and Russel refuges in the Pyrenees in 1911.

61. The *General Directory* was regularly published since 1891 and listed a growing number of hotels.

62. We could not get access to all the guides, but the 1909 edition does not mention this information, which can be found in the 1912 edition.

63. Larique, *L'Economie du tourisme*.

64. An exchange of letters between the TCF and the ministry of war published in the columns of the Club review shows that the TCF requested the creation of the military skiing school in the Vosges. The ministry replied that some officers had been temporarily detached to the Briançon ski school and that they would study the conditions of ski development in the region (*Revue mensuelle du TCF* (May 1909), 200–1).

65. *Revue mensuelle du TCF* (November 1910), 486–7.

66. *Revue mensuelle du TCF* (January 1909), 6.

67. Bouneau, 'Chemins de fer'.

68. *Revue mensuelle du TCF* (January 1914), 20.

69. *PLM Agenda,* Paris-Lyon-Méditerranée Railways, 1914.

70. Marc Boyer, *L'histoire de l'invention du tourisme* (La Tour d'Aygues: Edition de l'Aube, 2000).

71. Heating systems in luxury hotels in Switzerland were mentioned quite early (See L. Auscher, 'Winter Tourism and Winter Sports', *Revue mensuelle du TCF* (March 1908), 97–100).

72. Winter Tourism, *Revue mensuelle du TCF* (April 1909), 155.

73. Hotels in Winter Resorts, *Revue mensuelle du TCF* (November 1913), 492.

74. *Revue mensuelle du TCF* (October 1908), 440.

75. 100 pairs of Norwegian skis were purchased in 1908 (Winter Tourism Committee, sitting of 9 May 1908, *Revue mensuelle du TCF* (June 1908), 249).

76. The *Revue mensuelle du TCF* of December 1910 mentioned that prices ranged from 30 to 40 francs for Norwegian or Swiss skis on page 543.
77. A competition to make skis for children was organized during the winter of 1913–1914. The first prize and an order of 25 pairs of skis were attributed to Abel Rossignol from Voiron (*Revue mensuelle du TCF* (January 1914), 17).
78. M. Rousselet from Salins said that a single series of production was enough to supply equipment to the 28 people who were interested in skiing. M. Albert Mermet from Septmoncel and eight other people from surrounding villages made 62 pairs of skis with the TCF material. M. Lucien Lévigné, mayor of Vollore-Montagne, testified the manufacture of 20 pairs of skis for the villagers. M. Petitcolas, school teacher in Allarmont, declared that 15 local people were equipped with skis made following the instructions given by the TCF (different issues of *Revue mensuelle du TCF* between 1909 and 1914).
79. The first tourist office was created in Grenoble in 1889, one year before the creation of the TCF. Just before the Great War, there were 350 all over France.
80. *Revue mensuelle du TCF* (May 1909), 200.
81. Mountain Tourism Committee, sittings of 7 December 1910 and 16 January 1911, *Revue mensuelle du TCF* (March 1911), 105.
82. 133rd infantry regiment from Les Rousses (Lozère): subsidy (50 francs) and material for ski-making; 152nd infantry regiment from Gérardmer (Vosges): pairs of skis, subsidy (100 francs) and material for ski-making.
83. 10th mountain infantry regiment in Saint-Dié (Vosges): subsidy (100 francs); the 16th infantry regiment from Saint-Etienne (Loire): subsidy (100 francs); and the 35th infantry regiment from Belfort (Terrtioire-de-Belfort): subsidy (25 francs), five pairs of skis, and 25 fasteners.
84. The 3rd (Saint-Dié, Vosges), 5th (Remiremont, Vosges), 6th (Peira-Cava, Alpes-Maritimes), 17th Rambervilliers, Hautes-Alpes), 23rd (Beuil, Alpes-Maritimes) and 30th (Embrun, Hautes-Alpes) mountain infantry regiments; the 18th (Pau, Pyrénées-Atlantiques), 23rd (Bourg-en-Bresse, Ain), 42nd (Belfort, Territoire-de-Belfort), 44th (Bruyères, Vosges), 59th (Pamiers, Ariège), 97th (Chambéry, Savoie), 109th (Remiremont, Vosges), and 112th (Entrevaux, Alpes-de-Haute-Provence) infantry regiments and the 14th brigade in Isère.
85. Mountain Tourism Committee, 1908–1923, National Archives, 20000028/51.

Disclosure statement

No potential conflict of interest was reported by the author.

Stakeholders, Challenges and Issues at a Co-Hosted Youth Olympic Event: Lessons Learned from the European Youth Olympic Festival in 2015

Elsa Kristiansen, Anna-Maria Strittmatter and Berit Skirstad

ABSTRACT

The 12th European Youth Olympic Festival (EYOF) was arranged in Austria and Liechtenstein in January 2015. By using a stakeholder framework, the study aims to: (a) identify and differentiate between primary and secondary stakeholders based on their level of influence in planning, implementation and impact of the event; and (b) analyze the challenges and issues caused by the co-hosting. Qualitative data stemming from interviews, observations and document analysis indicate that EYOF is a less formalized event with a scaled down budget. The local stakeholders turned out to have most to gain and were willing to pay for such an event. Therefore, the Organizing Committee involved local sponsors, companies and communities, who became core or primary stakeholders, whereas the usual IOC core stakeholders played a reduced role. Major challenges in co-hosting were the coordination and administration of a border, two currencies, transportation and accommodation. EYOF as an international event might not have international influence, but it may have a sustainable impact on the communities due to the co-host. This implies that co-hosting is a good model for future Olympic hosts if one wants to attract smaller countries, and have the benefits of cost-reduction, strengthening the community and cross-border relations.

Introduction

'The European Winter Youth Olympic Festival (EYOF) jointly hosted by Austria and Liechtenstein …will serve as a historic guide to the Olympic Movement of how countries can share events', said chief executive Philipp Groborsch before the opening.[1]

The 12th winter EYOF was the first-ever Olympic event co-hosted by two countries and consequently had a dual organizing committee with representatives of both the Austrian Olympic Committee and the Olympic Committee of Lichtenstein. A previous instance of sharing was when the equestrian events of the Melbourne 1956 Summer Olympics had to take place in Stockholm because of quarantine regulations. UEFA also has had two countries organizing their European Football Championship three times (Belgium and the Netherlands in 2000; Austria and Switzerland in 2008; and Poland and Ukraine in 2012) and

FIFA has tried out the model once with South Korea and Japan hosting the World Cup in 2002. This co-hosting approach was pioneering in the history of the International Olympic Committee (IOC) and exemplifies the IOC's ongoing renewal of the Olympic Movement. With the adoption of Agenda 2020 at the 127th IOC Session in Monaco, the IOC approved 40 recommendations for the strategic roadmap of the Olympic Movement in the ensuing years. Subsequently, the dual host country approach is now accepted and encouraged after an ongoing public debate 'on costs versus benefits ... ensued'.[2] The focus on a lasting legacy from the Olympic event in the respective host city and nation has not only gained interest in the Olympic movement,[3] but also has become an increasing research interest among sport scholars.[4] As the co-hosting is a new phenomenon, in this paper we point out stakeholders, issues and challenges from the recently hosted 2015 Winter EYOF. By doing so, we draw on the impact on the local community present during the organization and implementation phase and look for a possible legacy caused by the dual host. While we know that an event organization is impacted by a large amount of stakeholders,[5] a co-hosted event might involve other stakeholders than single hosts which can be important for a positive outcome of the event. For this purpose, stakeholder theory serves as a conceptual framework enabling us to elaborate upon the dynamic stakeholder relationships and the evolving issues[6] with which the 2015 EYOF Organizing Committee had to deal with when hosting the event in two countries. The concept of Stakeholder theory has previously been found appropriate to study the organization of sport events.[7]

The paper is structured as follows. In the next section, we present relevant background information and statistics about EYOF 2015 and its hosts. Section three explains the conceptual framework of stakeholder theory followed by a presentation of the qualitative methods applied in this study. In the fourth section, we present the findings and discuss whether the organization of EYOF can serve as a model for future hosts of Olympic events. The article concludes with a summary of the main results and recommendations for further research.

Contextual Background: EYOF 2015 and the Host Region

The EYOF was launched in 1991 by an initiative of the former IOC President Rogge in order to promote Olympism among youth. The event is hosted biennially in a summer and a winter edition. The participants are between 14 and 18 years and nominated by their respective NOCs. In the period 25–30 January 2015, the 12th EYOF was arranged in Vorarlberg (Austria) and Liechtenstein. EYOF is organized on behalf of the European Olympic Committee (EOC) which has the exclusive rights to the event and is under the patronage of the IOC. For many young athletes EYOF is their first meeting with international competition,[8] and most of all, a multisport event with 45 participating nations. Only Albania, Azerbaijan, Israel and Kazakhstan of the EOC members did not send a team to the festival. For an entire week, 900 athletes, together with 600 officials, 1200 volunteers and 150 accredited media representatives were assembled.[9] Compared to other IOC organized events, the EOC-organized EYOF is a smaller and scaled down event with only eight sports: Alpine skiing (Malbun, Liechtenstein for individual competitions and St Gallenkirch, Austria for the mixed team); biathlon (Burserberg, Austria); cross-country (Steg, Liechtenstein); figure skating (Dornbirn, Austria); ice hockey (Tschagguns, Austria); Nordic combined (Gaschurn,

Austria); ski jumping (Tschagguns, Austria); and snowboard cross (Schruns, Austria). In addition, the Winter Youth Olympic Games (YOG) has bobsleigh, skeleton, curling, freestyle skiing and snowboarding, luge, short track and speed skating. Consequently, only four international sport federations were involved in EYOF. Table 1 shows a comparison with the other European multisport and IOC events.

The region, Vorarlberg and Liechtenstein, is embedded in the so-called countries-quadrangle bordering on Germany, Austria and Switzerland. Due to its location in the Alps, the region is a popular tourist destination. The official language is German. Vorarlberg is one of the nine states of the federal republic of Austria, located in the very west of the country with a population of 379,621 residing in an area of 2600 square kilometres. The other part of the region, Liechtenstein, is a constitutional hereditary monarchy based on a parliamentary democracy.[10] Liechtenstein has an area of 160 square kilometres, with the equivalent of one tenth of the population of Austria as of 30 June 2014.[11] Due to its small size, political as well as economic bonds with its neighbouring countries are important for Liechtenstein, reflecting its close relationship to Vorarlberg.[12] On the other side of the border, Vorarlberg has previously hosted several international sports events organized by the International Ski Federation (FIS). World Cups in Alpine, Snowboard cross and Freestyle snowboarding have been organized annually for several years. As a result, the OC met an experienced winter sports region.

Table 1. Differences between the IOC's two winter events, the 2014 Olympic Winter Games and the 2012 Winter Youth Olympic Games. The EOC winter event EYOF and the new EOC event, the European Games, are also presented.

	World organized		European organized	
	OG Sochi 2014	YOG Innsbruck 2012	EYOF Voralberg Liechtenstein 2015	European Games Baku 2015
Candidates cities (short list)	3	2	2	1
Olympic Villages	2	1	32 hotels	1
Participating NOCs	88	69	45	50
Medal winning NOCs	26	29	17	40
Int. federations	7	7	4	
Sports	15	15	8	20
Duration (days)	17	10	5	18
Medal events	98	63	30	98
Athletes	2566	1020	900	6000
Competition venues	12	6	9	18
Spectators*	1.1 million ticket holders & 4.1 billion television viewers	110,000	30,000	649,204 ticket holders & 600,000 tv viewers
Media/press representatives*	10,000	800	150	1248
Volunteers*	25,000	1357	1200	12,500
Costs	US$51 billion	€23.7 million	€6.5 million	

Note: Sources of information for the table are listed at EOC, 'Peace and Sport Together with 2015 Winter EYOF to Promote Olympic Values' (European Olympic Committee, 11 January 2015), http://www.eurolympic.org/en/news/2947-peace-and-sport-together-with-2015-winter-eyof-to-promote-olympic-values.html (accessed 23 March 2015); EYOF 2015, 'Schulungsunterlagen' (European Youth Olympic Festival 2015, 2014); EYOF 2015, 'Volunteer Training' (European Youth Olympic Festival 2015, 2014); IOC, 'Factsheet. Youth Olympic Games. Update December 2011' (International Olympic Committee, 2011), http://www.eurolympic.org/en/sports-events/the-european-games/baku-2015-facts-and-figures.html.
*Approximations.

Conceptual Framework

The conceptual framework is based on a stakeholder approach. Stakeholder theory allows for descriptive, instrumental and normative analyses of the stakeholders, that is, the various individuals, groups and organizations which affect or are impacted by the actions of a focal organization.[13] Stakeholder theory has been used by various sport event researchers to describe and analyze the event, the organizing committee and its stakeholders.[14] Additionally, Hanstad and colleagues have previously demonstrated that using a stakeholder approach helped to organize, analyze and develop an understanding of Youth Olympic Games compared to Olympic Games.[15] When analyzing the YOG, four key stakeholder groupings were found: the host core stakeholders (host governments, local communities in which the different competitions took place and the organizing committee); the international core stakeholders (the sport organizations and the delegations including athletes, coaches and other mission staff); the sponsors and media (primary for the OG but relatively absent from the YOG scene); and finally, parents and other stakeholders.[16]

To classify what type of stakeholder one is, Clarkson used the terms 'primary' and 'secondary' stakeholder:[17]

> A primary stakeholder group is one without whose continuing participation the corporation cannot survive as a going concern … Secondary stakeholder groups are defined as those who influence or affect, or are influenced or affected by, the corporation, but they are not engaged in transaction with the corporation and are not essential for its survival.[18]

It is quite possible for an organization to have more than one primary stakeholder and the relationship between the organization and its stakeholder is usually mutually beneficial.[19] Certain attributes have to be present in order to define whether a stakeholder is a primary or secondary stakeholder.[20] Mitchell et al. defined the characteristics as follows: (1) power could be coercive, utilitarian or normative; (2) legitimacy would be found when a stakeholder's claim is perceived as being appropriate, socially acceptable, expected based on individual, organizational or social norms; and (3) urgency would be felt when the stakeholder's claim is perceived as time sensitive and critical or highly important. They further underline that power is transitory; it can be acquired as well as lost. Latent power exists though, 'the exercise of stakeholder power is triggered by conditions that are manifest in the other two attributes of the relationship'.[21] Furthermore, it is important to understand that these attributes are not constant but are dynamic and changing in strength. Despite this, Freeman's definition still prevails where the stakeholder comprises 'any group or individual who can affect or is affected by the achievements of the organization's objectives'.[22] In sport, the stakeholders are interpreted very broadly to include, 'for example, media, fans, coaches, athletes, sponsors, and government, as well as 'members'.[23]

When reviewing the salience level of YOG stakeholders, Hanstad and colleagues concluded:

> The general list of OG stakeholders is the same as for YOG: host governments, community, organizing committee, delegations, sport organizations, sponsors, media, and other stakeholders. However, salience levels were found to differ. For example, main drivers of the OG – sponsors and the media – were not found to be as critical for YOG. This did not seem to affect the current survival of the event but it is not to say that the future survival of the event is not at stake without these stakeholders' resources.[24]

Since EYOF is part of the Olympic youth family, we assume that that the relative salience level is closer to YOG than the OG – but smaller due to the fewer number of sports involved, and therefore fewer International Federations (IFs) etc. Additionally, the ownership of the event is held by EOC, which is one of the five continental regions which comprise the IOC. EYOF is limited to European athletes compared to the YOG which is for youth from all over the world. Further, the co-hosting of EYOF is assumed to represent a difference compared to the YOG. EOC is what Fassin calls a 'real' stake owner, who has a legitimate claim in the organization and deserves a stake.[25] Researching stakeholders can be conducted on the basis of three different relationships: first, based on the organization itself; second, based on the stakeholders; and third, rooted in the relationship between organization and stakeholders.[26] Our study is based on the focal organization of EYOF, the OC, and looks at its operational and structural challenges as a co-host organization related to stakeholder issues.

Methods

We used a qualitative approach of the 2015 EYOF in this exploratory study of the first co-hosted Winter EYOF as we wanted to explore the event organizing committees and the other stakeholders' perspectives. The data collection consisted of observations, interviews and document analyses, and the techniques for the three sampling methods are described below.

Observations

The first two authors were present during the festival and had the opportunity to observe; one as solely a researcher while the other also worked as a venue operations coordinator volunteer at one of the venues. The aim of these observations was to see if a co-hosting created any observable challenges for the organizer. As a result, our collective role as observers was not limited to areas we could access with our accreditation level (competition sites, ceremonies and the congress centre) which gave us access to the general, spectator areas for these venues – but also to meetings with OC members of sports operations, venue operations, coaches meetings, jury of competition and volunteer trainings. As observers, we managed to collect data and experience the meaning of events as they occurred. Together, we visited all the competition sites in Austria and Liechtenstein, the opening and closing ceremonies, flower ceremonies and medal ceremonies. The field notes we assembled were important when preparing the interview guide since additional questions were included based on observations made during EYOF in order to explore, explain and/or verify observations.

Interviews

After obtaining approval from the Norwegian Research Council, informed consent to use material was obtained from all participants before conducting face-to-face interviews. At the beginning of each interview, participants were informed that the information they provided would remain anonymous, and that they could terminate the interviews at any time. We conducted a convenience and purposeful sampling procedure,[27] and interviewed six members of the organizing committee (including the CEO). Together they were responsible for the major operations of the OC. One NOC representative was also interviewed. In addition many informal conversations were held with different stakeholders involved in hosting this event. These informal talks offered a greater understanding of the research issue, and the result of spending time in the research situation provided insight into the daily operations which otherwise could be difficult. The interviews were conducted both during EYOF and later via Skype.

The semi-structured interview guide for the OC members focused on the issues and challenges of staging an event within two host countries, such as the bidding process, daily work within the OC, financial issues with two different currencies and money-flow, logistics (transport and accommodation), the nine venues, food and language issues. A flexible interview guide was used by researchers which allowed for reordering of questions in order to better probe participants' responses. Follow-up questions were used in order to elicit in-depth responses from the participants. The interviews ended with a process feedback question, 'What should I have asked you about, and do you have anything to add?'. Interviews lasted between 45 and 80 minutes. The interviews were conducted in English.

Documents

Documents provided by the OC such as the *Chefs de Mission Manual*, *Technical Manual* as well as volunteer training manuals provided a source of data about *inter alia* organizational and structural processes as well as policy procedures. These documents were a supplement to observations and interviews as well as providing the basis for further questions in interviews. In order to investigate the role of the media (one of the stakeholders), we searched for documents both in the national database for all Norwegian newspapers (called 'Retriever') and internationally, the daily website (Insidethegames) for EYOF in 2015. Little was written about the festival in the Norwegian media, and a total of 42 short notes/articles; 23 before and 19 after EYOF. None of these short notes/articles were in the nation-wide media, indicating the lack of public interest in the event. Many of the newspapers confused EYOF with the Youth Olympic Games.

Analysis

We used several methods to record our observations. Most important were the field notes where personal impressions were written down alongside reflective notes. Long reports were not written; rather, it was a process whereby seemingly different or important aspects of EYOF stood out, and would be noted and then discussed between the members of the research group. These notes were subsequently important for the interview guide for the post-Games interviews with members of the organizing committee. The interviews were tape recorded and transcribed. An examination through content analysis was deemed preferable when analyzing the additional interview data.[28] The coding of raw passages was carried out according to a classification scheme, and were used to unobtrusively explore large amounts of textual information in order to ascertain the trends and patterns of the words used, their relationships and the structures and discourses of communication.[29] We used the stakeholders identified from previous research as a starting point in the analysis.[30] The researchers read and coded the raw material in main categories based on topics in the interview guide, and elaborated subcategories. In an effort to ensure accuracy in data collection, two of the OC members received a first draft of the article which resulted in clarifications and additional information. Using data from several sources - observations, interviews and documents - increased the trustworthiness of the findings.

Results and Discussion

The discussion focuses around what we considered to be primary stakeholders of the event – the host core stakeholder represented by the OC and the local communities. The international core stakeholders play an important role for the OC but are less salient to the EYOF than they are to the YOG. The other two stakeholder groups found in YOG,[31] the sponsors and media, parents and other stakeholders were even less salient for this event compared to YOG by becoming secondary/involuntary EYOF stakeholders. This is examined in the second part of the discussion where EYOF is compared with the other multi events hosted by the IOC and EOC to present the context of EYOF under the Olympic system. Next we move on to the local community as a stakeholder with normative power for this event. In the final section we revisit some of the usual issues and challenges when hosting an event such as budget and finances, venues, accommodation and transportation.[32] Finally, we present some of the challenges presented by the OC members and the point of view from one NOC representative is added. In conclusion, implications of how the co-host experience by EYOF can serve as a model of good practice for future hosts will be outlined.

The Characteristics and the Uniqueness of a Co-Hosting OC

Since EYOF was co-hosted by two countries, both of these were represented at all structural levels of the OC. The host core stakeholders for the OC consisted of host governments and communities and the set-up was quite unique and more complex than if there had been only one host country as in the YOG.[33] Of these, the governments, both NOCs and the EOC had normative and coercive power which means that without them the event would not have taken place. The local communities were the stakeholder with normative power having high influence due to their economical contribution. According to one OC member, the idea to co-host the event came from the President of the NOC in Liechtenstein. He reached out to Austria because Lichtenstein was too small to host it alone, and the Host-City Contract was signed during the YOG in 2012. The operating company settled in June 2012 under the title *Europäisches Olympisches Jugendfestival Vorarlberg-Liechtenstein 2015 GmbH*, and functioned as the legal umbrella of the OC in Vorarlberg/Liechtenstein.[34] The General Assembly consisted of several stakeholders from the two countries with representatives from NOCs Austria and Liechtenstein, the Sport Ministry of Liechtenstein, the County of Vorarlberg, the Department of Sports Vorarlberg, the Cable Way Company and the mayors of Schruns and Tschagguns. Altogether Austria had 68% of the shares (Federal State of Vorarlberg 25%, Austrian Olympic Committee 17%, Schruns City 13%, and Tschagguns City 13%), and Liechtenstein 32% (Principality of Liechtenstein 15% and Liechtenstein Olympic Sports Association [LOSV] 17%). Under these was the supervisory board which made the final decision concerning finances as well as other items according to our interview with the CEO.

Even though Liechtenstein is represented in the top management of the OC, the organizational chart does not mirror the reality:

> On the organizational chart we wanted to show that Liechtenstein is also involved in the top management. In reality he [managing director from Liechtenstein] was not in the top management. The managing director from Liechtenstein was not responsible for the budget; he was not even present in the office. It was more a marketing move to put this position onto the organizational chart to show that both countries are equally represented. (OC member 1)

The two NOCs had very different powers. While Liechtenstein's NOC seemed to have a more passive role in the organization being guided by and under a kind of supervision of the Austria NOC, Liechtenstein's power can be interpreted as normative. The OC comprised 24 members, a rather small organization, but it functioned well as an operational unit. The administration, accounting and HR issues were under the direction of the CEO. The former managing director was replaced by a CEO, who came into the OC 10 months prior to the event. The OC, with a mean age of 32, had altogether experience from 16 Olympic Games.

With this event, the OC members found themselves compiling manuals where they drew upon their previous experiences with Sochi 2014 and Innsbruck 2012. As one OC member (2) said: 'We did everything the YOG way!'. Furthermore, and due to their experience, they 'increased the level of service because half of us had these function and experience from the 2012 YOG'. Apparently, an experienced staff is important when developing Olympic events even further, particularly when co-hosting.

The OC members emphasized that EYOF was a 'low budget event'. Due to the absence of important stakeholders as international sponsors, media/TV and spectators, the available funds were limited, and therefore they could not afford to hire senior event managers in the OC. Instead, the management decided to employ many young people with experience from previous Olympic events, such as the YOG. The importance of having experience from the YOG was stressed by all OC members. The experience of these 'Games gypsies' was important because of the restructuring which occurred immediately prior to the event, and the lack of money; all employees had to take on more tasks than intended at the beginning.[35]

As the main financial benefactor and as the more experienced country in hosting major sports events, Austria took the lead in the organization. Since Austria contributed €1.8 million and Liechtenstein 700,000 euro to the budget, the inequality was also reflected in the location of the venues (two in Liechtenstein and seven in Austria). This imbalance was accepted by both countries.

The International Core Stakeholders in the Scaled Down Event

The international core stakeholders previously found for YOG were the IFs and the delegations including athletes, coaches and other mission staff – and of course the IOC.[36] The IFs are also in this case as in other events responsible for the competitions following international rules, so they exercised normative and coercive power. As the IOC is a central stakeholder of YOG, so is EOC for EYOF, and they are both what Fassin labels as stake-owners without whose support these events would not be organized,[37] something which stresses their saliency towards the OC.[38] However, the EYOF is a smaller event in all ways, and the Olympic Charter which provides the rules and guidelines for the organization of the OG and YOG does not apply to an EOC event (see Table 1 for a comparison of these events).[39]

When interviewing the OC members about the importance of the different international stakeholders, only the EOC was mentioned – but more because of the EYOF Manager's role as a support person with normative knowledge rather than actual influence. Since there was no event manual provided by the EOC that the OC had to follow, the coercive power on the organization of the event is not as strong as the IOC's power over the YOG. The NOCs were naturally key clients, but their early concern raised before and after the event concerning the travel distance, did not affect the decisions based on the financial situation and their loyalty to the region. Nevertheless, their support and positive attitude towards the event was necessary for the OC and resulted in a successful event which classified the NOCs as primary stakeholders of both normative and coercive power. The athletes, who are also grouped as international stakeholders, were of course, visible at the different venues during the competitions. The OC admitted that they 'read Agenda 2020 carefully' [both OC members 4 and 5],[40] and had to rethink what they did in Innsbruck as this was an even smaller event with fewer stakeholders.

During EYOF, the four IFs of the eight participating winter sports were present; the International Ski Federation (FIS), International Skating Union (ISU), the International Ice Hockey Federation (IIHF) and the international Biathlon Union (IBU). Further international stakeholders were the athletes and the NOCs from 45 European countries which participated at EYOF. As can be seen in Table 1, the number of participating athletes is not that different from YOG, and this means that each sport can send a bigger team to EYOF compared to YOG. The legitimacy of the relationship between the international stakeholders and the OC, and the ability of the international stakeholders to influence the OC enables one to define the international stakeholders as moderately salient for the EYOF.[41]

According to the OC, there were 160 accredited journalists from 22 nations at the event. Nevertheless, we only observed a few in action at the venues. As well, few of them wrote for an international audience and many relied on what the organizers produced themselves. Additionally, the events were also covered by local newspapers and relied on the pictures that parents sent home to local news outlets. As with YOG, sponsors and media were secondary stakeholders at the festival.[42] They were not engaged in any transactions and therefore are not compellingly necessary for the survival of the organization,[43] and they did not see their task as reporting from the events because no one was willing to pay in order to see the competitions, and that is a signal to the wider society. We observed a journalist from one of the Norwegian Sports schools who had student-athletes participating in many sports. He covered the event and sent stories to their respective local newspapers for free. While some of the papers accepted this offer, the major newspapers were not even interested in a free story! No one really cared what was going on, therefore the media was not present and the sponsors also did not see what business it was for them. In contrast to the IOC-organized events, EYOF as an EOC event had more regional sponsors, which will be elaborated upon below.

Local Community and the Citizens as 'Core' Stakeholder

The local community and its citizens were mentioned as core clients in the interviews:

> We early realized that the communication to the citizens were of major importance for the OC and realization of the festival. They are our core group to plan for; it is not the parents or other spectators. We learned this in Innsbruck, so we put some effort into the music festival at the medal plaza [held in Schruns every evening], sport might not be not as interesting for the locals. So since EYOF is a festival, you need to include the other clients there and offer non-sporting activities too. (OC member 3)

The importance of the local population was a repeated theme in the interviews. In order to get the citizens to support the event, the OC had to sell the messages of the Olympic Movement, and they put lots of effort into communicating the notion that money which is spent by the local community would directly be an advantage for them, and that all new building constructions in the area were in synchronization with 'the already existing city planning' (OC member 1). For that reason, the OC involved citizens to actively help shape the event showing that spending the millions of Euro was of advantage to the area: 'We needed to deliver a good event for the athletes and for the citizens' (OC member 1). The OC strategically used local companies as sponsors:

> In the Olympic Games, there are many strong and resourceful partners, though; this is not the same here. As we had supportive providers in the local region, such as the local car owner, we chose to use them as sponsors. As a result we ended up with many minor local sponsors from the communities, which resulted in more paperwork and contract writing. (OC member 7)

Due to the tight budget of the OC, the dependency on the host region increased. As the main provider of resources came from the region, the saliency of the local community for the OC is very considerable. Based on Clarkson's classification of stakeholder salience stating that the relationship between an organization and its primary stakeholders is based on a high level of interdependence, we identify the local community as the core stakeholder of EYOF.[44] The fact that the OC gave priority to the local community's demands confirms our argument that the local community is of high salience towards the OC.[45] This argument is also proven by the coordination of accommodation within the region.

The strategic decision was to not have one Olympic village but to use the hotels along the Montafon valley as accommodation for all participants, visitors and staff of EYOF. The OC saw this move as an advantage since the hotel owners could function as 'multiplicators' for event communication and promotion. Further, profit would directly go to the citizens of the region which was important in strengthening local support for the OC. The inclusion of the region was also visible with the torch relay where the schools were very much involved in the organization of the event. The OC worked together with the schools to establishing the torch relay throughout the entire Montafon valley which resulted in a positive attitude towards the events among youth in the region.

In contrast to Innsbruck, where YOGOC's has easy access to international students,[46] the recruitment of the unpaid volunteers was more challenging. The OC received 3600 applications but required just 1200 people. The problem was that they needed bilingual volunteers who could speak both English and German. Three-quarters of the volunteers came from Voralberg. For the venues, the OC recruited experienced volunteers from the local communities who had worked with sports events in the Vorarlberg region before.[47] Furthermore, several schools sent pupils as volunteers to EYOF. While some classes were supervised by their teachers who also functioned as volunteers together with their class, some students could assign their work during EYOF as an internship which is mandatory in their school programme. The goal of the regional governments and the OC was to engage the local citizenry; the inhabitants of Vorarlberg and Liechtenstein played a very active part in shaping the event and making it a success. For many pupils it was very exciting to contribute to an Olympic event. If it had not been for the school children who were taken by bus to the events, there would not have been many spectators. The parents, together with the school children filled up the stadiums by way of free entrance. Altogether 30,000 people visited the Games during the five days of the event according to the organizer. However, the two observers among the authors doubt that this figure is correct.

The festival was not only seen as a boost for the local community but also as catalyst for strengthening the already-existing cross-border cooperation between Austria and Liechtenstein, and hopefully as a stimulus for sport and tourism. Even though the NOC from the two countries had already been co-operating for many years,[48] the cross-border relationship was reinforced. Austria took on the role of the 'big brother', taking the lead in the organization and pushing Liechtenstein up, in order to strengthen the whole Montafon region. For Austria's part, most of the responsibility was left to Voralberg, one of the nine Austrian regions:

> Originally, the region did not have really close ties, even though the distance in itself is only seven kilometers, but you have to go around the mountains with a car. Mountains divide people. They did not have a close relationship before, but this changed it. They had so many meetings that they feel more united now. (OC member 1)

EYOF seems to have strengthened cross-border relations in advance and during the event which was not taken for granted but required hard work by the OC. It is too early to judge whether this strong relationship will remain after the event, but the positive experience from the host region and the OC members enable us to assume that it will be so. In the following section we present the challenges that the OC as co-hosting organization had to face and cope with.

The Issues and Extra Challenges for a Co-Host (OC): The 'Invisible Border'

(a) Communication

The opening ceremony focused on the historic moment and the advantages that 'two nations and two different mindsets' hosted the festival together. The two national anthems played, two official opening speeches, and so on, and artists from both sides of the border contributed to the ceremony. The proximity of the two countries separated by mountains was obvious when present; hence, it was also pertinent that the challenges for the dual host organizing were mentioned with a smile in the opening. The host organization accredited their success to the cross-border *communication*. It was repeatedly stressed that two countries can host an event successfully if they communicate concerning the challenges such as the one elaborated upon above. However, when interviewing the members of OC, budget, venues, logistics, housing, transportation and the volunteers, were mentioned as challenges for the festival. Further, the fact that two countries were watching the work of the OC put pressure on the organization.

(b) Finances and Two Currencies

Budgets are always a major task for any OC.[49] This event was no exception, and the budget, money-flow and custom issues caused the OC hard times. EYOF had a total budget of €6.5 million provided by various partners and shareholders: Republic of Austria €1.8 million, County of Vorarlberg €1.8 million, Principality of Liechtenstein €0.7 million, Participation fees €1 million, Sponsors, EOC. In comparison, the 2012 YOG budget was €11 million. The new CEO was met with unsolved cash-flow issues, and a lack of money (€2 million). In addition, in January 2015 the Swiss National Bank suddenly changed the fixed currency exchange rate and no longer based it on the euro. For two countries with different currencies (Liechtenstein with CHF and Austria with the euro), this naturally created an unexpected situation. The OC did not foresee such a development, and it naturally affected all their budget points and they had to adjust to this new economic development. Another challenge was to get the money prior to the event from Liechtenstein:

> In Liechtenstein they have a different mindset. They did not understand that we needed cash before we could give them the invoice. But in order to organize such an event you need cash first and then you provide the invoices afterwards. It took many discussions with Liechtenstein to make them understand how the money flow works. (OC member 2)

What made the co-hosting particularly challenging was that Liechtenstein was not part of the European Union, and customs become an issue. When sending uniforms for volunteers from the headquarters in Schruns to Liechtenstein, they had to pay duty. Nevertheless, following the efforts of the CEO, reimbursements were made. This being a practical issue, a co-host organization nevertheless depends on both countries being equally involved in every part of the process.

(c) Venues

Another challenge was the venues, particularly deciding which of the many available venues to use for EYOF challenged the OC in the preparation of the event. As Liechtenstein infrastructure is best suited for hosting cross-country skiing and alpine skiing, these venues were easily agreed. While Austria paid two thirds of the total budget and Liechtenstein one third, this division was also decisive in that seven venues were assigned to Austria and two to Liechtenstein. However, it took until May 2014 before all the venues were agreed upon; in particular where to host the biathlon was a major issue.

There were also challenges for the venue managers and venue operations managers. Instead of purchasing services from bigger, well organized and renowned companies, the OC members tried to use local companies as much as possible:

> One major task at the beginning was to map the different local companies where the venues were situated because we wanted to use them. We wanted to support them and they know the area here. Every company here in Voralberg was uncertain whether the event was good for the region, so we had to convince them and sell in the festival. This process was time consuming. We tried to fill as many functions as possible with local ones first, but in the end we [i.e. OC] also had to use some outsiders as well (Vienna, Munich). The distance between the venues also made the job harder. (OC member 6)

A final stakeholder important to the smooth running of the venues was the military. Several OC members mentioned this as a resource that made their job possible, especially in the set-up of the venues when the area was affected by heavy snowfall in the beginning and during the event. Without the manpower of the military, venues would not have been in place in time after difficult weather conditions at the start of the event. The unpredicted challenges which came up made the OC dependent on the military which we therefore can interpret as stakeholders with urgency.

(d) Accommodation

'Accommodation was challenging from the start. We started working a year before the festival, and some even cancelled their internship because of the lack of place to stay' (OC member 5). First of all, the hired organizing committee of 24 individuals needed a place to stay for their year-long contract. The next step was to accommodate all the others, and it was underlined by the other member of the OC that it did not make it easier that it was the 'Montafon valley's busiest period'. Early on, a partnership with the Tourist Office Montafon was made which 'worked out great'. Montafon was completely booked during the festival.[50] The accommodation manager made contact with all the 32 hotels that housed the 45 national teams. Even though EYOF and YOG usually have Olympic Villages for the

NOCs to stay in such as with the OG,[51] the infrastructure in the Schruns-Tschagguns region made it almost impossible. Originally an Olympic Village in Schruns/Tschagguns within walking distance to the training and competition venues was included in the first bidding document for EYOF 2015[52]:

> Unfortunately for the athletes it changed, because there is no place to build it. I do not know how they come to the conclusion to use the hotels, but it was a better choice. In comparison, YOG is bigger, there was no place or reuse of such a building in the Montafon valley; we would not have the same sustainability or use of such a building after the games. (OC member 2)

The NOCs did not find this an optimal solution since the athletes, whom the competition actually is for, missed out on the Olympic atmosphere which so many athletes often encounter as the most memorable experience.[53] But when the OC went for this solution, the NOC representative admitted: 'The people at the hotel took really good care of us; they followed up on all our requests'.

(e) Transportation

The actual transportation logistics was solved by a team consisting of four persons, and from the interviews it became clear early that transportation was their 'baby':

> We had a lot of challenges, not only because we consisted of two countries, but we were a small team as well. The transfer between Liechtenstein and Austria had to go through a border which makes things harder as the customs involved a lot of paperwork. (OC member 5)

NOCs and volunteers had to cross the border daily. In order to make the crossing run more smoothly, their accreditation with pictures and pictogram functioned as a passport. 'As all parties were informed how this would work, this never became an issue' (OC member 3).

A hot topic before the festival started, was the distance between accommodation and venue – quite a distance for the athletes with the busiest schedules. Prior to the event, the NOCs raised concerns over this issue; some athletes actually had a two hour bus drive back and forth if they were competing in Liechtenstein (cross-country skiing in Steg and alpine skiing in Malbun). 'Transport is also a clear point where two countries so far away from the highway, but not so far in reality will struggle – you cannot move the mountains; two hours are two hours', was expressed by an OC member. The OC was aware of the concern, and they 'added cars for athletes' (OC member 2). Nevertheless, the sentiment was that the solutions were not optimal, and that the first co-hosted event needs to be improved if this is to be a tradition:

> We will give EOC a clear feedback on the transportation and logistics of this event. They cannot assign a championship to a host organizer who makes it so complicated. We did not find it acceptable, but we accepted it and stayed positive during the championship. But we left the hotel [at] 6 am and got back at 6 pm; we hardly saw each other – so we are concerned that the athletes did not have the experience we wanted them to have. Maybe the competitions should have been two days longer? (NOC Representative)

As observers, we experienced firsthand the traffic jam through Feldkirch when crossing the border. In addition, the travel distance made it very hard to attend more than one sport event a day for spectators. This also had consequences for the athletes due to a compact schedule filled with training, qualification and final days as well as single and team competitions who had limited time to watch each other. This has previously been pointed out as one of the best experiences for athletes during a multisport event.[54]

Conclusion and Implications: 'Think Before You Bid'

Informed by the stakeholder approach,[55] we first identified the primary stakeholders (i.e. local communities, NOCs of Austria and Liechtenstein), and secondary stakeholders (the sponsors and media, parents and other stakeholders) of EYOF 2015. In between, we grouped the international core stakeholders (NOCs and IFs) as salient to the OC but with limited influence on the event organization. A special role determines the EOC as stake owner.[56] In addition, an interesting finding was the importance of the local communities which turned out to be *core* or *primary* stakeholders with high salience towards the OC, in contrast to other Olympic events where local communities are less salient. This was caused by the scaled-down budget and lack of technical manuals for the EYOF which forced the 2015 EYOFOC to choose creative options and gave them the opportunity to obtain resources from local stakeholders. The local stakeholders were those who had most to gain and were willing to pay for such an event. Therefore, the OC involved the local sponsors, local companies and local community in order to create enthusiasm for the project.

The flip side of the local involvement was that the OC members had to deal with an increasing number of small stakeholders compared to events organized by the IOC where the usual core stakeholders had a reduced role. Hence, the local community appears to have more salience and power upon the EYOF than on YOG.[57] The voluntary and willing involvement of the citizens due to the strategically smart work of the OC led to region-wide success which will not disappear as quickly as it was formed. Even though the EOC as a responsible umbrella organization for the EYOF could be assumed to highly influence the OC, they did not coerce their power on the OC but rather served as adviser with normative knowledge. Since no one seemed to be interested in paying for the EYOF in order to watch the athletes competing, neither spectators, media nor sponsors had much salience for the OC.

The second aim of the investigation was to identify the challenges and issues the co-hosting EYOFOC had to deal with. The experience of junior staff (the event nomads) was a clear advantage when finding solutions for the issues and challenges which escalated since this was a co-hosted event. The major challenges in co-hosting were logistics with transportation, accommodation and the coordination and administration of two currencies and the EU border. As Jack recently pointed out: 'Multisport events are an expensive business!'.[58] Even worse, they are an intangible turn of investments. The 2015 EYOFOC addressed the issue of the 'escalating costs' of the Games elegantly,[59] though it was a process that made the CEO utter 'think before you bid' to future host nations. This goal was achieved by increasing the importance of several local communities in both countries, possibly to the cost of international stakeholders, though local criticism was reduced and an apparent local enthusiasm was amplified. The interviewees also emphasized that it was important to have just one leader, not two.

In conclusion, EYOF – as an international event – might not have international influence, but it may have a sustainable impact on the community and a possible legacy of cooperation between the two countries resulting from the co-host organization. The co-hosting of EYOF appears to be a good model for future Olympic hosts due to advantages such as cost-reduction, strengthening the local communities and cross-border relations.[60] The 2015 EYOFOC illustrated that smaller countries which would not otherwise be able to stage the event alone due to economic, logistic and resource issues may be successful hosts. The positive organization of the festival bounces positively back to the Olympic Movement, a big advantage for the heavily criticized organization.

Future research should investigate why nations continue to host and organize festivals where few want to travel to and take part in. We may claim the EYOF's purpose lies in being a laboratory rat for future Olympic events. Surely, host cities get money to rehabilitate their facilities and even get a few new venues as a reward for the hard work. Nevertheless, the actual contribution of the EYOF to youth sport development is to be questioned because the supply of Olympic events (especially for youth at the European level) is considerably higher than the public demand. The terrain gets even more complicated with the European Games, which were organized the first time in 2015 in Baku. The Baku organizer, who was the sole bidder, has promised to pay for 6000 athletes. This is not exactly in line with the moderation that IOC has suggested. To follow up with this kind of games will only be possible in an authoritarian state.

Notes

1. M. Rowbottom, 'Exclusive: Jointly Hosted Winter European Youth Olympic Festival is Historic Model for IOC, Says Chief Executive' (Inside the Games, 25 January 2015), http://www.insidethegames.biz/anoc/755-eoc/1025090-exclusive-jointly-hosted-european-winter-youth-olympic-festival-is-historic-model-for-ioc-says-chief-executive (accessed 23 March 2015).
2. IOC, 'Olympic Agenda 2020: Context and Background' (International Olympic Committee, 2014), 8.
3. B. Leopkey and M.M. Parent, 'Olympic Games Legacy: From General Benefits to Sustainable Long-Term Legacy', *The International Journal of the History of Sport* 29, no. 6 (2012), 924–923.
4. V. Girginov and L. Hills, 'A Sustainable Sports Legacy: Creating a Link between the London Olympics and Sports Participation', *The International Journal of the History of Sport* 25, no. 14 (2008), 2091–2116; C. Gratton and H. Preuss, 'Maximizing Olympic Impacts by Building Up Legacies', *The International Journal of the History of Sport* 25, no. 14 (2008), 1922–38; K. Homma and N. Masumoto, 'A Theoretical Approach for the Olympic Legacy Study Focusing on Sustainable Sport Legacy', *The International Journal of the History of Sport* 30, no. 12 (2013), 1455–71.
5. M.M. Parent, 'Evolution and Issue Patterns for Major-Sport-Event Organizing Committees and Stakeholders', *Journal of Sport Management* 22 (2008), 135–64.
6. Ibid.
7. D.V. Hanstad, M.M. Parent, and E. Kristiansen, 'The Youth Olympic Games: The Best of the Olympics or a Poor Copy?', *European Sport Management Quarterly* 13 (2013), 315–38; Parent, 'Evolution and Issue Patterns for Major-Sport-Event Organizing Committees and Stakeholders'; K. Toohey, 'The Sydney Olympics: Striving for Legacies – Overcoming Short-Term Disappointments and Long-Term Deficiencies', *The International Journal of the History of Sport* 25, no. 14 (2008), 1953–71.
8. E. Kristiansen and G.C. Roberts, 'Young Elite Athletes and Social Support: Coping with Competitive and Organizational Stress in "Olympic" Competition', *Scandinavian Journal of Medicine & Science in Sports* 20, no. 4 (2010), 686–95.
9. EYOF2015, 'Rock the Alps!', *EYOF2015*, 20 January, 2015, http://www.eyof2015.org/en-us/news/newsdetail.aspx?shmid=456&shact=62754479&shmiid=ElR74Dxn1HA__eql__.
10. Liechtenstein, 'Liechtenstein. Land Und Leute', 2015, http://www.liechtenstein.li/de/land-und-leute/ (accessed 3 March 2015).
11. Statistics Department of Liechtenstein, 'Bevölkerungsstatistik 30. Juni 2014 [Population Statistics 30 June 2014]', 2014.

12. EYOF2015, 'Rock the Alps!'; Liechtenstein, "Liechtenstein. Land Und Leute," 2015, http://www.liechtenstein.li/de/land-und-leute/ (accessed 3 March 2015).
13. T. Donaldson and L.E. Preston, 'The Stakeholder Theory of the Corporation: Concepts, Evidence, and Implications', *Academy of Management Journal* 20 (1995), 65–91; R.E. Freeman, *Strategic Management: A Stakeholder Approach* (Boston, MA: Pitman, 1984); R. Phillips, R.E. Freeman, and A. Wicks, 'What Stakeholder Theory is Not', *Business Ethics Quarterly* 13 (2003), 479–502.
14. Parent, 'Evolution and Issue Patterns for Major-Sport-Event Organizing Committees and Stakeholders'; e.g. Toohey, 'The Sydney Olympics'.
15. Hanstad, Parent, and Kristiansen, 'The Youth Olympic Games'.
16. Ibid.
17. M.E. Clarkson, 'A Stakeholder Framework for Analyzing and Evaluating Corporate Social Performance', *Academy of Management Review* 20 (1995), 92–117.
18. Ibid, 106–107.
19. J.E. Post, L.E. Preston, and S. Sachs, *Redefining the Corporation: Stakeholder Management and Organizational Wealth* (Stanford, CA: Stanford University Press, 2002).
20. R.K. Mitchell, B.R. Agle, and D.J. Wood, 'Toward a Theory of Stakeholder Identification and Salience: Defining the Principle of Who and What Really Counts', *Academy of Management Review* 22, no. 4 (1997), 853–86.
21. Ibid., 868.
22. Freeman, *Strategic Management*, 46.
23. Y. Fassin, 'Stakeholder Management, Reciprocity and Stakeholder Responsibility', *Journal of Business Ethics* 109, no. 1 (2012), 83–96.
24. Hanstad, Parent, and Kristiansen, 'The Youth Olympic Games', 332.
25. Fassin, 'Stakeholder Management, Reciprocity and Stakeholder Responsibility'.
26. M.M. Parent, *Large-Scale Sporting Events: Organizing Committees and Stakeholders* (Edmonton: University of Alberta, Faculty of Physical Education & Recreation, 2005).
27. A. Strauss and J. Corbin, *Basics of Qualitative Research: Grounded Theory Procedures and Techniques* (Thousand Oaks, CA: Sage Publications, 1998).
28. N.L. Kondracki, N.S. Wellman, and D. Amundson, 'Content Analysis: Review of Methods and Their Application in Nutrition Education', *Journal of Nutrition Education and Behavior* 34 (2002), 224–30.
29. C. Grbich, *Qualitative Data Analysis. An Introduction* (London: Sage, 2007).
30. Hanstad, Parent, and Kristiansen, 'The Youth Olympic Games'.
31. Ibid.; M.M. Parent et al., 'The Sustainability of the Youth Olympic Games: Stakeholder Networks and Institutional Perspectives', *The International Review for the Sociology of Sport* 50 (2015), 326–348.
32. M.M. Parent and S. Smith-Swan, *Managing Major Sports Events: Theory and Practice* (London: Routledge, 2012).
33. Hanstad, Parent, and Kristiansen, 'The Youth Olympic Games'.
34. EYOF2015, 'Chefs de Mission Manual, 2nd Edition' (European Youth Olympic Festival 2015 Voralberg and Liechtenstein, December 2014).
35. Parent and Smith-Swan *Managing Major Sports Events*, 9, define a Games gypsy as 'one who has been bitten by the Games bug, and seeks that Games-time adrenaline-rush experience by going from one Games to another (Olympic or otherwise)'.
36. Hanstad, Parent, and Kristiansen, 'The Youth Olympic Games'.
37. Fassin, 'Stakeholder Management, Reciprocity and Stakeholder Responsibility'.
38. Mitchell, Agle, and Wood, 'Toward a Theory of Stakeholder Identification and Salience'.
39. IOC, 'Olympic Charter, in Force as from 8 July 2011' (International Olympic Committee, 2011).
40. IOC, 'Olympic Agenda 2020'.
41. Mitchell, Agle, and Wood, 'Toward a Theory of Stakeholder Identification and Salience'.
42. Hanstad, Parent, and Kristiansen, 'The Youth Olympic Games'.

43. Clarkson, 'A Stakeholder Framework for Analyzing and Evaluating Corporate Social Performance'.
44. Ibid.
45. Mitchell, Agle, and Wood, 'Toward a Theory of Stakeholder Identification and Salience'.
46. Hanstad, Parent, and Kristiansen, 'The Youth Olympic Games'.
47. Candidate File, 'EYOF 2015 Voralberg and Liechtenstein: Where Winter is at Home' (Candidate WINTER EYOF 2015 & Vorarlberg & Liechtenstein, 2009).
48. D. Etchells, 'Two-Nation European Youth Olympic Festival Has Worked But Olympic Games is Different Story, Warns Hickey', *Insidethegames*, 30 January 2015, http://www.insidethegames.biz/anoc/755-eoc/1025233-two-nation-european-youth-olympic-festival-has-worked-but-olympic-games-is-different-story-warns-hickey (accessed 2 April 2015).
49. Parent and Smith-Swan, *Managing Major Sports Events*.
50. EYOF2015, 'Rock the Alps!'.
51. E. Kristiansen, S.S. Andersen, and D.V. Hanstad, 'The Mundanity of Olympic Housing: Norwegian Athletes at the 2010 Winter Games', *International Journal of Applied Sports Sciences* 25, no. 2 (2013), 147–58.
52. Candidate File, 'EYOF 2015 Voralberg and Liechtenstein'.
53. E. Kristiansen, 'Competing for Culture: Young Olympians' Narratives from the First Winter Youth Olympic Games', *International Journal of Sport & Exercise Psychology* 13, no. 1 (2015), 29–42.
54. Ibid.
55. Donaldson and Preston, 'The Stakeholder Theory of the Corporation'; Freeman, *Strategic Management*; Phillips, Freeman, and Wicks, 'What Stakeholder Theory is Not'.
56. Fassin, 'Stakeholder Management, Reciprocity and Stakeholder Responsibility'.
57. Hanstad, Parent, and Kristiansen, 'The Youth Olympic Games'.
58. 'A Consultant's View: Future of Multi-Sport Games: More or Different?' (PlaytheGame, 1 April 2015), http://www.playthegame.org/news/comments/2015/005_a-consultants-view-future-of-multi-sport-games-more-or-different/ (accessed 17 March 2015).
59. IOC, 'Olympic Agenda 2020', 14.
60. Ibid.

Disclosure statement

No potential conflict of interest was reported by the authors.

Historical Frameworks and Sporting Research

Gary James

ABSTRACT

In recent years, there has been a wealth of research into how the game of association football developed. However, rather than establishing a common theme this research has led to competing theories with the debate dividing opinion on how the game of football was developed and propagated. While debate is healthy, the approach taken by some could lead to fellow academics looking to those engaged in sport history as unprofessional. This paper seeks to propose a way forward with academics working towards an all-encompassing history of the sport, by suggesting the adoption of a framework based on the work of Fernand Braudel, where indepth analysis of individual events is combined with the identification of transformational cycles. The paper concludes by suggesting that historians interested in soccer's early history work together within the framework to develop a more detailed and all-encompassing early history of the sport. This framework will not claim that either the orthodox or revisionist view is accurate, instead it will determine how best to work those debates into an all-encompassing approach while searching for detailed evidence on what was actually occurring at local levels.

Introduction

By 1985, it was recognized that an historian's focus on sport history was of value and that research in our field had gained a 'new respectability' after the publication of several important studies.[1] The field has since developed considerably with research focusing on a variety of sports, countries, regions and individuals, as well as consideration of sport's place within topics such as class, gender, race, fashion, media and so on.[2] Leading academics working in our field have urged us to focus on writing good history, without worrying whether sport history is any more or less valuable than other sub-disciplines.[3] Our field has developed significantly and, as a community, we have considered methodologies utilized in our research and have sought to develop ideas and encourage others to engage with methodological debates.[4] Throughout the last three decades of sport history's own acceptance, or attempts at acceptance, into the mainstream of history academia, there have been challenges to our way of thinking. Researchers have begun to question some of sport's long-established 'truths' and this has led to healthy debate and occasionally unhelpful criticism or even ridicule.[5] Consider the origins of football debate that has been raging

161

for several years, particularly within the pages of this journal.[6] It was not too long ago that historians and the general public felt they knew how association football was 'born', developed and propagated around the country. We believed there had been mob football, followed by a rediscovery of the game via the public schools whose pupils subsequently travelled around the country promoting the sport to communities. This explanation was chronicled extensively, but then historians researching sport at a local level started to question the earlier findings, leading to a wealth of valuable research in recent publications.[7] However, rather than establishing a common theme, this research has led to competing theories with some historians believing in the 'orthodox' position, keeping faith with the traditional view, while 'revisionists' argued that the public schools were not as influential as traditionalists believed and that the lower middle-classes were more relevant in the game's ultimate development.[8] This has resulted in some researchers publishing academic articles listing every occurrence of the word football they have identified in online newspaper archives, with the intention that presenting a wealth of material in this manner will lead to the agreement that their preferred viewpoint is the right one. Of course, researchers on all sides of the debate could apply similar logic and, in all probability, discover material that suggests their version of the game's development is unequivocally the right one. Rather than regurgitate a particular view or present a wealth of material highlighting when the word 'football' appeared in digitized archives within this article, the decision has been taken to consider how the various versions of the game's roots could be brought together into an all-encompassing framework, detailing association football's evolution.

Much has been written about the game's origins, even if academics have differing views on what constitutes the birth of the game, with some focusing on the establishment of the Football Association as the pivotal moment, while others consider the influence of the Sheffield region. Some talk of the arrival of professionalism, while others consider the public schools and their adherence to their first rules. Some have talked of the footballing bans implemented at various points, suggesting that the sport had a role in daily life several hundred years before the sport's first known formal rules. If these varying interpretations are anything to go by, then it seems that we are no nearer to establishing the true development of the sport than we were a century ago. Back then, the early chroniclers of the game believed they had the answers, while today we know of the limitations they worked to. The debate between historians has at times appeared to become personal and often our academic papers appear to conflict and, in some cases, ridicule others for their mistakes or for conclusions we disagree with.[9] There is a great need for academic rigour, of course, and we should challenge each other's findings, but when we are arguing over minor mentions of the word football and what they mean then this can be damaging. It could lead to fellow academics looking to those engaged in sport history as unprofessional with, perhaps, a return to the days when the social history of sport was looked upon as 'just another discrete historical ghetto where fans with typewriters practice their esoteric craft with little contact with the historical mainstream'.[10] Discussion is healthy but the way the origins of football debate has been developing could be looked upon critically by fellow historians and, indeed, the wider public. At a time when academia needs to engage more than ever with the public, it is vital we also engage with each other and find ways to cooperate rather than criticize. We have powerful stories of social change to highlight and to inform the wider public, and the story of football's development can be utilized to establish good audiences for academia and prove the worth of our work and discipline.

This paper proposes the adoption of a framework based on the work of Fernand Braudel, and comprises five sections with the first outlining Braudel's work; the second considering how Braudel's framework could be adapted to prove of value to sport history, the third section considering analysis of data, the fourth providing examples, and the fifth suggesting how the proposed framework could then be applied. The paper concludes by suggesting that historians interested in soccer's early history work together, within the framework to develop a more detailed and all-encompassing early history of the sport. This framework will not claim that either the orthodox or revisionist view is accurate, instead it will determine how best to work those debates into an all-encompassing approach while searching for detailed evidence on what was actually occurring at local levels.

Braudel's Concept

To consider the framework being suggested it is important to consider the research of French historian Fernand Braudel. Braudel was not a sports historian but, as with most football historians today, he actively researched archives to search for material that may help provide new ways of considering history's dilemmas. In 1958, his research led to the publication of the Longue durée,[11] where he argued that historians should consider three categories of social time – the Longue durée, Moyenne durée and Courte durée. Although these are not direct translations, it is fair to suggest that these three categories can be understood as the long-term, cyclical history and the history of events.[12] It should be stressed however that cyclical history does not mean that this is a repetitive process, rather that this definition refers to the fact that activities at that level are cycles within a larger timeframe. Each definition is explored further later, but for the purpose of this section it is important to consider these periods at a high level with the Longue durée itself an embracing concept, providing the unifying element of human history.[13] Braudel aimed to show that the historian's focus solely on event led history was flawed and that only by considering the long-term, and indeed the cyclical, or middle level, could we hope to establish a true understanding of the manner in which a society was established. He argued that over the long-term our collective behaviour is established alongside our enduring societal structures, while the cyclical level includes periods of major change. Some of these cycles may last for several decades or even centuries, while others last a few years, but each one adds to the overall progression. He believed that his views were marginalized by 'old-fashioned historians who emphasized political events and personalities',[14] and, ironically, short-term history has again dominated in recent decades.[15] Braudel's three time periods can be explained further:

Longue Durée

The Longue durée is typically perceived as a period of hundreds, if not thousands, of years. Usually considered to be boundless time,[16] or the full history of something, such as a nation or an organization, and in Braudel's own work he published, for example, on geographical regions such as the Mediterranean.[17] He believed that change is possible through human action overcoming the limits of the structures around them, including geographical and mental constraints.[18] Braudel claimed that, for historians, the Longue durée is a structure that 'travels through vast tracts of time without changing; if it deteriorates during the long journey, it simply restores itself as it goes along and regains its health, and in the final analysis its characteristics alter only very slowly'.[19] He believed this approach allowed historians a framework for them to observe and evaluate historical events and contextualize them within longer time frames.

Moyenne Durée

This level of time can be considered a period of development within the longer timeframe, and is often seen as measured in decades or potentially a century or more.[20] It is a period where it is possible to discern a trend or a particular cycle such as the Industrial Revolution. It contains a series of events that, when considered as a whole, demonstrate societal change. Dramatic fluctuations or attention grabbing events can be better interpreted within these cycles, with the trend becoming apparent the more we understand the individual events and the circumstances that surround them.[21] Each cycle has its own causal explanations for how that cycle developed and these can include environmental conditions; for example, the opportunity to use a field for sport; legislation, such as the banning of football activity; employment needs, such as longer working hours in a growing industrial city; or a multitude of other factors.

Courte Durée

Often understood to be a period of hours, days, weeks or maybe a year or so, this period is simply the time of an event or episode. In footballing parlance that could be an incident within a game, the match itself or even a particular season. The history of events was not an area Braudel often focused on, preferring instead to consider the medium and long-term,[22] and this was often perceived as a weakness of Longue durée theorists. Much of the criticism of Braudel's work focused on his perceived lack of interest in events and the limited volume of research into them by students of his and the Annales school.[23] Braudel has documented his belief that events were the dust of time,[24] with many events selected either retrospectively, once a pattern is known, or by those who have something to gain from highlighting an event at the expense of another. This is a criticism that could be levelled at some involved with the origins of football debate or at some of the early chroniclers of football. Wallerstein questioned the validity of historians utilizing an event that occurred in one year, but was not reported until later years, as he questioned whether this was truthful and whether it was any more significant than an event that was never chronicled.[25] In the origins debate, significance has been placed on villagers signing up to a football club in 1871 based on a booklet written some 38 years after the event was alleged to have taken place, written by a man with a vested interest.[26] It seems plausible that Braudel and Wallerstein would have taken issue with judgements made on that individual event, especially as others claim that particular club's formation as occurring the following year.[27] Braudel would have looked for the event's significance within the overall pattern.[28]

Proposed Framework for Association Football

Although the Longue durée encompasses the full history of a subject,[29] it is worth considering how the framework is relevant to football. The full history of the sport could be told using an adapted version of Braudel's framework, with this section detailing how this could be applied. Accepting the Longue durée as the full history of football is fine, however to ensure the approach can be utilized to improve our analysis of soccer and development of our research it is important that clarity of the method and process is documented. In this section, an adapted version of Braudel's concept is proposed, one which provides clarity and will benefit the work of academic historians working in the field of sport history. It is suggested that three separate levels of time do exist within sport history and, whereas many traditional sports historians may suggest that Braudel's concept is too vague, these can help to describe sport's development through critical analysis of archival sources. The following sections explain the three adapted levels of time.

Full Time

No game is complete until the final whistle is blown, and it is only then that points are allocated and winners can celebrate as they have a complete understanding of the game's life. Contestants, spectators and the game's chroniclers have experienced the full length of the contest and analysis can be made of the full time of the match, its twists and turns, teams' periods of dominance, possession, goals scored, corners taken, injuries suffered and so on. Each game has phases of play and specific incidents that shape its direction. As we all understand the concept of a game's full duration, it seems sensible to consider the entire history of soccer as one of 'Full Time' where every moment leads to its development. The sport continues to grow and develop, which means that football has not yet reached its final whistle, but it is safe to assume that, as with sports media outlets, we can assess what we have experienced so far and reach conclusions on the developments along the way.

For the purpose of this paper, Full Time is the term utilized for the full duration of the sport, including the period before the first rules were formulated. On its own, this macro history level is important but it is only when it is combined with more detailed time frames at lower levels that we can start to seriously consider the complete picture. At full time in an ordinary game, scores are known, but only analysis within that game will show how that score was achieved, and the same is true for the Full Time history of football. Full Time allows us to contextualize events and their significance over the life of the sport and, of course, this approach could apply to sports clubs, competitions and so on.

Transformational Level

This level is characterized by periods where the sport has developed or been transformed in some way. As Braudel suggests the way these middle level time periods, the cycles, are organized provides the structure. They provide the 'coherent and fairly fixed series of relationships between realities and social masses'.[30] Those cycles, with their influences, outputs and inputs, demonstrate the general tendencies of sporting activity over time without being obscured by the attention-grabbing individual events. An individual game may be significant, but in terms of football's history it is the general pattern demonstrated within cycles that proves whether the individual game is part of a wider development or simply a one-off based on local influences. Our role as historians is to question why did the sport develop in the manner it did during this period and how did it change? What were the agents? We must identify the inputs, outputs, actions and consequences of each transformational period. We must also recognize that we may identify transformational periods that vary in significance on the Full Time development of the sport. Some transformational periods may only have significance on a local basis, like the establishment and life of a soccer club in Manchester in 1863,[31] but ultimately may have little bearing on the national development of the sport. In an ideal world, we would create a Full Time history of soccer for every town, city, region, nation and internationally, but until we do so, we should construct a national picture based on what has already been researched and the regions academics are currently focusing on. The aim of this level is to determine links and comparisons with individual episodes acting as rungs in a ladder moving the development of the sport onwards.

Episodal Level

Event-led history is often perceived as important to sports historians where we can, and do, fixate on specific games, goals, trophy successes and so on. In the debate on the origins of football, some researchers have focused on finding events to add to their argument. However, it is important to remember that events on their own are not the 'story' and it may be that data, particularly that unearthed during an online search of a digitized newspaper, is abused if it is considered in isolation.[32] The role of the historian as a challenging, interpretive analyst of all that is uncovered remains central to our work and, with so much data available via digitized material, it is important to ensure that we consider all angles. To interpret sport's development it is important to look underneath, on top and alongside events to search for those events' true significance, and we must not abuse or misuse the record of the past.[33] Successful historians analyze the study of events against the other two time periods to aid understanding of the deeper running trend.[34] It has been suggested that those focusing wholly on data gathering seem unable to appreciate this,[35] and it is true that some historians can be prone to focus on individual episodes without performing true critical analysis of intellectual substance. Moving to a Full Time framework does not mean we reduce our efforts to investigate and analyze in detail, instead our role is to identify, measure and interpret the significance of individual events and interactions. We must seek out those events, connections and interactions that are hidden, and we must rescue from oblivion those whose voices and stories have not been heard.[36] We need to consider if an event is relevant to a wider theme; a Eureka moment; or an inconsequential occurrence, giving careful consideration when we are questioning the significance of data and participating in a debate, such as the origins of football, where our academic community is divided by competing mythologies and disagreements over relevant context.[37]

It was suggested that Braudel's work lacked investigation of the effects of individual action on the creation of structures,[38] and this is where the approach proposed in this paper develops his concept further, strengthening and appropriately recording the role of the event in sport's Full Time history. It is the investigation of the events at the Episodal Level that adds to transformational cycles at the next level. We need to interrogate these episodes to understand if and how they progress the sport, or play a part in a transformational cycle. Braudel believed the past presented a series of paradoxes for us to attempt to resolve with one such paradox being the inherent difficulties of recording and integrating immediate, short-term human experiences of the moment with the long-range developments,[39] but this is possible within a Longue durée framework, certainly within sport. Consider recent research into Manchester's earliest known club, Hulme Athenaeum,[40] and the suggestion made that the club is not significant as it struggled for opponents and did not progress beyond 1863–1872.[41] Looking at purely the individual events for that club could indeed suggest little significance, however, that view completely misses the point that a community was developed via that club which, over 30 years later, saw at least one founding member of that earliest known Mancunian club, still playing a leading role in developing and promoting regional football.[42] His club may have died, but he and some of his colleagues remained leading footballing figures in the region for the rest of their lives. The interactions of both the individual and the team tell us a great deal about how football in Manchester developed and it is that level of detail, analysis and interpretation required in all regions that this paper hopes to promote via the proposed framework. Events at the Episodal Level are as important as the wider analysis because without these, the detail is lacking, but it is vital sports historians have a critical reading of the information discovered. This reading, by experts in their subject areas or regions, is what takes the individual moment and establishes its significance within a wider, transformational cycle and interactions can become clear by studying these episodes. These webs of social activity help us to consider their influence on the wider history of the sport, assisting in our determination of transformational cycles. Social interactions lead to invention and innovation and help progress the Longue durée of a topic.[43]

Analysis

To ensure the framework fits with our research needs, it is worth considering the process of analysis. Analysis of detail is important in understanding the Full Time of an activity, and in recent decades it has been claimed that the focus of 'babyboomer historians' has been on the micro-history of subjects such as class and race, while some long-range historians have ignored detail in favour of the overall trend.[44] This may be appropriate for their studies. However, to understand long-range history, it is important to investigate, analyze and interpret the detail as well as the general theme. The knowledge of individual events shapes and informs each transformational cycle and they in turn help the Full Time of an activity to develop. It is the understanding of how episodes interrelate that shapes a cycle and it is these complex relationships that we need to understand if we are to map the full history of a sport or, indeed, its origins. Each episode on its own may not be significant, even if some historians view a solitary reference to the word 'football' as being important, but it is the identification of whether these single events are turning points, or merely an isolated episode that is important. Some historians researching football's origins have focused on online newspaper mentions in digitized archives which, as Johnes and Nicholson have highlighted, can lead to misinterpretation and a lack of knowledge of the wider context of the piece.[45] The availability of digital archives has allowed historians to unearth a plethora of episodes or events and for those of us who cut our research teeth by poring over micro-filmed newspapers in the 1980s, the opportunities are endless. However, it should be remembered that these archives are indicative of activity rather than conclusive as they provide evidence that needs to be analyzed and questioned, but not the answer. We must remain vigilant and recognize that some footballing activity was never reported; some was reported but not in sufficient detail; some reports were lost; some records withheld and so on. There is also the issue of how newspapers were selected to be digitized. We should question what has been made available, why, by whom, the funding and so on, as this may provide answers to other questions about how we perceive history, news and national significance. The British

Library's digitization project, for example, paid little attention to sporting newspapers until recently, while some universities have sought to digitize sporting collections which will aid their own priority projects.[46]

As with any historical research, critical analysis by experts in their subject areas is required. We need to search for the evidence of what occurred and we need to interpret it by placing it into context. There should be nothing new about this process as all academic historians have been trained to do this through their own educational systems and research experience. Take a simple report such as one which talks of 12 or 13 people 'playing of football' on the frozen Serpentine in Hyde Park, reported in 1840.[47] The report focuses on the rescue of some of the people and the death of one of the party but, from a sports context, some historians could utilize that report to suggest that football was being played in all conditions in central London. That would be a conclusion that seems extreme, but it is exactly what we appear to be getting at times in the origins of soccer debate. What we should actually be doing is straightforward investigative work and we need to ask why were they playing on ice? Where did they get the ball? Was it sold locally, and if so how many balls were sold each week and what size and shape were they? Was it significant that the number of players was 12 or 13? How did they balance the teams? Did they have teams or was it a general kickabout? What were their aims? Why play on the ice in the first place? The questioning, of course, must continue until we uncover enough answers to establish the event's true significance, and it may be that we simply cannot find enough answers to make a valuable assumption about the activity being performed. The individual episodes have to be considered for how they relate to each other – the themes, processes and significance. It is not necessary to make every individual episode fit within the theme of a transformational cycle, but it is vital to consider whether the episode is part of a cycle or is it merely a one-off event, an outlier, or of no significance whatsoever.

Once we have identified enough episodes to see a pattern emerge, then we must consider whether that pattern is strong enough to be perceived as a transformational cycle. Within a transformational cycle, we must see a clear development or change from the previous cycle. As an example, consider the move towards professionalism in English soccer during the 1880s. Our research of that period needs to identify the key episodes that led to the sport allowing professionalism across the country; the debates; the threatened breakaway by northern clubs; the meetings held; and every instance of player payment we can find. We will then need to analyze these episodes and search for their significance, and will need to consider what the inputs into this transformational cycle and the outputs are, such as the establishment of competitions for professionals and amateurs; wage constraints; increased movement between clubs; impact on admission charges; and so on. That transformational cycle can then be appropriately placed in the Full Time history of the sport. If researchers can focus on their specialist areas and identify the events, circumstances and cycles that matter to them, documenting how events form cycles and how those cycles transform into the following cycle, then we will produce an all-encompassing history of football. Of course, this approach requires academics to collaborate and for some to act as stewards, signposting the way around the three time levels and helping others to formulate their own research questions, mapping and cycles as they uncover the micro detail necessary to understand what was happening at a local level, alongside identification of transformational cycles, and within the Full Time of the sport. This approach will help to make the history of football's development comprehensible and based on fact, rigorously assessed with each episode identified for what it is, whether that be as part of a wider transformational period, or simply a one-off episode. We must review each other's work and look for similarities and agreements to inform the wider picture. Where we disagree, we must consider why we hold the views we do and look for a means of bridging those disagreements. By focusing on commonality, we will be able to establish a historical truth, one that adds value and can be further researched and analyzed. Cooperation is necessary,[48] but alongside this we must communicate our findings positively and support each other in bringing our research to the wider public. Soccer matters to people and provides an opportunity for valid, genuine, thought-provoking history to be discussed by academics and non-academics alike. The proposed framework allows us to share ideas and encourages debate, it is not simply about re-introducing an old idea and making it fit with the modern world, as it allows us to question the significance of the smallest football reference, to search for sequences, to establish the transformational nature of cycles and to create an all-encompassing history of the sport. We need to combine low-level detail, identified through in-depth archival research and local knowledge, within a Full Time history, while identifying transformational cycles and all their associated inputs and outputs. This approach will allow historians to engage with each other and with the public in a manner that can only benefit our discipline. It gives us both the micro-history that we have become accustomed to in recent decades and an understanding of how that detail has shaped our sport's development over centuries. It provides the best of both worlds – deep plundering of the archives with the critical analysis of what shapes society over the long-term. Searches of digitized records provide opportunity but they do not provide the answer on their own. Instead we need to immerse ourselves in the data and interpret it wisely, searching for patterns of activity, community development and progression. It is essential we provide informative answers to the questions of how football became established as a sport; how it developed and where it was played.

The Full Time history of football's development would include current events of course, and this is where weaknesses can occur because, while we are still experiencing and living the sport's development, we will find it difficult to analyze and identify transformational cycles developing at the moment, although the game's globalization has already received some focus as part of a 'world system'.[49]

Examples

To help explain the proposed framework further, the following examples have been provided of well-known footballing moments to demonstrate how these events can be interpreted within a Full Time framework of soccer. The first is a modern example. In 2012, Sergio Agüero scored a goal in the dying seconds of the final game of the season to win the Premier League in 2012. The goal has been replayed frequently and is seen as 'the' story of the 2011–2012 soccer season. Using this as an example of Full Time history, that goal was an event within the Episodal Level, important but not the full story. The Transformational Level could be said to be the 2011–2012 season itself or, more appropriately when considering the significance of this level, it could be interpreted as a period characterized by overseas ownership of Premier League clubs. A period that for Agüero's club, Manchester City, started in 2007, but for the Premier League goes back further with, of course, Chelsea being perceived as one of the earliest clubs to benefit from the patronage of an overseas investor. As the Agüero example demonstrates, this framework provides a method to formulate questions about change. Here, we question why was Agüero playing for Manchester City and, with the right questioning we trace back to the investment in the club by Sheikh Mansour and on to the overseas ownership of clubs. We do not simply state that Agüero's goal won the League. We analyze every aspect of that event and see that it is merely one episode within a more significant transformational cycle, where overseas ownership of Premier League clubs became prevalent.

Looking further back, there is the example of the First Division of the Football League being increased from 20 clubs to 22 in 1919.[50] This move was agreed at a special meeting of the League and it has been suggested that this increase was to ensure London clubs remained in the top flight to prevent a breakaway of southern clubs.[51] However, the special meeting of the League was merely one event within a much longer debate that stretched back to April 1915. Reports of the Football League discussions in 1919 show that the decision to increase the size of the First Division had come as a protective measure following a fixed game between Liverpool and Manchester United on Good Friday 1915. That game resulted in a dubious victory to Manchester United and, after investigation, it was proved that players from both clubs had agreed to fix the match as part of a betting scandal. The points accrued by United were enough to ensure that at the season's end the club would not be relegated, and that Chelsea would be, although the match fix was not proven to have been an attempt at saving United from relegation. The debates surrounding the fixed game rumbled on throughout the war and, when officials decided to increase the League, there were protests from other clubs including Everton who held the view that the League should not be increased and that Manchester United should be relegated as the guilty party.[52] The significance of these comments are that a simple episode, such as the increase in membership of the Football League, is merely one event within a sequence of events at the Episodal Level and that, in this case, analysis of each League meeting and an interrogation of material, reveals a broader series of episodes. The increase in League is often shown from the perspective of the Arsenal promotion and Tottenham relegation, but had the Liverpool–United match fixing scandal never occurred then the prospect of saving Chelsea from the punishment of relegation may never have been discussed. The mood of those meetings was that Chelsea were hard done by, with little said about Tottenham's plight, but this often gets overlooked today as we consider the apparent injustice of Tottenham being relegated from a division that is about to be increased, for Arsenal. There is a significance to that, of course, and this adds to the need to research and document the Full Time history of football, with patterns identified at the Transformational Level and individual events at the Episodal Level. In the case of the League's expansion, that is clearly a Transformational cycle containing a series of episodes such as the Liverpool–United game and the various meetings along the way.

Another example concerns an event that has been raised by those with opposing views in the origins debate. This is a game of football advertized in Ashton-under-Lyne during the 1840s.[53] This match may or may not have occurred, leading to differing interpretations from modern day historians with some suggesting that the advertizement means little, while others use it as evidence that a footballing culture was in existence.[54] On its own the newspaper advertizement for the game can indeed be interpreted either way, but what it actually demonstrates is that our knowledge of the circumstances peculiar to that event is not yet sufficient enough to provide a definitive answer. What is needed is a full investigation into the environment around Ashton-under-Lyne at that time, along with analysis of the named individuals, groups and locations, to understand whether the pattern within that locality adds to evidence that can then be interpreted as part of a transformational period of activity. Research into the eight miles that surround Manchester has identified that the Ashton area had multiple teams in existence by the end of the 1870s, with other footballing activity reported between 1846 and the 1870s, and this suggests that the 1846 advertized game may well have been a key episode in the development of the sport locally,[55] but further investigation is required.

At present, we cannot say whether the Ashton game is an outlier, statistical evidence of activity that was not part of an overall pattern or whether it represents a much stronger community of activity than previously understood. The suggestion is that it followed, and was followed by, other evidence of footballing action in the Ashton locality, and if we could prove that subsequent footballing activity in the Ashton area involved some of the people mentioned in the advertizement, then clearly that is of more significance. This framework allows historians to question what an event or period actually meant to the long-term development and encourages historians to 'look underneath it and see it in terms of the long-term, asking was it epiphenomenal? Was it momentary? Was it a kind of flash? Or did it really make a difference?'[56] This approach enables us to take a more considered approach when analyzing an event's significance. One event, such as the formation of a football club, is only significant to the overall story if that club's establishment tells us something that influences our understanding at the Transformational Level and, indeed, within the Full Time history. This means that to truly understand the development of football, we need to consider each level in turn and so, rather than this framework appearing to be a vague overarching explanation for football's development, it actually becomes a precise analysis of data and phenomena. In this proposed framework, the work of dedicated researchers is vital but instead of simply looking for events at the Episodal Level and, for example, considering whether they support the orthodox or revisionist viewpoints, researchers need to consider the three levels of time to improve our overall understanding.

Suggested Research and the Transformational Level

If we accept this framework and recognize that three separate time periods exist, then the logical way forward is to gain a global understanding of what occurred within each transformational cycle. We need to agree what those cycles are, research them and document the inputs, influences and outputs of each cycle. Identifying these cycles and producing a descriptive analysis of what occurred within each cycle, and of how each cycle transforms into another, will allow historians to produce a history of football that is all encompassing.[57] One-off events and games will be important in our research but not necessarily significant in the overall history of the sport. As the origins debate has demonstrated, recognizing the specifics behind the formation of a cycle can be complex but it is an activity worth pursuing. The first step would be for high-level analysis to be made breaking the Full Time history of the sport down into transformational cycles. This would allow historians to focus on their own specialities within a wider framework with the aim of filling in the gaps to make their research add real value to the determining of the key episodes within a transformational cycle. The need for in-depth, local research is vital, but where this differs from what has been happening so far is that historians will work together focusing on micro-history to inform, via the suggested framework, the Full Time history of our sport. Combining micro-historical research with a macro-historical framework can prove the value of our work, provide real meaning to our conclusions and can bring consensus on what really matters.[58]

For the purposes of this proposal, it is essential to give an indication of the type of Transformational cycles that appear to exist. These should be debated, but they have been presented here to help progress the adoption of a Full Time framework for soccer. Analysis so far suggests 11 broad Transformational periods,[59] including four periods focusing on what could be described as the origins of the game: Mob Football; Early Forms of Football; Establishment of Clubs and Competitions; and Professionalism. An analysis of Manchester's association football development up to 1919 is to be published utilizing this Full Time framework, with research for that publication identifying appropriate transformational cycles for that region.[60] Figure 1 provides a basic overview of the first six Manchester transformational cycles, as an indication of how the three levels coexist. Although in-depth research in Manchester has identified time periods, it would be unwise at this stage to place a time frame alongside any of the national transformational periods, as detailed analysis is required. The significance being to search for the events of the game's past and consider how they link together to form a pattern of activity. By focusing in this way we can interpret how events have shaped the sport while also understanding the circumstances that enabled or prevented the sport's progression. The position at the start of each transformational cycle and at the end needs to be documented, as do the individual mentions of football within each cycle, some of which will progress the sport, some will have no impact whatsoever, and some will add a geographical perspective on where footballing activity was occurring. Outliers are of interest of course, but it is the cycle that aids our overall understanding. Once we have

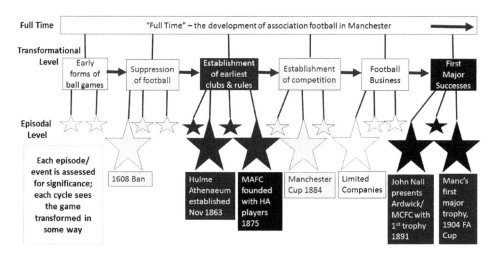

Figure 1. Research into Manchester's Full Time history of association football has identified six transformational cycles, which chronicle the early development of the sport in the region. Each event and newspaper reference identified has been analyzed at the Episodal Level to determine its significance, and to consider whether patterns of activity have emerged. Where a significant progression has been observed, further analysis has determined how those events have influenced a transformational cycle. The events listed are merely to give an indication of the type of event considered within each cycle. This research has, for example, helped identify the significance of Hulme Athenaeum with its first secretary in 1863, John Nall, directly linked with the formative years of both Manchester City and United, and he continued to play a significant role in the development of regional soccer through to his death in 1897.

identifiable transformational periods, we can then understand how these link together to form the game's history. Many factors, including environmental and political, have helped shape sport, and it is clear that all of these factors need to be considered alongside the simple events identified at the Episodal Level.

To develop this framework, we need more regional studies; agreement of transformational cycles (possibly with bespoke regional cycles); to map the full growth of the sport; and to agree on the inputs and outputs for each cycle. Instead of looking for differences, which many historians can be guilty of, we should pay more attention to similarities.[61] We can take the regional research already performed and combine it all within the proposed framework to identify patterns, consistencies and trends, while also taking steps to encourage research into the areas where gaps exist. Causal explanations can be complex and often not easily identified, but it should be apparent that for any sport to develop there needs to be a series of factors that come about perfectly to create a Goldilocks 'just right' opportunity. Understandably, some will consider that this framework is simply 'history', however the suggested framework is more about making sense of the Full Time history of the sport and its transformational phases, rather than focusing on the eureka moments. It is an embracing theory, and is a subtle change in the way we think, but it could have a significant impact on our understanding and interpretation of how the game developed. Historians have an important role to play in ensuring our findings are fact based, comprehensive and comprehendible and it is vital we question our approaches and develop standards and frameworks that help us come to terms with the modern, digitized world of academia where information overload could make our community appear in conflict and disjointed with little of worth to add.[62] We must not stand still or worse, retreat into our own particular comfort zone, while criticizing those that disagree with us. We must embrace each other's work and join forces to create a comprehensive history, within a framework that makes sense of it all, while developing roles to provide critical assessment of how the data uncovered in the Episodal Level fits into a transformational cycle and, ultimately, into the Full Time of the sport.

The author intends to organize a conference where historians genuinely interested in moving towards this Full Time framework can collaborate with the aim of establishing an all-encompassing history. As part of this collaboration, the work of historians may vary, with some focusing on the detail and others providing critical consideration of how the data fits into the proposed levels of time, but all will help seek agreement on the development of the game. It is apparent that each period of substantial development has its own unique series of events and its own particular explanatory forces in a manner suggested by Bober when considering economic cycles.[63] Economists and scientists recognize the concept of cycles,[64] supporting the concept of the Transformational Level. Although each cycle has its own experience, they are outgrowths of processes from the preceding cycle,[65] which means that as we identify the inputs to a cycle, we will be able to recognize the constants in existence from the previous cycle. The development from mob football to public school and rule-based football is hotly debated at present. What this framework will help to demonstrate is exactly what footballing activity continued across those two transformational periods, along with, hopefully, the details of communities that continued to participate and the individuals who promoted the sport's development. For sports historians, the Transformational Level with its periods of change provides the opportunity to identify continuities and shifts in sports development.

Conclusion

Historians are fully aware that extensive research is vital in understanding how our sports developed, but it is also clear that providing a framework within which gaps can be identified is also important. Guldi and Armitage have claimed that since the 1960s academia has encouraged students to focus on narrow time frames and on the local,[66] and this appears to be true for the sport history community. We have tended to focus on regional histories and restrictive timeframes without much consideration of the Full Time history of our subject. We have perhaps fooled ourselves into thinking that our own limited time periods, and focus on local issues, will provide answers to the wider picture but in truth, by not properly positioning our research within a longer duration and wider framework, we have limited the possibility of reaching conclusions that genuinely answer our questions. Instead we have, particularly in the origins of football debate, provided multiple views of how the game developed, with some historians taking great delight in challenging those who have disagreed with their own perceptions. This has led to historians focusing on their own specialist area and their role in the debate, limiting their public engagement and readership in the process in a manner suggested by Guldi and Armitage.[67] Historians need to engage with each other and, perhaps more importantly, with non-specialist readers if their work is to be of value, rather than exhibit a 'my research is better than yours' approach which has, at times, appeared to be the motive in some academic papers on the origins of football. This is unhealthy. It does not mean that historians working in a narrow field and time frame have nothing to offer, or that their work is of less value – far from it. Detailed research of this nature is absolutely vital, but it has to be recognized that, in many cases, the material identified is at the Episodal Level of time, and that it requires consideration at both the Transformational Level and within the sport's Full Time.

By collaborating on the propagation of a Full Time framework, as proposed earlier, it will allow all of our regional and time restricted studies to be included within a wider analysis and will move the debate forward. The aim is to take the small detail to help create the bigger picture, and that is surely worth achieving? Cannadine believed that historians were producing increasing amounts of academic history that 'fewer and fewer people' were actually reading and, if the altmetrics and read figures for some papers on the origins of football are to be utilized as a barometer, his view appears to be true for most, but not all, football origins papers.[68] By suggesting historians collaborate on the development of this framework, this paper concludes with the view that this overarching approach will enable historians to combine both the orthodox and revisionist research identified to date to develop a robust historiography of the sport. Some sports historians, such as McDowell, have documented the need to identify the phases and themes in the historiography of sport. Indeed, McDowell has published a critical assessment of the research into Scottish football still required based around phases which is, in essence, the beginning of establishing a Full Time history of Scottish football.[69] McDowell's approach has added value and, if we work together to utilize the proposed framework, we can provide an all-encompassing view of the history of football, based on the widest range of material and theorizing, providing a credible approximation of the topic's history.[70]

The discipline of sport history could be improved if we followed a framework, such as that proposed, and added proper context to it by interpreting episodes and archival records correctly, while explaining our findings together to as wide an audience as possible. Let us not spend our time arguing in academic journals and instead seek ways to understand why any differences exist. Johnes talked of the opportunity for historians to attract people to historical study, for universities to become embedded in their communities, and called for sports historians to recognize the need to engage more if our role is to prove valuable in the future, and his views should be considered.[71] Other historians, such as McKibbin,[72] have questioned the position of sport history and what developments we need to make, adding to the view that there remains some uncertainty of the direction of the field. The Full Time framework proposed here provides an opportunity for those researching football's formative years to demonstrate real value, leading to the establishment of a universal history of football which considers all of our findings, starting with the origins of football, and then disseminate it to our communities. A common approach will allow us to engage with a non-academic audience at varying levels to ensure we inform non-specialists about the Full Time history of our sport, transformational cycles, individual 'headline grabbing' episodes and our regional position within the sport's full narrative. Other areas of history have recognized that we must engage with the public by 'developing a longue-duree contextual background against which archival information, events and sources can be interpreted',[73] and as Vamplew has stated, sport is no different from other areas of history.[74] It is time for us to adopt a framework and processes that we can all work toward. We have the tools and the technological means to overcome many of the traditional objections to considering long-term history.[75] This approach will produce a more critical, intensive and valuable synthesis of material and will ensure that each regional study adds to the whole, rather than appearing as a rival position.

Full Time history can be applied to any aspect of a sport's existence, and while this paper has focused on soccer origins it could equally apply to other sports, individual clubs, international competition and so on. The beauty of this framework is that it allows us to think both big and small, to consider the lowest level of detail, alongside the widest possible theme. There is a place for all to contribute their local, regional and specific research within the Full Time history of the sport, without our topics being confined or, as Sherratt commented, 'ghettoised'.[76] Any aspect of sport can be researched within this framework by considering a series of successive developments, regionally, nationally and internationally, looking for the individual moments and understanding how they influence that particular developmental period. This may require a different approach within the supervision and education of students but, with the right amount of training, there is no reason why historians cannot approach the proposed framework with optimism, hope and ambition. McDowell asked whether there were historians who desired a different route for Scottish football's historiography, and this paper concludes with a similar question.[77] Do we want to work together to produce an all-encompassing history of our sport, one which will help us engage with the general public, or do we want to demonstrate to the outside world our differences and squabbles?

The author is keen to hear from academics researching in this field with a desire to collaborate on defining the Full Time history of association football.

Notes

1.   Karen J. Winkler, 'A Lot More Than Trading Baseball Cards: Sport History Gains a New Respectability', *Chronicle of Higher Education*, 5 June 1985, 5–9.

2. Reviewing the article titles in the latest issues of journals such as the *Journal of Sport History, The International Journal of the History of Sport* and *Soccer and Society* demonstrates the breadth and variety of topics.

3. Wray Vamplew, 'Sporting a Handicap: Mainstreaming Sports History', International Sports and Leisure History (Spleish), 'Future for Sports and Leisure History' Symposium, http://www.cheshire.mmu.ac.uk/sport-history/blogs.php (accessed 10 August 2015).

4. For example, Samantha-Jayne Oldfield, 'Narrative Methods in Sport History Research: Biography, Collective Biography, and Prosopography', *The International Journal of the History of Sport* 32, no. 15 (2016), 1855–82; Duncan Stone, John Hughson and Rob Eliis (eds), *New Directions in Sport History* (Abingdon: Routledge, 2015); and Mike Huggins, 'The Visual in Sport History: Approaches, Methodologies and Sources', *The International Journal of the History of Sport* 32, no. 15 (2015), 1813–30.

5. Examples include Peter Swain, 'Early Football and the Emergence of Modern Soccer: A Reply to Tony Collins', *The International Journal of the History of Sport* 33, no. 5 (2016), 251–71; Graham Curry and Eric Dunning, *Association Football: A Study in Figurational Sociology* (Abingdon: Routledge, 2015), 155–74; R.W. Lewis, 'Innovation Not Invention: A Reply to Peter Swain Regarding the Professionalization of Association Football in England and its Diffusion', *Sport in History* 30, no. 3 (2010), 475–88; Peter Swain, 'Cultural Continuity and Football in Nineteenth Century Lancashire', *Sport in History* 28, no. 4 (2008), 566–82; Adrian Harvey, 'Curate's Egg Pursued by Red Herrings: A Reply to Eric Dunning and Graham Curry', *The International Journal of the History of Sport* 21, no. 1 (2004), 127–31; and Adrian Harvey, 'The Curate's Egg Put Back Together: Comments on Eric Dunning's Response to an Epoch in the Annals of National Sport', *The International Journal of the History of Sport* 19, no. 4 (2002), 191–9.

6. Articles include Tony Collins, 'Early Football and the Emergence of Modern Soccer, c.1840–1880', *The International Journal of the History of Sport* 32, no. 9 (2015), 1127–42; Gary James, 'Manchester's Footballing Pioneers, 1863–1904: A Collective Biography', *The International Journal of the History of Sport* 32, no. 9 (2015), 1143–59; Peter Swain and Adrian Harvey, 'On Bosworth Field or the Playing Fields of Eton and Rugby? Who Really Invented Modern Football?', *The International Journal of the History of Sport* 29, no. 10 (2012), 1425–45; Gavin Kitching, '"Old" Football and the "New" Codes: Some Thoughts on the Origins of "Football" Debate and Suggestions for Further Research', *The International Journal of the History of Sport* 28, no. 13 (2011), 1733–49; and Robert Lewis, 'The Genesis of Professional Football: Bolton–Blackburn–Darwen, the Centre of Innovation, 1878–85', *The International Journal of the History of Sport* 14, no. 1 (1997), 21–54.

7. In addition to those mentioned elsewhere in this article, these include Curry and Dunning, *Association Football*; Gavin Kitching, 'The Origins of Football: History, Ideology and the Making of "The People's Game"', *History Workshop Journal* 79, no. 1 (2015), 127–53; Graham Curry and Eric Dunning, 'The "Origins of Football Debate" and the Early Development of the Game in Nottinghamshire', *Soccer and Society* (2015). doi: 10.1080/14660970.2015.1067801; Gary James and Dave Day, 'The Emergence of an Association Football Culture in Manchester, 1840–1884', *Sport in History* 34, no. 1 (2014), 49–74; Matthew L. McDowell, *A Cultural History of Association Football in Scotland, 1865–1902* (Lampeter: Edwin Mellen Press, 2013); Swain, 'Cultural Continuity'; Thomas John Preston, 'The Origins and Development of Association Football in the Liverpool District, c.1879 until c.1915' (PhD thesis, University of Central Lancashire, Preston, 2007); Neal Garnham, *Association Football and Society in Pre-Partition Ireland* (Belfast: Ulster Historical Foundation, 2004); Ian Nannestad, 'From Sabbath Breakers to Respectable Sportsmen: The Development of Football in Lincolnshire ca. 1855 to ca. 1881' (MA thesis, De Montfort University, Leicester, 2003); Martin Johnes, *Soccer and Society in South Wales, 1900–1939* (Cardiff: University of Wales Press, 2002); Adrian Harvey, 'An Epoch in the Annals of National Sport: Football in Sheffield and the Creation of Modern Soccer and Rugby', *The International Journal of the History of Sport* 18, no. 4 (2001), 53–87; and John Goulstone, 'The Working Class Origins of Modern Football', *The International Journal of the History of Sport* 17, no. 1 (2000), 135–43.

8. For historiography, see the following recent papers: Collins, 'Early Football and the Emergence of Modern Soccer'; Kitching, 'The Origins of Football'; and Curry and Dunning, 'The "Origins of Football Debate" and the Early Development of the Game in Nottinghamshire'.
9. Examples include Swain, 'Early Football and the Emergence of Modern Soccer'; Peter Swain and Robert Lewis, 'Manchester and the Emergence of an Association Football Culture: An Alternative Viewpoint', *The International Journal of the History of Sport* 32, no. 9 (2015), 1160–80; Lewis, 'Innovation Not Invention'; Swain, 'Cultural Continuity and Football in Nineteenth Century Lancashire'; Harvey, 'Curate's Egg Pursued by Red Herrings'; and Harvey, 'The Curate's Egg Put Back Together'.
10. Tony Mason, 'Writing The History of Sport', unpublished seminar paper, Centre for the Study of Social History, University of Warwick, 10 October 1991, quoted in Jeffrey Hill, 'British Sports History: A Post-Modern Future?', *Journal of Sport History* 23, no. 1 (1996), 2.
11. Fernand Braudel, 'Histoire et Science Sociale: La Longue Durée', *Annales* 13, no. 4 (1958), 725–53.
12. Immanuel Wallerstein, *Unthinking Social Science* (Philadelphia, PA: Temple University Press, 2001), 136.
13. Dale Tomich, 'The Order of Historical Time: The Longue durée and Micro-History', in Richard E. Lee (ed.), *The Longue durée and World-Systems Analysis* (Binghamton: Binghampton University, 2008), 2.
14. William H. McNeill, 'Fernand Braudel, Historian', *Journal of Modern History* 73, no. 1 (2001), 133.
15. Jo Guldi and David Armitage, *The History Manifesto* (Cambridge: Cambridge University Press, 2014), 63.
16. Owen Hufton, 'Fernand Braudel', *Past & Present* 112 (1986), 112.
17. Fernand Braudel, *The Mediterranean and the Mediterranean World in the Age of Philip II* (London: Harper and Row, 1972).
18. Ulysses Santamaria and Anne M. Bailey, 'A Note on Braudel's Structure as Duration', *History and Theory* 23, no. 1 (1984), 82.
19. Fernand Braudel, *On History* (Chicago: University of Chicago Press, 1982), 75.
20. Santamaria and Bailey, 'A Note on Braudel's Structure as Duration', 81.
21. Peter Stanfield, '"Pix Biz Spurts with War Fever": Film and the Public Sphere – Cycles and Topicality', *Film History: An International Journal* 25, nos 1–2 (2013), 222.
22. Santamaria and Bailey, 'A Note on Braudel's Structure as Duration', 81.
23. Ibid.
24. Michael Ermarth, 'On History. By Fernand Braudel', *Business History Review* 56, no. 1 (1982), 90.
25. Immanuel Wallerstein, *Unthinking Social Science*, 137.
26. William Thomas Dixon, *History of Turton Football Club and Souvenir of Carnival and Sports* (Bolton: Unknown Publisher, 1909), 5.
27. C.E. Sutcliffe and F. Hargreaves, *The History of the Lancashire Football Association* (Blackburn: Geo. Toulmin and Sons, 1928), 32.
28. Fernand Braudel, *The Mediterranean and the Mediterranean World in the Age of Philip II*, vol. II, 901.
29. Fernand Braudel, 'History and the Social Sciences: the Longue durée', in Richard E. Lee (ed.), *The Longue durée and World Systems Analysis* (Albany: State University of New York, 2012), 241–76.
30. Fernand Braudel, *On History*, 30–1.
31. James and Day, 'The Emergence of an Association Football Culture in Manchester'.
32. Guldi and Armitage, *The History Manifesto*, 71.
33. Richard Aldrich, 'The Three Duties of the Historian of Education', *History of Education: Journal of the History of Education Society* 32, no. 2 (2010), 136.
34. Jan Vansina, 'For Oral Tradition (But Not Against Braudel)', *History in Africa*, no. 5 (1978), 351–2.

35. Geoffrey M. Hodgson, 'Darwin, Veblen and the Problem of Causality in Economics', *History and Philosophy of the Life Sciences* 23 (2001), 385–423.
36. Guldi and Armitage, *The History Manifesto*, 29; and Aldrich, 'The Three Duties of the Historian of Education', 135.
37. Guldi and Armitage, *The History Manifesto*, 115.
38. Santamaria and Bailey, 'A Note on Braudel's Structure as Duration', 82.
39. Richard A. Gould, 'Ethnoarchaeology and the Past: Our Search for the "Real Thing"', *Fennoscandia archaeologica* VI (1989), 7.
40. James and Day, 'The Emergence of an Association Football Culture in Manchester', 56–9; and James, 'Manchester's Footballing Pioneers'.
41. Swain and Lewis, 'Manchester and the Emergence of an Association Football Culture'.
42. James, 'Manchester's Footballing Pioneers', 1149–55.
43. Arthur P. Molella, 'The Longue durée of Abbott Payson Usher: A. P. Usher, A History of Mechanical Inventions', *Technology and Culture* 46, no. 4 (2005), 796.
44. Guldi and Armitage, *The History Manifesto*, 29.
45. Martin Johnes and Bob Nicholson, 'Sport History and Digital Archives in Practice', in Gary Osmond and Murray G. Phillips (eds), *Sport History in the Digital Era* (Urbana: University of Illinois Press, 2015), 53–5.
46. A limited run of the *Athletic News* was added to the British Newspaper Archive's digital collection in the early months of 2016, but there are significant gaps, while the International Sport & Leisure History group at Manchester Metropolitan University established a project in 2015 to digitize three leading sports newspapers produced in Manchester.
47. 'Miscellaneous', *Manchester Times*, 26 December 1840, 2.
48. Ignacio Olabarri, '"New" New History: A Longue durée Structure', *History and Theory* 34, no. 1 (1995), 7.
49. Yuan Bi, 'Integration or Resistance: The Influx of Foreign Capital in British Football in the Transnational Age', *Soccer & Society* 16, no. 1 (2015), 17–41.
50. 'Four New Clubs Elected', *Yorkshire Post*, 11 March 1919.
51. Matthew Taylor, *The Leaguers: The Making of Professional Football in England, 1900–1939* (Liverpool: Liverpool University Press, 2005), 15–17.
52. 'Four New Clubs Elected', *Yorkshire Post*, 11 March 1919.
53. *Bell's Life*, 20 December 1846, 7.
54. John Goulstone, *Football's Secret History* (Upminster: 3–2 Books, 2001); Adrian Harvey, *Football: The First Hundred Years The Untold Story* (Abingdon: Routledge, 2005), 76; and Curry and Dunning, *Association Football*, 158–9.
55. James and Day, 'The Emergence of an Association Football Culture in Manchester', 54–6.
56. Immanuel Wallerstein et al., 'Discussion', *Review* 1 (1978), 98.
57. Stanley Bober, *The Economics of Cycles and Growth* (New York: Wiley, 1968), 44–5.
58. Guldi and Armitage, *The History Manifesto*, 133.
59. In addition to the four documented within the main text, the other seven broad Transformational periods are Dominance of League Football; Mass Spectator Sport; England's Isolation; World Cup and European Success; Disasters, Demonstrations and Hooliganism; Premier League Birth; and Overseas Ownership/Globalization of the English Game.
60. Gary James, *The Emergence of Footballing Cultures: Manchester, 1840–1919* (Manchester: Manchester University Press, forthcoming).
61. Olabarri, '"New" New History', 1.
62. Guldi and Armitage, *The History Manifesto*, 119.
63. Bober, *The Economics of Cycles and Growth*, 44.
64. Gould, 'Ethnoarchaeology and the Past', 7.
65. Bober, *The Economics of Cycles and Growth*, 44–5.
66. Guldi and Armitage, *The History Manifesto*, 38–60.
67. Ibid., 63.

68. David Cannadine, 'British History: Past, Present – And Future?', *Past and Present*, no. 116 (1987), 176–7. Altmetrics and read figures can be read on the Taylor and Francis website, tandfonline.com, for all their journal articles.
69. Matthew L. McDowell, 'The Field of Play: Phases and Themes in the Historiography of Pre-1914 Scottish Football', *The International Journal of the History of Sport*, 31 no. 17 (2014), 2121–40. Students at the University of Maryland, most notably Sam Clevenger, have also been considering applying longue durée principles in their research. See https://thecorpus.wordpress.com/2015/07/17/report-the-history-manifesto-april-20th-2015/#more-725 (accessed 8 June 2016).
70. Gould, 'Ethnoarchaeology and the Past', 20.
71. Martin Johnes, 'What's the Point of Sports History?', *The International Journal of the History of Sport* 30, no. 1 (1995), 102–8.
72. Ross McKibbin, 'Sports History: Status, Definitions and Meanings', *Sport in History* 31, no. 2 (2011), 167–74.
73. Guldi and Armitage, *The History Manifesto*, 117.
74. Vamplew, 'Sporting a Handicap'.
75. David Armitage, 'What's the Big Idea? Intellectual History and the Longue durée', *History of European Ideas* 38, no. 4 (2012), 493–507.
76. Andrew Sherratt, 'Reviving the Grand Narrative: Archaeology and Long-term Change. The Second David L. Clarke Memorial Lecture', *Journal of European Archaeology* 3, no. 1 (2013), 5.
77. McDowell, 'The Field of Play', 2134.

Disclosure statement

No potential conflict of interest was reported by the author.

Index

www.ingramcontent.com/pod-product-compliance
Ingram Content Group UK Ltd.
Pitfield, Milton Keynes, MK11 3LW, UK
UKHW010020280225
455677UK00023B/701